The Diary Of Samuel Pepys

1665

The Echo Library 2006

Published by

The Echo Library

Echo Library
131 High St.
Teddington
Middlesex TW11 8HH

www.echo-library.com

Please report serious faults in the text to complaints@echo-library.com

ISBN 1-84702-968-X

THE DIARY OF SAMUEL PEPYS M.A. F.R.S.
CLERK OF THE ACTS AND SECRETARY TO THE ADMIRALTY
TRANSCRIBED FROM THE SHORTHAND MANUSCRIPT IN THE
PEPYSIAN LIBRARY MAGDALENE COLLEGE CAMBRIDGE BY THE
REV. MYNORS BRIGHT M.A. LATE FELLOW
AND PRESIDENT OF THE COLLEGE
(Unabridged)
WITH LORD BRAYBROOKE'S NOTES
EDITED WITH ADDITIONS BY
HENRY B. WHEATLEY F.S.A.

DIARY OF SAMUEL PEPYS.

1665 N.S.

JANUARY 1664-1665

January 1st (Lord's day). Lay long in bed, having been busy late last night, then up and to my office, where upon ordering my accounts and papers with respect to my understanding my last year's gains and expense, which I find very great, as I have already set down yesterday. Now this day I am dividing my expense, to see what my clothes and every particular hath stood me in: I mean all the branches of my expense. At noon a good venison pasty and a turkey to ourselves without any body so much as invited by us, a thing unusuall for so small a family of my condition: but we did it and were very merry. After dinner to my office again, where very late alone upon my accounts, but have not brought them to order yet, and very intricate I find it, notwithstanding my care all the year to keep things in as good method as any man can do. Past 11 o'clock home to supper and to bed.

2nd. Up, and it being a most fine, hard frost I walked a good way toward White Hall, and then being overtaken with Sir W. Pen's coach, went into it, and with him thither, and there did our usual business with the Duke. Thence, being forced to pay a great deale of money away in boxes (that is, basins at White Hall), I to my barber's, Gervas, and there had a little opportunity of speaking with my Jane alone, and did give her something, and of herself she did tell me a place where I might come to her on Sunday next, which I will not fail, but to see how modestly and harmlessly she brought it out was very pretty. Thence to the Swan, and there did sport a good while with Herbert's young kinswoman without hurt, though they being abroad, the old people. Then to the Hall, and there agreed with Mrs. Martin, and to her lodgings which she has now taken to lie in, in Bow Streete, pitiful poor things, yet she thinks them pretty, and so they are for her condition I believe good enough. Here I did 'ce que je voudrais avec' her most freely, and it having cost 2s. in wine and cake upon her, I away sick of her impudence, and by coach to my Lord Brunker's, by appointment, in the Piazza, in Covent-Guarding; where I occasioned much mirth with a ballet I brought with me, made from the seamen at sea to their ladies in town; saying Sir

W. Pen, Sir G. Ascue, and Sir J. Lawson made them. Here a most noble French dinner and banquet, the best I have seen this many a day and good discourse. Thence to my bookseller's and at his binder's saw Hooke's book of the Microscope,

> ["Micrographia: or some physiological descriptions of minute bodies made by Magnifying Glasses. London, 1665," a very remarkable work with elaborate plates, some of which have been used for lecture illustrations almost to our own day. On November 23rd, 1664, the President of the Royal Society was "desired to sign a licence for printing of Mr. Hooke's microscopical book." At this time the book was mostly printed, but it was delayed, much to Hooke's disgust, by the examination of several Fellows of the Society. In spite of this examination the council were anxious that the author should make it clear that he alone was responsible for any theory put forward, and they gave him notice to that effect. Hooke made this clear in his dedication (see Birch's "History," vol. i., pp. 490-491)]

which is so pretty that I presently bespoke it, and away home to the office, where we met to do something, and then though very late by coach to Sir Ph. Warwicke's, but having company with him could not speak with him. So back again home, where thinking to be merry was vexed with my wife's having looked out a letter in Sir Philip Sidney about jealousy for me to read, which she industriously and maliciously caused me to do, and the truth is my conscience told me it was most proper for me, and therefore was touched at it, but tooke no notice of it, but read it out most frankly, but it stucke in my stomach, and moreover I was vexed to have a dog brought to my house to line our little bitch, which they make him do in all their sights, which, God forgive me, do stir my jealousy again, though of itself the thing is a very immodest sight. However, to cards with my wife a good while, and then to bed.

3rd. Up, and by coach to Sir Ph. Warwicke's, the streete being full of footballs, it being a great frost, and found him and Mr. Coventry walking in St. James's Parke. I did my errand to him about the felling of the King's timber in the forests, and then to my Lord of Oxford, Justice in Eyre, for his consent thereto, for want whereof my Lord Privy Seale stops the whole business. I found him in his lodgings, in but an ordinary furnished house and roome where he was, but I find him to be a man of good discreet replys. Thence to the Coffee-house, where certain newes that the Dutch have taken some of our colliers to the North; some say four, some say seven. Thence to the 'Change a while, and so home to dinner and to the office, where we sat late, and then I to write my letters, and then to Sir W. Batten's, who is going out of towne to Harwich to-morrow to set up a light-house there, which he hath lately got a patent from the King to set up, that will turne much to his profit. Here very merry, and so to my office again, where very late, and then home to supper and to bed, but sat up with my wife at cards till past two in the morning.

4th. Lay long, and then up and to my Lord of Oxford's, but his Lordshipp was in bed at past ten o'clock: and, Lord helpe us! so rude a dirty family I never saw in my life. He sent me out word my business was not done, but should against the afternoon. I thence to the Coffee-house, there but little company, and so home to the 'Change, where I hear of some more of our ships lost to the Northward. So to Sir W. Batten's, but he was set out before I got thither. I sat long talking with my lady, and then home to dinner. Then come Mr. Moore to see me, and he and I to my Lord of Oxford's, but not finding him within Mr. Moore and I to "Love in a Tubb," which is very merry, but only so by gesture, not wit at all, which methinks is beneath the House. So walked home, it being a very hard frost, and I find myself as heretofore in cold weather to begin to burn within and pimples and pricks all over my body, my pores with cold being shut up. So home to supper and to cards and to bed.

5th. Up, it being very cold and a great snow and frost tonight. To the office, and there all the morning. At noon dined at home, troubled at my wife's being simply angry with Jane, our cook mayde (a good servant, though perhaps hath faults and is cunning), and given her warning to be gone. So to the office again, where we sat late, and then I to my office, and there very late doing business. Home to supper and to the office again, and then late home to bed.

6th. Lay long in bed, but most of it angry and scolding with my wife about her warning Jane our cookemayde to be gone and upon that she desires to go abroad to-day to look a place. A very good mayde she is and fully to my mind, being neat, only they say a little apt to scold, but I hear her not. To my office all the morning busy. Dined at home. To my office again, being pretty well reconciled to my wife, which I did desire to be, because she had designed much mirthe to-day to end Christmas with among her servants. At night home, being twelfenight, and there chose my piece of cake, but went up to my viall, and then to bed, leaving my wife and people up at their sports, which they continue till morning, not coming to bed at all.

7th. Up and to the office all the morning. At noon dined alone, my wife and family most of them a-bed. Then to see my Lady Batten and sit with her a while, Sir W. Batten being out of town, and then to my office doing very much business very late, and then home to supper and to bed.

8th (Lord's day). Up betimes, and it being a very fine frosty day, I and my boy walked to White Hall, and there to the Chappell, where one Dr. Beaumont' preached a good sermon, and afterwards a brave anthem upon the 150 Psalm, where upon the word "trumpet" very good musique was made. So walked to my Lady's and there dined with her (my boy going home), where much pretty discourse, and after dinner walked to Westminster, and there to the house where Jane Welsh had appointed me, but it being sermon time they would not let me in, and said nobody was there to speak with me. I spent the whole afternoon walking into the Church and Abbey, and up and down, but could not find her, and so in the evening took a coach and home, and there sat discoursing with my wife, and by and by at supper, drinking some cold drink I think it was, I was forced to go make water, and had very great pain after it, but was well by and by and continued so, it being only I think from the drink, or from my straining at stool to do more than my body would. So after prayers to bed.

9th. Up and walked to White Hall, it being still a brave frost, and I in perfect good health, blessed be God! In my way saw a woman that broke her thigh, in her heels slipping up upon the frosty streete. To the Duke, and there did our usual worke. Here I saw the Royal Society bring their new book, wherein is nobly writ their charter' and laws, and comes to be signed by the Duke as a Fellow; and all the Fellows' hands are to be entered there, and lie as a monument; and the King hath put his with the word Founder. Thence I to Westminster, to my barber's, and found occasion to see Jane, but in presence of her mistress, and so could not speak to her of her failing me yesterday, and then to the Swan to Herbert's girl, and lost time a little with her, and so took coach, and to my Lord Crew's and dined with him, who receives me with the greatest respect that could be, telling me that he do much doubt of the successe of this warr with Holland, we going about it, he doubts, by the instigation of persons that do not enough apprehend the consequences of the danger of it, and therein I do think with him. Holmes was this day sent to the Tower,--[For taking New York from the Dutch]--but I perceive it is made matter of jest only; but if the Dutch should be our masters, it may come to be of earnest to him, to be given over to them for a sacrifice, as Sir W. Rawly [Raleigh] was. Thence to White Hall to a Tangier Committee, where I was accosted and most highly complimented by my Lord Bellasses,

[John Belasyse, second son of Thomas, first Viscount Fauconberg, created Baron Belasyse of Worlaby, January 27th, 1644, Lord Lieutenant of the East Riding of Yorkshire, and Governor of Hull. He was appointed Governor of Tangier, and Captain of the Band of Gentlemen Pensioners. He was a Roman Catholic, and therefore was deprived of all his appointments in 1672 by the provisions of the Test Act, but in 1684 James II. made him First Commissioner of the Treasury. He died 1689.]

our new governor, beyond my expectation, or measure I could imagine he would have given any man, as if I were the only person of business that he intended to rely on, and desires my correspondence with him. This I was not only surprized at, but am well pleased with, and may make good use of it. Our patent is renewed, and he and my Lord Barkeley, and Sir Thomas Ingram put in as commissioners. Here some business happened which may bring me some profit. Thence took coach and calling my wife at her tailor's (she being come this afternoon to bring her mother some apples, neat's tongues, and wine); I home, and there at my office late with Sir W. Warren, and had a great deal of good discourse and counsel from him, which I hope I shall take, being all for my good in my deportment in my office, yet with all honesty. He gone I home to supper and to bed.

10th. Lay long, it being still very cold, and then to the office, where till dinner, and then home, and by and by to the office, where we sat and were very late, and I writing letters till twelve at night, and then after supper to bed.

11th. Up, and very angry with my boy for lying long a bed and forgetting his lute. To my office all the morning. At noon to the 'Change, and so home to dinner. After dinner to Gresham College to my Lord Brunker and Commissioner Pett, taking, Mr. Castle with me there to discourse over his draught of a ship he is to build for us. Where I first found reason to apprehend Commissioner Pett to be a man of an ability extraordinary in any thing, for I found he did turn and wind Castle like a chicken in his business, and that most pertinently and mister-like, and great pleasure it was to me to hear them discourse, I, of late having studied something thereof, and my Lord Brunker is a very able person also himself in this sort of business, as owning himself to be a master in the business of all lines and Conicall Sections: Thence home, where very late at my office doing business to my content, though [God] knows with what ado it was that when I was out I could get myself to come home to my business, or when I was there though late would stay there from going abroad again. To supper and to bed. This evening, by a letter from Plymouth, I hear that two of our ships, the Leopard and another, in the Straights, are lost by running aground; and that three more had like to have been so, but got off, whereof Captain Allen one: and that a Dutch fleete are gone thither; which if they should meet with our lame ships, God knows what would become of them. This I reckon most sad newes; God make us sensible of it! This night, when I come home, I was much troubled to hear my poor canary bird, that I have kept these three or four years, is dead.

12th. Up, and to White Hall about getting a privy seal for felling of the King's timber for the navy, and to the Lords' House to speak with my Lord Privy Seale about it, and so to the 'Change, where to my last night's ill news I met more. Spoke with a Frenchman who was taken, but released, by a Dutch man-of-war of thirty-six guns (with seven more of the like or greater ships), off the North Foreland, by Margett. Which is a strange attempt, that they should come to our teeth; but the wind being easterly, the wind that should bring our force from Portsmouth, will carry them away home. God preserve us against them, and pardon our making them in our discourse so contemptible an enemy! So home and to dinner, where Mr. Hollyard with us dined. So to the office, and there late till 11 at night and more, and then home to supper and to bed.

13th. Up betimes and walked to my Lord Bellasses's lodgings in Lincolne's Inne Fieldes, and there he received and discoursed with me in the most respectfull manner that could be, telling me what a character of my judgment, and care, and love to Tangier he had received of me, that he desired my advice and my constant correspondence, which he much valued, and in my courtship, in which, though I understand his designe very well, and that it is only a piece of courtship, yet it is a comfort to me that I am become so considerable as to have him need to say that to me, which, if I did not do something in the world, would never have been. Here well satisfied I to Sir Ph. Warwicke, and there did some business with him; thence to Jervas's and there spent a little idle time with him, his wife, Jane, and a sweetheart of hers. So to the Hall awhile and thence to the Exchange, where yesterday's newes confirmed, though in a little different manner; but a couple of ships in the Straights we have lost, and the Dutch have been in Margaret [Margate] Road. Thence home to dinner and so abroad and alone to the King's house, to a play, "The Traytor," where, unfortunately, I met with Sir W. Pen, so that I must be forced to confess it to my wife, which troubles me. Thence walked home, being ill-satisfied with the present actings of the House, and prefer the other House before this infinitely. To my Lady Batten's, where I find Pegg Pen, the first time that ever I saw her to wear spots. Here very merry, Sir W. Batten being looked for to-night, but is not yet come from Harwich. So home to supper and to bed.

14th. Up and to White Hall, where long waited in the Duke's chamber for a Committee intended for Tangier, but none met, and so I home and to the office, where we met a little, and then to the 'Change, where our late ill newes confirmed in loss of two ships in the Straights, but are now the Phoenix and Nonsuch! Home to dinner, thence with my wife to the King's house, there to see "Vulpone," a most excellent play; the best I think I ever saw, and well, acted. So with Sir W. Pen home in his coach, and then to the office. So home, to supper, and bed, resolving by the grace of God from this day to fall hard to my business again, after some weeke or fortnight's neglect.

15th (Lord's day). Up, and after a little at my office to prepare a fresh draught of my vowes for the next yeare, I to church, where a most insipid young coxcomb preached. Then home to dinner, and after dinner to read in "Rushworth's Collections" about the charge against the late Duke of Buckingham, in order to the fitting me to speak and understand the discourse anon before the King about the suffering the Turkey merchants to send out their fleete at this dangerous time, when we can neither spare them ships to go, nor men, nor King's ships to convoy them. At four o'clock with Sir W. Pen in his coach to my Lord Chancellor's, where by and by Mr. Coventry, Sir W. Pen, Sir J. Lawson, Sir G. Ascue, and myself were called in to the King, there being several of the Privy Council, and my Lord Chancellor lying at length upon a couch (of the goute I suppose); and there Sir W. Pen begun, and he had prepared heads in a paper, and spoke pretty well to purpose, but with so much leisure and gravity as was tiresome; besides, the things he said were but very poor to a man in his trade after a great consideration, but it was to purpose, indeed to dissuade the King from letting these Turkey ships to go out: saying (in short) the King having resolved to have 130 ships out by the spring, he must have above 20 of them merchantmen. Towards which, he in the whole River could find but 12 or 14, and of them the five ships taken up by these merchants were a part, and so could not be spared. That we should need 30,000 [sailors] to man these 130 ships, and of them in service we have not above 16,000; so we shall need 14,000 more. That these ships will with their convoys carry above 2,000 men, and those the best men that could be got; it being the men used to the Southward that are the best men for warr, though those bred in the North among the colliers are good for labour. That it will not be safe for the merchants, nor honourable for the King, to expose these rich ships with his convoy of six ships to go, it not being enough to secure them against the Dutch, who, without doubt, will have a great fleete in the Straights. This, Sir J. Lawson enlarged upon. Sir G. Ascue he chiefly spoke that the warr and trade could not be supported together, and, therefore, that trade must stand still to give way to them. This Mr. Coventry seconded, and showed how the medium of the men the King hath one year with another employed in his Navy since his coming, hath not been above 3,000 men, or at most 4,000 men; and now having occasion of 30,000, the remaining 26,000 must be found out of the trade of the nation. He showed how the cloaths, sending by these merchants to Turkey, are already bought and paid for to the workmen, and are as many as they would send these twelve months or more; so the poor do not suffer by their not going, but only the merchant, upon whose hands they lit dead; and so the inconvenience is the less. And yet for them he propounded, either the King should, if his Treasure would suffer it, buy them, and showed the losse would not be so great to him: or, dispense with the Act of Navigation, and let them be carried out by strangers; and ending that he doubted not but when the merchants saw there was no remedy, they would and could find ways of sending them abroad to their profit. All ended with a conviction (unless future discourse with the merchants should alter it) that it was not fit for them to go out, though the ships be loaded. The King in discourse did ask me two or three questions about my newes of Allen's loss in the Streights, but I said nothing as to the business, nor am not much sorry for it, unless the King had spoke to me as he did to them, and then I could have said something to the purpose I think. So we withdrew, and the merchants were called in. Staying without, my Lord Fitz Harding come thither, and fell to discourse of Prince Rupert, and made nothing to say that his disease was the pox and that he must be fluxed, telling the horrible degree of the disease upon him with its breaking out on his head. But above all I observed how he observed from the Prince, that courage is not what men take it to be, a contempt of death; for, says he, how chagrined the Prince was the other day when he thought he should die, having no more mind to it than another man. But, says he, some men are more apt to think they shall escape than another man in fight, while another is doubtfull he shall be hit. But when the first man is sure he shall die, as now the Prince is, he is as much troubled and apprehensive of it as any man else; for, says he, since we told [him] that we believe he would overcome his disease, he is as merry, and swears and laughs and curses, and do all the things of a [man] in health, as ever he did in his life; which, methought, was a most extraordinary saying before a great many persons there of quality. So by and by with Sir W. Pen home again, and after supper to the office to finish my vows, and so to bed.

16th. Up and with Sir W. Batten and Sir W. Pen to White Hall, where we did our business with the Duke. Thence I to Westminster Hall and walked up and down. Among others Ned Pickering met me and tells me how active my Lord is at sea, and that my Lord Hinchingbroke is now at Rome, and, by all report, a very noble and hopefull gentleman. Thence to Mr. Povy's, and there met Creed, and dined well after his old manner of plenty and curiosity. But I sat in pain to think whether he would begin with me again after dinner with his enquiry after my bill, but he did not, but fell into other discourse, at which I was glad, but was vexed this morning meeting of Creed at some bye questions that he demanded of me about some such thing, which made me fear he meant that very matter, but I perceive he did not. Thence to visit my Lady Sandwich and so to a Tangier Committee, where a great company of the new Commissioners, Lords, that in behalfe of my Lord Bellasses are very loud and busy and call for Povy's accounts, but it was a most sorrowful thing to see how he answered to questions so little to the purpose, but to his owne wrong. All the while I sensible how I am concerned in my bill of L100 and somewhat more. So great a trouble is fear, though in a case that at the worst will bear enquiry. My Lord Barkeley was very violent against Povy. But my Lord Ashly, I observe, is a most clear man in matters of accounts, and most ingeniously did discourse and explain all matters. We broke up, leaving the thing to a Committee of which I am one. Povy, Creed, and I staid discoursing, I much troubled in mind seemingly for the business, but indeed only on my own behalf, though I have no great reason for it, but so painfull a thing is fear. So after considering how to order business, Povy and I walked together as far as the New Exchange and so parted, and I by coach home. To the office a while, then to supper and to bed. This afternoon Secretary Bennet read to the Duke of Yorke his letters, which say that Allen

[Among the State Papers is a letter from Captain Thomas Allin to Sir Richard Fanshaw, dated from "The Plymouth, Cadiz Bay," December 25th, 1664, in which he writes: "On the 19th attacked with his seven ships left, a Dutch fleet of fourteen, three of which were men-of-war; sunk two vessels and took two others, one a rich prize from Smyrna; the others retired much battered. Has also taken a Dutch prize laden with iron and planks, coming from Lisbon ("Calendar," Domestic, 1664-65, p. 122).]

has met with the Dutch Smyrna fleet at Cales,--[The old form of the name Cadiz.]--and sunk one and taken three. How true or what these ships are time will show, but it is good newes and the newes of our ships being lost is doubted at dales and Malaga. God send it false!

17th. Up and walked to Mr. Povy's by appointment, where I found him and Creed busy about fitting things for the Committee, and thence we to my Lord Ashly's, where to see how simply, beyond all patience, Povy did again, by his many words and no understanding, confound himself and his business, to his disgrace, and rendering every body doubtfull of his being either a foole or knave, is very wonderfull. We broke up all dissatisfied, and referred the business to a meeting of Mr. Sherwin and others to settle, but here it was mighty strange methought to find myself sit herein Committee with my hat on, while Mr. Sherwin stood bare as a clerke, with his hat off to his Lord Ashlyand the rest, but I thank God I think myself never a whit the better man for all that. Thence with Creed to the 'Change and Coffee-house, and so home, where a brave dinner, by having a brace of pheasants and very merry about Povy's folly. So anon to the office, and there sitting very late, and then after a little time at Sir W. Batten's, where I am mighty great and could if I thought it fit continue so, I to the office again, and there very late, and so home to the sorting of some of my books, and so to bed, the weather becoming pretty warm, and I think and hope the frost will break.

18th. Up and by and by to my bookseller's, and there did give thorough direction for the new binding of a great many of my old books, to make my whole study of the same binding, within very few. Thence to my Lady Sandwich's, who sent for me this morning. Dined with her, and it was to get a letter of hers conveyed by a safe hand to my Lord's owne hand at Portsmouth, which I did undertake. Here my Lady did begin to talk of what she had heard concerning Creed, of his being suspected to be a fanatique and a false fellow. I told her I thought he was as shrewd and cunning a man as any in England, and one that I would feare first should outwit me in any thing. To which she readily concurred. Thence to Mr. Povy's by agreement, and there with Mr. Sherwin, Auditor Beale, and Creed and I hard at it very late about Mr. Povy's accounts, but such accounts I never did see, or hope again to see in my days. At night, late, they gone, I did get him to put out of this account our sums that are in posse only yet, which he approved of when told, but would never have stayed it if I had been gone. Thence at 9 at night home, and so to supper vexed and my head akeing and to bed.

19th. Up, and it being yesterday and to-day a great thaw it is not for a man to walk the streets, but took coach and to Mr. Povy's, and there meeting all of us again agreed upon an answer to the Lords by and by, and thence we did come to Exeter House, and there was a witness of most [base] language against Mr. Povy, from my Lord Peterborough, who is most furiously angry with him, because the other, as a foole, would needs say that the L26,000 was my Lord Peterborough's account, and that he had nothing to do with it. The Lords did find fault also with our answer, but I think really my Lord Ashly would fain have the outside of an Exchequer,--[This word is blotted, and the whole sentence is confused.]--but when we come better to be examined. So home by coach, with my Lord Barkeley, who, by his discourse, I find do look upon Mr. Coventry as an enemy, but yet professes great justice and pains. I at home after dinner to the office, and there sat all the afternoon and evening, and then home to supper and to bed. Memorandum. This day and yesterday, I think it is the change of the weather, I have a great deal of pain, but nothing like what I use to have. I can hardly keep myself loose, but on the contrary am forced to drive away my pain. Here I am so sleepy I cannot hold open my eyes, and therefore must be forced to break off this day's passages more shortly than I would and should have done. This day was buried (but I could not be there) my cozen Percivall Angier; and yesterday I received the newes that Dr. Tom Pepys is dead, at Impington, for which I am but little sorry, not only because he would have been troublesome to us, but a shame to his family and profession; he was such a coxcomb.

20th. Up and to Westminster, where having spoke with Sir Ph. Warwicke, I to Jervas, and there I find them all in great disorder about Jane, her mistress telling me secretly that she was sworn not to reveal anything, but she was undone. At last for all her oath she told me that she had made herself sure to a fellow that comes to their house that can only fiddle for his living, and did keep him company, and had plainly told her that she was sure to him never to leave him for any body else. Now they were this day contriving to get her presently to marry one Hayes that was there, and I did seem to persuade her to it. And at last got them to suffer me to advise privately, and by that means had her company and think I shall meet her next Sunday, but I do really doubt she will be undone in marrying this fellow. But I did give her my advice, and so let her do her pleasure, so I have now and then her company. Thence to the Swan at noon, and there sent for a bit of meat and dined, and had my baiser of the fille of the house there, but nothing plus. So took coach and to my Lady Sandwich's, and so to my bookseller's, and there took home Hooke's book of microscopy, a most excellent piece, and of which I am very proud. So home, and by and by again abroad with my wife about several businesses, and met at the New Exchange, and there to our trouble found our pretty Doll is gone away to live they say with her father in the country, but I doubt something worse. So homeward, in my way buying a hare and taking it home, which arose upon my discourse to-day with Mr. Batten, in Westminster Hall, who showed me my mistake that my hare's foote hath not the joynt to it; and assures me he never had his cholique since he carried it about him: and it is a strange thing how fancy works, for I no sooner almost handled his foote but my belly began to be loose and to break wind, and whereas I was in some pain yesterday and t'other day and in fear of more to-day, I became very well, and so continue. At home to my office a while, and so to supper, read, and to cards, and to bed.

21st. At the office all the morning. Thence my Lord Brunker carried me as far as Mr. Povy's, and there I 'light and dined, meeting Mr. Sherwin, Creed, &c., there upon his accounts. After dinner they parted and Mr. Povy carried me to Somersett House, and there showed me the Queene-Mother's chamber and closett, most beautiful places for furniture and pictures; and so down the great stone stairs to the garden, and tried the brave echo upon the stairs; which continues a voice so long as the singing three notes, concords, one after another, they all three shall sound in consort together a good while most pleasantly. Thence to a Tangier Committee at White Hall, where I saw nothing ordered by judgment, but great heat and passion and faction now in behalf of my Lord Bellasses, and to the reproach of my Lord Tiviott, and dislike as it were of former proceedings. So away with Mr. Povy, he carrying me homeward to Mark Lane in his coach, a simple fellow I now find him, to his utter shame in his business of accounts, as none but a sorry foole would have discovered himself; and yet, in little, light, sorry things very cunning; yet, in the principal, the most ignorant man I ever met with in so great trust as he is. To my office till past 12, and then home to supper and to bed, being now mighty well, and truly I cannot but impute it to my fresh hare's foote. Before I went to bed I sat up till two o'clock in my chamber reading of Mr. Hooke's Microscopicall Observations, the most ingenious book that ever I read in my life.

22nd (Lord's day). Up, leaving my wife in bed, being sick of her months, and to church. Thence home, and in my wife's chamber dined very merry, discoursing, among other things, of a design I have come in my head this morning at church of making a match between Mrs. Betty Pickering and Mr. Hill, my friend the merchant, that loves musique and comes to me a'Sundays, a most ingenious and sweet-natured and highly accomplished person. I know not how their fortunes may agree, but their disposition and merits are much of a sort, and persons, though different, yet equally, I think, acceptable. After dinner walked to Westminster, and after being at the Abbey and heard a good anthem well sung there, I as I had appointed to the Trumpett, there expecting when Jane Welsh should come, but anon comes a maid of the house to tell me that her mistress and master would not let her go forth, not knowing of my being here, but to keep her from her sweetheart. So being defeated, away by coach home, and there spent the evening prettily in discourse with my wife and Mercer, and so to supper, prayers, and to bed.

23rd. Up, and with Sir W. Batten and Sir W. Pen to White Hall; but there finding the Duke gone to his lodgings at St. James's for all together, his Duchesse being ready to lie in, we to him, and there did our usual business. And here I met the great newes confirmed by the Duke's own relation, by a letter from Captain Allen. First, of our own loss of two ships, the Phoenix and Nonesuch, in the Bay of Gibraltar: then of his, and his seven ships with him, in the Bay of Cales, or thereabouts, fighting with the 34 Dutch Smyrna fleete; sinking the King Salamon, a ship worth a L150,000 or more, some say L200,000, and another; and taking of three merchant-ships. Two of our ships were disabled, by the Dutch unfortunately falling against their will against them; the Advice, Captain W. Poole, and Antelope, Captain Clerke: The Dutch men-of-war did little service. Captain Allen did receive many shots at distance before he would fire one gun, which he did not do till he come within pistol-shot of his enemy. The Spaniards on shore at Cales did stand laughing at the Dutch, to see them run away and flee to the shore, 34 or thereabouts, against eight Englishmen at most. I do purpose to get the whole relation, if I live, of Captain Allen himself. In our loss of the two ships in the Bay of Gibraltar, it is observable how the world do comment upon the misfortune of Captain Moone of the Nonesuch (who did lose, in the same manner, the Satisfaction), as a person that hath ill-luck attending him; without considering that the whole fleete was ashore. Captain Allen led the way, and Captain Allen himself writes that all the masters of the fleete, old and young, were mistaken, and did carry their ships aground. But I think I heard the Duke say that Moone, being put into the Oxford, had in this conflict regained his credit, by sinking one and taking another. Captain Seale of the Milford hath done his part very well, in boarding the King Salamon, which held out half an hour after she was boarded; and his men kept her an hour after they did master her, and then she sunk, and drowned about 17 of her men. Thence to Jervas's, my mind, God forgive me, running too much after some folly, but 'elle' not being within I away by coach to the 'Change, and thence home to dinner. And finding Mrs. Bagwell waiting at the office after dinner, away she and I to a cabaret where she and I have eat before, and there I had her company 'tout' and had 'mon plaisir' of 'elle'. But strange to see how a woman, notwithstanding her greatest pretences of love 'a son mari' and religion, may be 'vaincue'. Thence to the Court of the Turkey Company at Sir Andrew Rickard's to treat about carrying some men of ours to Tangier, and had there a very civil reception, though a denial of the thing as not practicable with them, and I think so too. So to my office a little and to Jervas's again, thinking 'avoir rencontrais' Jane, 'mais elle n'etait pas dedans'. So I back again and to my office, where I did with great content 'ferais' a vow to mind my business, and 'laisser aller les femmes' for a month, and am with all my heart glad to find myself able to come to so good a resolution, that thereby I may follow my business, which and my honour thereby lies a bleeding. So home to supper and to bed.

24th. Up and by coach to Westminster Hall and the Parliament House, and there spoke with Mr. Coventry and others about business and so back to the 'Change, where no news more than that the Dutch have, by consent of all the Provinces, voted no trade to be suffered for eighteen months, but that they apply themselves wholly to the warr.

> [This statement of a total prohibition of all trade, and for so long a period as eighteen months, by a government so essentially commercial as that of the United Provinces, seems extraordinary. The fact was, that when in the beginning of the year 1665 the States General saw that the war with England was become inevitable, they took several vigorous measures, and determined to equip a formidable fleet, and with a view to obtain a sufficient number of men to man it, prohibited all navigation, especially in the great and small fisheries as they were then called, and in the whale fishery. This measure appears to have resembled the embargoes so commonly resorted to in this country on similar occasions, rather than a total prohibition of trade.--B.]

And they say it is very true, but very strange, for we use to believe they cannot support themselves without trade. Thence home to dinner and then to the office, where all the afternoon, and at night till very late, and then home to supper and bed, having a great cold, got on Sunday last, by sitting too long with my head bare, for Mercer to comb my hair and wash my eares.

25th. Up, and busy all the morning, dined at home upon a hare pye, very good meat, and so to my office again, and in the afternoon by coach to attend the Council at White Hall, but come too late, so back with Mr. Gifford, a merchant, and he and I to the Coffee-house, where I met Mr. Hill, and there he tells me that he is to be Assistant to the Secretary of the Prize Office (Sir Ellis Layton), which is to be held at Sir Richard Ford's, which, methinks, is but something low, but perhaps may bring him something considerable; but it makes me alter my opinion of his being so rich as to make a fortune for Mrs. Pickering. Thence home and visited Sir J. Minnes, who continues ill, but is something better; there he told me what a mad freaking fellow Sir Ellis Layton hath been, and is, and once at Antwerp was really mad. Thence to my office late, my cold troubling me, and having by squeezing myself in a coach hurt my testicles, but I hope will cease its pain without swelling. So home out of order, to supper and to bed.

26th. Lay, being in some pain, but not much, with my last night's bruise, but up and to my office, where busy all the morning, the like after dinner till very late, then home to supper and to bed. My wife mightily troubled with the tooth ake, and my cold not being gone yet, but my bruise yesterday goes away again, and it chiefly occasioned I think now from the sudden change of the weather from a frost to a great rayne on a sudden.

27th. Called up by Mr. Creed to discourse about some Tangier business, and he gone I made me ready and found Jane Welsh, Mr. Jervas his mayde, come to tell me that she was gone from her master, and is resolved to stick to this sweetheart of hers, one Harbing (a very sorry little fellow, and poor), which I did in a word or two endeavour to dissuade her from, but being unwilling to keep her long at my house, I sent her away and by and by followed her to the Exchange, and thence led her about down to the 3 Cranes, and there took boat for the Falcon, and at a house looking into the fields there took up and sat an hour or two talking and discoursing . . . . Thence having endeavoured to make her think of making herself happy by staying out her time with her master and other counsels, but she told me she could not do it, for it was her fortune to have this man, though she did believe it would be to her ruine, which is a strange, stupid thing, to a fellow of no kind of worth in the world and a beggar to boot. Thence away to boat again and landed her at the Three Cranes again, and I to the Bridge, and so home, and after shifting myself, being dirty, I to the 'Change, and thence to Mr. Povy's and there dined, and thence with him and Creed to my Lord Bellasses', and there debated a great while how to put things in order against his going, and so with my Lord in his coach to White Hall, and with him to my Lord Duke of Albemarle, finding him at cards. After a few dull words or two, I away to White Hall again, and there delivered a letter to the Duke of Yorke about our Navy business, and thence walked up and down in the gallery, talking with Mr. Slingsby, who is a very ingenious person, about the Mint and coynage of money. Among other things, he argues that there being L700,000 coined in the Rump time, and by all the Treasurers of that time, it being their opinion that the Rump money was in all payments, one with another, about a tenth part of all their money. Then, says he, to my question, the nearest guess we can make is, that the money passing up and down in business is L7,000,000. To another question of mine he made me fully understand that the old law of prohibiting bullion to be exported, is, and ever was a folly and an injury, rather than good. Arguing thus, that if the exportations exceed importations, then the balance must be brought home in money, which, when our merchants know cannot be carried out again, they will forbear to bring home in money, but let it lie abroad for trade, or keepe in foreign banks: or if our importations exceed our exportations, then, to keepe credit, the merchants will and must find ways of carrying out money by stealth, which is a most easy thing to do, and is every where done; and therefore the law against it signifies nothing in the world. Besides, that it is seen, that where money is free, there is great plenty; where it is restrained, as here, there is a great want, as in Spayne. These and many other fine discourses I had from him. Thence by coach home (to see Sir J. Minnes first), who is still sick, and I doubt worse than he seems to be. Mrs. Turner here took me into her closet, and there did give me a glass of most pure water, and shewed me her Rocke, which indeed is a very noble thing but a very bawble. So away to my office, where late, busy, and then home to supper and to bed.

28th. Up and to my office, where all the morning, and then home to dinner, and after dinner abroad, walked to Paul's Churchyard, but my books not bound, which vexed me. So home to my office again, where very late about business, and so home to supper and to bed, my cold continuing in a great degree upon me still. This day I received a good sum of money due to me upon one score or another from Sir G. Carteret, among others to clear all my matters about Colours,--[Flags]--wherein a month or two since I was so embarrassed and I thank God I find myself to have got clear, by that commodity, L50 and something more; and earned it with dear pains and care and issuing of my owne money, and saved the King near L100 in it.

29th (Lord's day). Up and to my office, where all the morning, putting papers to rights which now grow upon my hands. At noon dined at home. All the afternoon at my business again. In the evening come Mr. Andrews and Hill, and we up to my chamber and there good musique, though my great cold made it the less pleasing to me. Then Mr. Hill (the other going away) and I to supper alone, my wife not appearing, our discourse upon the particular vain humours of Mr. Povy, which are very extraordinary indeed. After supper I to Sir W. Batten's, where I found him, Sir W. Pen, Sir J. Robinson, Sir R. Ford and Captain Cocke and Mr. Pen, junior. Here a great deal of sorry disordered talk about the Trinity House men, their being exempted from land service. But, Lord! to see how void of method and sense their discourse was, and in what heat, insomuch as Sir R. Ford (who we judged, some of us, to be a little foxed) fell into very high terms with Sir W. Batten, and then with Captain Cocke. So that I see that no man is wise at all times. Thence home to prayers and to bed.

30th. This is solemnly kept as a Fast all over the City, but I kept my house, putting my closett to rights again, having lately put it out of order in removing my books and things in order to being made clean. At this all day, and at night to my office, there to do some business, and being late at it, comes Mercer to me, to tell me that my wife was in bed, and desired me to come home; for they hear, and have, night after night, lately heard noises over their head upon the leads. Now it is strange to think how, knowing that I have a great sum of money in my house, this puts me into a most mighty affright, that for more than two hours, I could not almost tell what to do or say, but feared this and that, and remembered that this evening I saw a woman and two men stand suspiciously in the entry, in the darke; I calling to them, they made me only this answer, the woman said that the men came to see her; but who she was I could not tell. The truth is, my house is mighty dangerous, having so many ways to be come to; and at my windows, over the stairs, to see who goes up and down; but, if I escape to-night, I will remedy it. God preserve us this night safe! So at almost two o'clock, I home to my house, and, in great fear, to bed, thinking every running of a mouse really a thiefe; and so to sleep, very brokenly, all night long, and found all safe in the morning.

31st. Up and with Sir W. Batten to Westminster, where to speak at the House with my Lord Bellasses, and am cruelly vexed to see myself put upon businesses so uncertainly about getting ships for Tangier being ordered, a servile thing, almost every day. So to the 'Change, back by coach with Sir W. Batten, and thence to the Crowne, a taverne hard by, with Sir W. Rider and Cutler, where we alone, a very good dinner. Thence home to the office, and there all the afternoon late. The office being up, my wife sent for me, and what was it but to tell me how Jane carries herself, and I must put her away presently. But I did hear both sides and find my wife much in fault, and the grounds of all the difference is my wife's fondness of Tom, to the being displeased with all the house beside to defend the boy, which vexes me, but I will cure it. Many high words between my wife and I, but the wench shall go, but I will take a course with the boy, for I fear I have spoiled him already. Thence to the office, to my accounts, and there at once to ease my mind I have made myself debtor to Mr. Povy for the L117 5s. got with so much joy the last month, but seeing that it is not like to be kept without some trouble and question, I do even discharge my mind of it, and so if I come now to refund it, as I fear I shall, I shall now be ne'er a whit the poorer for it, though yet it is some trouble to me to be poorer by such a sum than I thought myself a month since. But, however, a quiet mind and to be sure of my owne is worth all. The Lord be praised for what I have, which is this month come down to L1257. I staid up about my accounts till almost two in the morning.

DIARY OF SAMUEL PEPYS.

FEBRUARY 1664-1665

February 1st. Lay long in bed, which made me, going by coach to St. James's by appointment to have attended the Duke of Yorke and my Lord Bellasses, lose the hopes of my getting something by the hire of a ship to carry men to Tangier. But, however, according to the order of the Duke this morning, I did go to the 'Change, and there after great pains did light of a business with Mr. Gifford and Hubland [Houblon] for bringing me as much as I hoped for, which I have at large expressed in my stating the case of the "King's Fisher," which is the ship that I have hired, and got the Duke of Yorke's agreement this afternoon after much pains and not eating a bit of bread till about 4 o'clock. Going home I put in to an ordinary by Temple Barr and there with my boy Tom eat a pullet, and thence home to the office, being still angry with my wife for yesterday's foolery. After a good while at the office, I with the boy to the Sun behind the Exchange, by agreement with Mr. Young the flag-maker, and there was met by Mr. Hill, Andrews, and Mr. Hubland, a pretty serious man. Here two very pretty savoury dishes and good discourse. After supper a song, or three or four (I having to that purpose carried Lawes's book), and staying here till 12 o'clock got the watch to light me home, and in a continued discontent to bed. After being in bed, my people come and say there is a great stinke of burning, but no smoake. We called up Sir J. Minnes's and Sir W. Batten's people, and Griffin, and the people at the madhouse, but nothing could be found to give occasion to it. At this trouble we were till past three o'clock, and then the stinke ceasing, I to sleep, and my people to bed, and lay very long in the morning.

2nd. Then up and to my office, where till noon and then to the 'Change, and at the Coffee-house with Gifford, Hubland, the Master of the ship, and I read over and approved a charter-party for carrying goods for Tangier, wherein I hope to get some money. Thence home, my head akeing for want of rest and too much business. So to the office. At night comes, Povy, and he and I to Mrs. Bland's to discourse about my serving her to helpe her to a good passage for Tangier. Here I heard her kinswoman sing 3 or 4 very fine songs and in good manner, and then home and to supper. My cook mayd Jane and her mistresse parted, and she went away this day. I vexed to myself, but was resolved to have no more trouble, and so after supper to my office and then to bed.

3rd. Up, and walked with my boy (whom, because of my wife's making him idle, I dare not leave at home) walked first to Salsbury court, there to excuse my not being at home at dinner to Mrs. Turner, who I perceive is vexed, because I do not serve her in something against the great feasting for her husband's Reading--[On his appointment as Reader in Law.]--in helping her to some good penn'eths, but I care not. She was dressing herself by the fire in her chamber, and there took occasion to show me her leg, which indeed is the finest I ever saw, and she not a little proud of it. Thence to my Lord Bellasses; thence to Mr. Povy's, and so up and down at that end of the town about several businesses, it being a brave frosty day and good walking. So back again on foot to the 'Change, in my way taking my books from binding from my bookseller's. My bill for the rebinding of some old books to make them suit with my study, cost me, besides other new books in the same bill, L3; but it will be very handsome. At the 'Change did several businesses, and here I hear that newes is come from Deale, that the same day my Lord Sandwich sailed thence with the fleete, that evening some Dutch men of warr were seen on the back side of the Goodwin, and, by all conjecture, must be seen by my Lord's fleete; which, if so, they must engage. Thence, being invited, to my uncle Wight's, where the Wights all dined; and, among the others, pretty Mrs. Margaret, who indeed is a very pretty lady; and though by my vowe it costs me 12d. a kiss after the first, yet I did adventure upon a couple. So home, and among other letters found one from Jane, that is newly gone, telling me how her mistresse won't pay her her Quarter's wages, and withal tells me how her mistress will have the boy sit 3 or 4 hours together in the dark telling of stories, but speaks of nothing but only her indiscretion in undervaluing herself to do it, but I will remedy that, but am vexed she should get some body to write so much because of making it publique. Then took coach and to visit my Lady Sandwich, where she discoursed largely to me her opinion of a match, if it could be thought fit by my Lord, for my Lady Jemimah, with Sir G. Carteret's eldest son; but I doubt he hath yet no settled estate in land. But I will inform myself, and give her my opinion. Then Mrs. Pickering (after private discourse ended, we going into the other room) did, at my Lady's command, tell me the manner of a masquerade

[The masquerade at Court took place on the 2nd, and is referred to by Evelyn, who was present, in his Diary. Some amusing incidents connected with the entertainment are related in the "Grammont Memoirs" (chapter vii.).]

before the King and Court the other day. Where six women (my Lady Castlemayne and Duchesse of Monmouth being two of them) and six men (the Duke of Monmouth and Lord Arran and Monsieur Blanfort, being three of them) in vizards, but most rich and antique dresses, did dance admirably and most gloriously. God give us cause to continue the mirthe! So home, and after awhile at my office to supper and to bed.

4th. Lay long in bed discoursing with my wife about her mayds, which by Jane's going away in discontent and against my opinion do make some trouble between my wife and me. But these are but foolish troubles and so not to be set to heart, yet it do disturb me mightily these things. To my office, and there all the morning. At noon being invited, I to the Sun behind the 'Change, to dinner to my Lord Belasses, where a great deal of discourse with him, and some good, among others at table he told us a very handsome passage of the King's sending him his message about holding out the town of Newarke, of which he was then governor for the King. This message he sent in a sluggbullet, being writ in cypher, and wrapped up in lead and swallowed. So the messenger come to my

Lord and told him he had a message from the King, but it was yet in his belly; so they did give him some physique, and out it come. This was a month before the King's flying to the Scotts; and therein he told him that at such a day, being the 3d or 6th of May, he should hear of his being come to the Scotts, being assured by the King of France that in coming to them he should be used with all the liberty, honour, and safety, that could be desired. And at the just day he did come to the Scotts. He told us another odd passage: how the King having newly put out Prince Rupert of his generallshipp, upon some miscarriage at Bristoll, and Sir Richard Willis

[Sir Richard Willis, the betrayer of the Royalists, was one of the "Sealed Knot." When the Restoration had become a certainty, he wrote to Clarendon imploring him to intercede for him with the king (see Lister's "Life of Clarendon," vol. iii., p. 87).]

of his governorship of Newarke, at the entreaty of the gentry of the County, and put in my Lord Bellasses, the great officers of the King's army mutinyed, and come in that manner with swords drawn, into the market-place of the towne where the King was; which the King hearing, says, "I must to horse." And there himself personally, when every body expected they should have been opposed, the King come, and cried to the head of the mutineers, which was Prince Rupert, "Nephew, I command you to be gone." So the Prince, in all his fury and discontent, withdrew, and his company scattered, which they say was the greatest piece of mutiny in the world. Thence after dinner home to my office, and in the evening was sent to by Jane that I would give her her wages. So I sent for my wife to my office, and told her that rather than be talked on I would give her all her wages for this Quarter coming on, though two months is behind, which vexed my wife, and we begun to be angry, but I took myself up and sent her away, but was cruelly vexed in my mind that all my trouble in this world almost should arise from my disorders in my family and the indiscretion of a wife that brings me nothing almost (besides a comely person) but only trouble and discontent. She gone I late at my business, and then home to supper and to bed.

5th (Lord's day). Lay in bed most of the morning, then up and down to my chamber, among my new books, which is now a pleasant sight to me to see my whole study almost of one binding. So to dinner, and all the afternoon with W. Hewer at my office endorsing of papers there, my business having got before me much of late. In the evening comes to see me Mr. Sheply, lately come out of the country, who goes away again to-morrow, a good and a very kind man to me. There come also Mr. Andrews and Hill, and we sang very pleasantly; and so, they being gone, I and my wife to supper, and to prayers and bed.

6th. Up and with Sir J. Minnes and Sir W. Pen to St. James's, but the Duke is gone abroad. So to White Hall to him, and there I spoke with him, and so to Westminster, did a little business, and then home to the 'Change, where also I did some business, and went off and ended my contract with the "Kingfisher" I hired for Tangier, and I hope to get something by it. Thence home to dinner, and visited Sir W. Batten, who is sick again, worse than he was, and I am apt to think is very ill. So to my office, and among other things with Sir W. Warren 4 hours or more till very late, talking of one thing or another, and have concluded a firm league with him in all just ways to serve him and myself all I can, and I think he will be a most usefull and thankfull man to me. So home to supper and to bed. This being one of the coldest days, all say, they ever felt in England; and I this day, under great apprehensions of getting an ague from my putting a suit on that hath lain by without ayring a great while, and I pray God it do not do me hurte.

7th. Up and to my office, where busy all the morning, and at home to dinner. It being Shrove Tuesday, had some very good fritters. All the afternoon and evening at the office, and at night home to supper and to bed. This day, Sir W. Batten, who hath been sicke four or five days, is now very bad, so as people begin to fear his death; and I am at a loss whether it will be better for me to have him die, because he is a bad man, or live, for fear a worse should come.

8th. Up and by coach to my Lord Peterborough's, where anon my Lord Ashly and Sir Thomas Ingram met, and Povy about his accounts, who is one of the most unhappy accountants that ever I knew in all my life, and one that if I were clear in reference to my bill of L117 he should be hanged before I would ever have to do with him, and as he understands nothing of his business himself, so he hath not one about him that do. Here late till I was weary, having business elsewhere, and thence home by coach, and after dinner did several businesses and very late at my office, and so home to supper and to bed.

9th. Up and to my office, where all the morning very busy. At noon home to dinner, and then to my office again, where Sir William Petty come, among other things to tell me that Mr. Barlow

> [Thomas Barlow, Pepys's predecessor as Clerk of the Acts, to whom he paid part of the salary. Barlow held the office jointly with Dennis Fleeting.]

is dead; for which, God knows my heart, I could be as sorry as is possible for one to be for a stranger, by whose death he gets L100 per annum, he being a worthy, honest man; but after having considered that when I come to consider the providence of God by this means unexpectedly to give me L100 a year more in my estate, I have cause to bless God, and do it from the bottom of my heart. So home late at night, after twelve o'clock, and so to bed.

10th. Up and abroad to Paul's Churchyard, there to see the last of my books new bound: among others, my "Court of King James,"

> ["The Court and Character of King James, written and taken by Sir Anthony Weldon, being an eye and eare witnesse," was published in 1650, and reprinted in 1651 under the title of "Truth brought to Light" Weldon's book was answered in a work entitled "Aulicus Coquinariae."

Both the original book and the answer were reprinted in "The Secret History of the Court of King James," Edinburgh, 1811, two vols. (edited by Sir Walter Scott).]

and "The Rise and Fall of the Family of the Stewarts;" and much pleased I am now with my study; it being, methinks, a beautifull sight. Thence (in Mr. Grey's coach, who took me up), to Westminster, where I heard that yesterday the King met the Houses to pass the great bill for the L2,500,000. After doing a little business I home, where Mr. Moore dined with me, and evened our reckonings on my Lord Sandwich's bond to me for principal and interest. So that now on both there is remaining due to me L257. 7s., and I bless God it is no more. So all the afternoon at my office, and late home to supper, prayers, and to bed.

11th. Up and to my office, where all the morning. At noon to 'Change by coach with my Lord Brunkard, and thence after doing much business home to dinner, and so to my office all the afternoon till past 12 at night very busy. So home to bed.

12th (Lord's day). Up and to church to St. Lawrence to hear Dr. Wilkins, the great scholar, for curiosity, I having never heard him: but was not satisfied with him at all, only a gentleman sat in the pew I by chance sat in, that sang most excellently, and afterward I found by his face that he had been a Paul's scholler, but know not his name, and I was also well pleased with the church, it being a very fine church. So home to dinner, and then to my office all the afternoon doing of business, and in the evening comes Mr. Hill (but no Andrews) and we spent the evening very finely, singing, supping and discoursing. Then to prayers and to bed.

13th. Up and to St. James's, did our usual business before the Duke. Thence I to Westminster and by water (taking Mr. Stapely the rope-maker by the way), to his rope-ground and to Limehouse, there to see the manner of stoves and did excellently inform myself therein, and coming home did go on board Sir W. Petty's "Experiment," which is a brave roomy vessel, and I hope may do well. So went on shore to a Dutch [house] to drink some mum, and there light upon some Dutchmen, with whom we had good discourse touching stoveing

[Stoveing, in sail-making, is the heating of the bolt-ropes, so as to make them pliable.--B.]

and making of cables. But to see how despicably they speak of us for our using so many hands more to do anything than they do, they closing a cable with 20, that we use 60 men upon. Thence home and eat something, and then to my office, where very late, and then to supper and to bed. Captain Stokes, it seems, is at last dead at Portsmouth.

14th (St. Valentine). This morning comes betimes Dicke Pen, to be my wife's Valentine, and come to our bedside. By the same token, I had him brought to my side, thinking to have made him kiss me; but he perceived me, and would not; so went to his Valentine: a notable, stout, witty boy. I up about business, and, opening the door, there was Bagwell's wife, with whom I talked afterwards, and she had the confidence to say she came with a hope to be time enough to be my Valentine, and so indeed she did, but my oath preserved me from loosing any time with her, and so I and my boy abroad by coach to Westminster, where did two or three businesses, and then home to the 'Change, and did much business there. My Lord Sandwich is, it seems, with his fleete at Alborough Bay. So home to dinner and then to the office, where till 12 almost at night, and then home to supper and to bed.

15th. Up and to my office, where busy all the morning. At noon with Creed to dinner to Trinity-house, where a very good dinner among the old sokers, where an extraordinary discourse of the manner of the loss of the "Royall Oake" coming home from Bantam, upon the rocks of Scilly, many passages therein very extraordinary, and if I can I will get it in writing. Thence with Creed to Gresham College, where I had been by Mr. Povy the last week proposed to be admitted a member;

> [According to the minutes of the Royal Society for February 15th, 1664-65, "Mr. Pepys was unanimously elected and admitted." Notes of the experiments shown by Hooke and Boyle are given in Birch's "History of the Royal Society," vol. ii., p. 15.]

and was this day admitted, by signing a book and being taken by the hand by the President, my Lord Brunkard, and some words of admittance said to me. But it is a most acceptable thing to hear their discourse, and see their experiments; which were this day upon the nature of fire, and how it goes out in a place where the ayre is not free, and sooner out where the ayre is exhausted, which they showed by an engine on purpose. After this being done, they to the Crowne Taverne, behind the 'Change, and there my Lord and most of the company to a club supper; Sir P. Neale, Sir R. Murrey, Dr. Clerke, Dr. Whistler, Dr. Goddard, and others of most eminent worth. Above all, Mr. Boyle to-day was at the meeting, and above him Mr. Hooke, who is the most, and promises the least, of any man in the world that ever I saw. Here excellent discourse till ten at night, and then home, and to Sir W. Batten's, where I hear that Sir Thos. Harvy intends to put Mr. Turner out of his house and come in himself, which will be very hard to them, and though I love him not, yet for his family's sake I pity him. So home and to bed.

16th. Up, and with Mr. Andrews to White Hall, where a Committee of Tangier, and there I did our victuallers' business for some more money, out of which I hope to get a little, of which I was glad; but, Lord! to see to what a degree of contempt, nay, scorn, Mr. Povy, through his prodigious folly, hath brought himself in his accounts, that if he be not a man of a great interest, he will be kicked out of his employment for a foole, is very strange, and that most deservedly that ever man was, for never any man, that understands accounts so little, ever went through so much, and yet goes through it with the greatest shame and yet with confidence that ever I saw man in my life. God deliver me in my owne business of my bill out of his hands, and if ever I foul my fingers with him again let me suffer for it! Back to the 'Change, and thence home to dinner, where Mrs. Hunt dined with me, and poor Mrs. Batters; who brought her little daughter with her, and a letter from her husband, wherein, as a token, the foole presents me very seriously with his daughter for me to take the charge of bringing up for him, and to make my owne. But I took no notice to her at all of the substance of the letter, but fell to discourse, and so went away to the office, where all the afternoon till almost one in the morning, and then home to bed.

17th. Up, and it being bitter cold, and frost and snow, which I had thought had quite left us, I by coach to Povy's, where he told me, as I knew already, how he was handled the other day, and is still, by my Lord Barkeley, and among other things tells me, what I did not know, how my Lord Barkeley will say openly, that he hath fought more set fields--[Battles or actions]--than any man in England hath done. I did my business with him, which was to get a little sum of money paid, and so home with Mr. Andrews, who met me there, and there to the office. At noon home and there found Lewellin, which vexed me out of my old jealous humour. So to my office, where till 12 at night, being only a little while at noon at Sir W. Batten's to see him, and had some high words with Sir J. Minnes about Sir W. Warren, he calling him cheating knave, but I cooled him, and at night at Sir W. Pen's, he being to go to Chatham to-morrow. So home to supper and to bed.

18th. Up, and to the office, where sat all the morning; at noon to the 'Change, and thence to the Royall Oake taverne in Lumbard Streete, where Sir William Petty and the owners of the double-bottomed boat (the Experiment) did entertain my Lord Brunkard, Sir R. Murrey, myself, and others, with marrow bones and a chine of beefe of the victuals they have made for this ship; and excellent company and good discourse: but, above all, I do value Sir William Petty. Thence home; and took my Lord Sandwich's draught of the harbour of Portsmouth down to Ratcliffe, to one Burston, to make a plate for the King, and another for the Duke, and another for himself; which will be very neat. So home, and till almost one o'clock in the morning at my office, and then home to supper and to bed. My Lord Sandwich, and his fleete of twenty-five ships in the Downes, returned from cruising, but could not meet with any Dutchmen.

19th. Lay in bed, it being Lord's day, all the morning talking with my wife, sometimes pleased, sometimes displeased, and then up and to dinner. All the afternoon also at home, and Sir W. Batten's, and in the evening comes Mr. Andrews, and we sung together, and then to supper, he not staying, and at supper hearing by accident of my mayds their letting in a rogueing Scotch woman that haunts the office, to helpe them to washe and scoure in our house, and that very lately, I fell mightily out, and made my wife, to the disturbance of the house and neighbours, to beat our little girle, and then we shut her down into the cellar, and there she lay all night. So we to bed.

20th. Up, and with Sir J. Minnes to attend the Duke, and then we back again and rode into the beginning of my Lord Chancellor's new house, near St.

James's; which common people have already called Dunkirke-house, from their opinion of his having a good bribe for the selling of that towne. And very noble I believe it will be. Near that is my Lord Barkeley beginning another on one side, and Sir J. Denham on the other. Thence I to the House of Lords and spoke with my Lord Bellasses, and so to the 'Change, and there did business, and so to the Sun taverne, haling in the morning had some high words with Sir J. Lawson about his sending of some bayled goods to Tangier, wherein the truth is I did not favour him, but being conscious that some of my profits may come out by some words that fell from him, and to be quiet, I have accommodated it. Here we dined merry; but my club and the rest come to 7s. 6d., which was too much. Thence to the office, and there found Bagwell's wife, whom I directed to go home, and I would do her business, which was to write a letter to my Lord Sandwich for her husband's advance into a better ship as there should be occasion. Which I did, and by and by did go down by water to Deptford, and then down further, and so landed at the lower end of the town, and it being dark 'entrer en la maison de la femme de Bagwell', and there had 'sa compagnie', though with a great deal of difficulty, 'neanmoins en fin j'avais ma volont d'elle', and being sated therewith, I walked home to Redriffe, it being now near nine o'clock, and there I did drink some strong waters and eat some bread and cheese, and so home. Where at my office my wife comes and tells me that she hath hired a chamber mayde, one of the prettiest maydes that ever she saw in her life, and that she is really jealous of me for her, but hath ventured to hire her from month to month, but I think she means merrily. So to supper and to bed.

21st. Up, and to the office (having a mighty pain in my forefinger of my left hand, from a strain that it received last night) in struggling 'avec la femme que je' mentioned yesterday, where busy till noon, and then my wife being busy in going with her woman to a hot-house to bathe herself, after her long being within doors in the dirt, so that she now pretends to a resolution of being hereafter very clean. How long it will hold I can guess. I dined with Sir W. Batten and my Lady, they being now a'days very fond of me. So to the 'Change, and off of the 'Change with Mr. Wayth to a cook's shop, and there dined again for discourse with him about Hamaccos

[Or hammock-battens: cleats or battens nailed to the sides of a vessel's beams, from which to suspend the seamen's hammocks.]

and the abuse now practised in tickets, and more like every day to be. Also of the great profit Mr. Fen makes of his place, he being, though he demands but 5 per cent. of all he pays, and that is easily computed, but very little pleased with any man that gives him no more. So to the office, and after office my Lord Brunkerd carried me to Lincolne's Inne Fields, and there I with my Lady Sandwich (good lady) talking of innocent discourse of good housewifery and husbands for her daughters, and the luxury and looseness of the times and other such things till past 10 o'clock at night, and so by coach home, where a little at my office, and so to supper and to bed. My Lady tells me how my Lord

Castlemayne is coming over from France, and is believed will be made friends with his Lady again. What mad freaks the Mayds of Honour at Court have: that Mrs. Jenings, one of the Duchesses mayds, the other day dressed herself like an orange wench, and went up and down and cried oranges; till falling down, or by such accident, though in the evening, her fine shoes were discerned, and she put to a great deale of shame; that such as these tricks being ordinary, and worse among them, thereby few will venture upon them for wives: my Lady Castlemayne will in merriment say that her daughter (not above a year old or two) will be the first mayde in the Court that will be married. This day my Lord Sandwich writ me word from the Downes, that he is like to be in towne this week.

22nd. Lay last night alone, my wife after her bathing lying alone in another bed. So cold all night. Up and to the office, where busy all the morning. At noon at the 'Change, busy; where great talk of a Dutch ship in the North put on shore, and taken by a troop of horse. Home to dinner and Creed with me. Thence to Gresham College, where very noble discourse, and thence home busy till past 12 at night, and then home to supper and to bed. Mrs. Bland come this night to take leave of me and my wife, going to Tangier.

23rd. This day, by the blessing of Almighty God, I have lived thirty-two years in the world, and am in the best degree of health at this minute that I have been almost in my life time, and at this time in the best condition of estate that ever I was in-the Lord make me thankfull. Up, and to the office, where busy all the morning. At noon to the 'Change, where I hear the most horrid and astonishing newes that ever was yet told in my memory, that De Ruyter with his fleete in Guinny hath proceeded to the taking of whatever we have, forts, goods, ships, and men, and tied our men back to back, and thrown them all into the sea, even women and children also. This a Swede or Hamburgher is come into the River and tells that he saw the thing done.

> [Similar reports of the cruelty of the English to the Dutch in Guinea were credited in Holland, and were related by Downing in a letter to Clarendon from the Hague, dated April 14th, 1665 (Lister's "Life of Clarendon," vol. iii., p. 374).]

But, Lord! to see the consternation all our merchants are in is observable, and with what fury and revenge they discourse of it. But I fear it will like other things in a few days cool among us. But that which I fear most is the reason why he that was so kind to our men at first should afterward, having let them go, be so cruel when he went further. What I fear is that there he was informed (which he was not before) of some of Holmes's dealings with his countrymen, and so was moved to this fury. God grant it be not so! But a more dishonourable thing was never suffered by Englishmen, nor a more barbarous done by man, as this by them to us. Home to dinner, and then to the office, where we sat all the afternoon, and then at night to take my finall leave of Mrs. Bland, who sets out to-morrow for Tangier, and then I back to my office till past 12, and so home to supper and to bed.

24th. Up, and to my office, where all the morning upon advising again with some fishermen and the water bayliffe of the City, by Mr. Coventry's direction, touching the protections which are desired for the fishermen upon the River, and I am glad of the occasion to make me understand something of it. At noon home to dinner, and all the afternoon till 9 at night in my chamber, and Mr. Hater with me (to prevent being disturbed at the office), to perfect my contract book, which, for want of time, hath a long time lain without being entered in as I used to do from month to month. Then to my office, where till almost 12, and so home to bed.

25th. Up, and to the office, where all the morning. At noon to the 'Change; where just before I come, the Swede that had told the King and the Duke so boldly this great lie of the Dutch flinging our men back to back into the sea at Guinny, so particularly, and readily, and confidently, was whipt round the 'Change: he confessing it a lie, and that he did it in hopes to get something. It is said the judges, upon demand, did give it their opinion that the law would judge him to be whipt, to lose his eares, or to have his nose slit but I do not hear that anything more is to be done to him. They say he is delivered over to the Dutch Embassador to do what he pleased with him. But the world do think that there is some design on one side or other, either of the Dutch or French, for it is not likely a fellow would invent such a lie to get money whereas he might have hoped for a better reward by telling something in behalf of us to please us. Thence to the Sun taverne, and there dined with Sir W. Warren and Mr. Gifford, the merchant: and I hear how Nich. Colborne, that lately lived and got a great estate there, is gone to live like a prince in the country, and that this Wadlow, that did the like at the Devil by St. Dunstane's, did go into the country, and there spent almost all he had got, and hath now choused this Colborne out of his house, that he might come to his old trade again. But, Lord! to see how full the house is, no room for any company almost to come into it. Thence home to the office, where dispatched much business; at night late home, and to clean myself with warm water; my wife will have me, because she do herself, and so to bed.

26th (Sunday). Up and to church, and so home to dinner, and after dinner to my office, and there busy all the afternoon, till in the evening comes Mr. Andrews and Hill, and so home and to singing. Hill staid and supped with me, and very good discourse of Italy, where he was, which is always to me very agreeable. After supper, he gone, we to prayers and to bed.

27th. Up and to St. James's, where we attended the Duke as usual. This morning I was much surprized and troubled with a letter from Mrs. Bland, that she is left behind, and much trouble it cost me this day to find out some way to carry her after the ships to Plymouth, but at last I hope I have done it. At noon to the 'Change to inquire what wages the Dutch give in their men-of-warr at this day, and I hear for certain they give but twelve guilders at most, which is not full 24s., a thing I wonder at. At home to dinner, and then in Sir J. Minnes's coach, my wife and I with him, and also Mercer, abroad, he and I to White Hall, and he would have his coach to wait upon my wife on her visits, it being the first time my wife hath been out of doors (but the other day to bathe her) several weeks. We to a Committee of the Council to discourse concerning pressing of men; but, Lord! how they meet; never sit down: one comes, now another goes, then comes another; one complaining that nothing is done, another swearing that he hath been there these two hours and nobody come. At last it come to this, my Lord Annesly, says he, "I think we must be forced to get the King to come to every committee; for I do not see that we do any thing at any time but when he is here." And I believe he said the truth and very constant he is at the council table on council-days; which his predecessors, it seems, very rarely did; but thus I perceive the greatest affair in the world at this day is likely to be managed by us. But to hear how my Lord Barkeley and others of them do cry up the discipline of the late times here, and in the former Dutch warr is strange, wishing with all their hearts that the business of religion were not so severely carried on as to discourage the sober people to come among us, and wishing that the same law and severity were used against drunkennesse as there was then, saying that our evil living will call the hand of God upon us again. Thence to walk alone a good while in St. James's Parke with Mr. Coventry, who I perceive is grown a little melancholy and displeased to see things go as they do so carelessly. Thence I by coach to Ratcliffe highway, to the plate-maker's, and he has begun my Lord Sandwich's plate very neatly, and so back again. Coming back I met Colonell Atkins, who in other discourse did offer to give me a piece to receive of me 20 when he proves the late news of the Dutch, their drowning our men, at Guinny, and the truth is I find the generality of the world to fear that there is something of truth in it, and I do fear it too. Thence back by coach to Sir Philip Warwicke's; and there he did contract with me a kind of friendship and freedom of communication, wherein he assures me to make me understand the whole business of the Treasurer's business of the Navy, that I shall know as well as Sir G. Carteret what money he hath; and will needs have me come to him sometimes, or he meet me, to discourse of things tending to the serving the King: and I am mighty proud and happy in becoming so known to such a man. And I hope shall pursue it. Thence back home to the office a little tired and out of order, and then to supper and to bed.

28th: At the office all the morning. At noon dined at home. After dinner my wife and I to my Lady batten's, it being the first time my wife hath been there, I think, these two years, but I had a mind in part to take away the strangenesse, and so we did, and all very quiett and kind. Come home, I to the taking my wife's kitchen accounts at the latter end of the month, and there find 7s. wanting, which did occasion a very high falling out between us, I indeed too angrily insisting upon so poor a thing, and did give her very provoking high words, calling her beggar, and reproaching her friends, which she took very stomachfully and reproached me justly with mine; and I confess, being myself, I cannot see what she could have done less. I find she is very cunning, and when she least shews it hath her wit at work; but it is an ill one, though I think not so bad but with good usage I might well bear with it, and the truth is I do find that my being over-solicitous and jealous and froward and ready to reproach her do make her worse. However, I find that now and then a little difference do no hurte, but too much of it will make her know her force too much. We parted after many high words very angry, and I to my office to my month's accounts, and find myself worth L1270, for which the Lord God be praised! So at almost 2 o'clock in the morning I home to supper and to bed, and so ends this month, with great expectation of the Hollanders coming forth, who are, it seems, very high and rather more ready than we. God give a good issue to it!

THE DIARY OF SAMUEL PEPYS M.A. F.R.S.
CLERK OF THE ACTS AND SECRETARY TO THE ADMIRALTY
TRANSCRIBED FROM THE SHORTHAND MANUSCRIPT IN THE
PEPYSIAN LIBRARY
MAGDALENE COLLEGE CAMBRIDGE BY THE REV. MYNORS
BRIGHT M.A. LATE FELLOW
AND PRESIDENT OF THE COLLEGE
(Unabridged)
WITH LORD BRAYBROOKE'S NOTES
EDITED WITH ADDITIONS BY
HENRY B. WHEATLEY F.S.A.

DIARY OF SAMUEL PEPYS.

MARCH & APRIL 1664-1665

March 1st. Up, and this day being the day than: by a promise, a great while ago, made to my wife, I was to give her L20 to lay out in clothes against Easter, she did, notwithstanding last night's falling out, come to peace with me and I with her, but did boggle mightily at the parting with my money, but at last did give it her, and then she abroad to buy her things, and I to my office, where busy all the morning. At noon I to dinner at Trinity House, and thence to Gresham College, where Mr. Hooke read a second very curious lecture about the late Comett; among other things proving very probably that this is the very same Comett that appeared before in the year 1618, and that in such a time probably it will appear again, which is a very new opinion; but all will be in print. Then to the meeting, where Sir G. Carteret's two sons, his owne, and Sir N. Slaning, were admitted of the society: and this day I did pay my admission money, 40s. to the society. Here was very fine discourses and experiments, but I do lacke philosophy enough to understand them, and so cannot remember them. Among others, a very particular account of the making of the several sorts of bread in France, which is accounted the best place for bread in the world. So home, where very busy getting an answer to some question of Sir Philip Warwicke touching the expense of the navy, and that being done I by coach at 8 at night with my wife and Mercer to Sir Philip's and discoursed with him (leaving them in the coach), and then back with them home and to supper and to bed.

2nd. Begun this day to rise betimes before six o'clock, and, going down to call my people, found Besse and the girle with their clothes on, lying within their bedding upon the ground close by the fireside, and a candle burning all night, pretending they would rise to scoure. This vexed me, but Besse is going and so she will not trouble me long. Up, and by water to Burston about my Lord's plate, and then home to the office, so there all the morning sitting. At noon dined with Sir W. Batten (my wife being gone again to-day to buy things, having bought nothing yesterday for lack of Mrs. Pierces company), and thence to the office again, where very busy till 12 at night, and vexed at my wife's staying out so late, she not being at home at 9 o'clock, but at last she is come home, but the reason of her stay I know not yet. So shut up my books, and home to supper and to bed.

3rd. Up, and abroad about several things, among others to see Mr. Peter Honiwood, who was at my house the other day, and I find it was for nothing but to pay me my brother John's Quarterage. Thence to see Mrs. Turner, who takes it mighty ill I did not come to dine with the Reader, her husband, which, she says, was the greatest feast that ever was yet kept by a Reader, and I believe it was well. But I am glad I did not go, which confirms her in an opinion that I am growne proud. Thence to the 'Change, and to several places, and so home to dinner and to my office, where till 12 at night writing over a discourse of mine to Mr. Coventry touching the Fishermen of the Thames upon a reference of the business by him to me concerning their being protected from presse. Then home to supper and to bed.

4th. Up very betimes, and walked, it being bitter cold, to Ratcliffe, to the plate-maker's and back again. To the office, where we sat all the morning, I, with being empty and full of ayre and wind, had some pain to-day. Dined alone at home, my wife being gone abroad to buy some more things. All the afternoon at the office. William Howe come to see me, being come up with my Lord from sea: he is grown a discreet, but very conceited fellow. He tells me how little respectfully Sir W. Pen did carry it to my Lord onboard the Duke's ship at sea; and that Captain Minnes, a favourite of Prince Rupert's, do shew my Lord little respect; but that every body else esteems my Lord as they ought. I am sorry for the folly of the latter, and vexed at the dissimulation of the former. At night home to supper and to bed. This day was proclaimed at the 'Change the war with Holland.

5th (Lord's day). Up, and Mr. Burston bringing me by order my Lord's plates, which he has been making this week. I did take coach and to my Lord Sandwich's and dined with my Lord; it being the first time he hath dined at home since his coming from sea: and a pretty odd demand it was of my Lord to my Lady before me: "How do you, sweetheart? How have you done all this week?" himself taking notice of it to me, that he had hardly seen her the week before. At dinner he did use me with the greatest solemnity in the world, in carving for me, and nobody else, and calling often to my Lady to cut for me; and all the respect possible. After dinner looked over the plates, liked them mightily, and indeed I think he is the most exact man in what he do in the world of that kind. So home again, and there after a song or two in the evening with Mr. Hill, I to my office, and then home to supper and to bed.

6th. Up, and with Sir J. Minnes by coach, being a most lamentable cold day as any this year, to St. James's, and there did our business with the Duke. Great preparations for his speedy return to sea. I saw him try on his buff coat and hatpiece covered with black velvet. It troubles me more to think of his venture, than of anything else in the whole warr. Thence home to dinner, where I saw Besse go away; she having of all wenches that ever lived with us received the greatest love and kindnesse and good clothes, besides wages, and gone away with the greatest ingratitude. I then abroad to look after my Hamaccoes, and so home, and there find our new chamber-mayde, Mary, come, which instead of handsome, as my wife spoke and still seems to reckon, is a very ordinary wench, I think, and therein was mightily disappointed. To my office, where busy late, and then home to supper and to bed, and was troubled all this night with a pain in my left testicle, that run up presently into my left kidney and there kept akeing all night. In great pain.

7th. Up, and was pretty well, but going to the office, and I think it was sitting with my back to the fire, it set me in a great rage again, that I could not continue till past noon at the office, but was forced to go home, nor could sit down to dinner, but betook myself to my bed, and being there a while my pain begun to abate and grow less and less. Anon I went to make water, not dreaming of any thing but my testicle that by some accident I might have bruised as I used to do, but in pissing there come from me two stones, I could feel them, and caused my water to be looked into; but without any pain to me in going out, which makes me think that it was not a fit of the stone at all; for my pain was asswaged upon my lying down a great while before I went to make water. Anon I made water again very freely and plentifully. I kept my bed in good ease all the evening, then rose and sat up an hour or two, and then to bed and lay till 8 o'clock, and then,

8th. Though a bitter cold day, yet I rose, and though my pain and tenderness in my testicle remains a little, yet I do verily think that my pain yesterday was nothing else, and therefore I hope my disease of the stone may not return to me, but void itself in pissing, which God grant, but I will consult my physitian. This morning is brought me to the office the sad newes of "The London," in which Sir J. Lawson's men were all bringing her from Chatham to the Hope, and thence he was to go to sea in her; but a little a'this side the buoy of the Nower, she suddenly blew up. About 24 [men] and a woman that were in the round-house and coach saved; the rest, being above 300, drowned: the ship breaking all in pieces, with 80 pieces of brass ordnance. She lies sunk, with her round-house above water. Sir J. Lawson hath a great loss in this of so many good chosen men, and many relations among them. I went to the 'Change, where the news taken very much to heart. So home to dinner, and Mr. Moore with me. Then I to Gresham College, and there saw several pretty experiments, and so home and to my office, and at night about 11 home to supper and to bed.

9th. Up and to the office, where we sat all the afternoon. At noon to dinner at home, and then abroad with my wife, left her at the New Exchange and I to Westminster, where I hear Mrs. Martin is brought to bed of a boy and christened Charles, which I am very glad of, for I was fearful of being called to be a godfather to it. But it seems it was to be done suddenly, and so I escaped. It is strange to see how a liberty and going abroad without purpose of doing anything do lead a man to what is bad, for I was just upon going to her, where I must of necessity [have] broken my oath or made a forfeit. But I did not, company being (I heard by my porter) with her, and so I home again, taking up my wife, and was set down by her at Paule's Schoole, where I visited Mr. Crumlum at his house; and, Lord! to see how ridiculous a conceited pedagogue he is, though a learned man, he being so dogmaticall in all he do and says. But among other discourse, we fell to the old discourse of Paule's Schoole; and he did, upon my declaring my value of it, give me one of Lilly's grammars of a very old impression, as it was in the Catholique times, which I shall much set by. And so, after some small discourse, away and called upon my wife at a linen draper's shop buying linen, and so home, and to my office, where late, and home to supper and to bed. This night my wife had a new suit of flowered ash-coloured silke, very noble.

10th. Up, and to the office all the morning. At noon to the 'Change, where very hot, people's proposal of the City giving the King' another ship for "The London," that is lately blown up, which would be very handsome, and if well managed, might be done; but I fear if it be put into ill hands, or that the courtiers do solicit it, it will never be done. Home to dinner, and thence to the Committee of Tangier at White Hall, where my Lord Barkely and Craven and others; but, Lord! to see how superficially things are done in the business of the Lottery, which will be the disgrace of the Fishery, and without profit. Home, vexed at my loss of time, and thereto my office. Late at night come the two Bellamys, formerly petty warrant Victuallers of the Navy, to take my advice about a navy debt of theirs for the compassing of which they offer a great deal of money, and the thing most just. Perhaps I may undertake it, and get something by it, which will be a good job. So home late to bed.

11th. Up and to the office, at noon home to dinner, and to the office again, where very late, and then home to supper and to bed. This day returned Sir W. Batten and Sir J. Minnes from Lee Roade, where they have been to see the wrecke of "The London," out of which, they say, the guns may be got, but the hull of her will be wholly lost, as not being capable of being weighed.

12th (Lord's day). Up, and borrowing Sir J. Minnes's coach, to my Lord Sandwich's, but he was gone abroad. I sent the coach back for my wife, my Lord a second time dining at home on purpose to meet me, he having not dined once at home but those times since his coming from sea. I sat down and read over the Bishop of Chichester's' sermon upon the anniversary of the King's death, much cried up, but, methinks, but a mean sermon. By and by comes in my Lord, and he and I to talke of many things in the Navy, one from another, in general, to see how the greatest things are committed to very ordinary men, as to parts and experience, to do; among others, my Lord Barkeley. We talked also of getting W. Howe to be put into the Muster-Mastershipp in the roome of Creed, if Creed will give way, but my Lord do it without any great gusto, calling Howe a proud coxcomb in passion. Down to dinner, where my wife in her new lace whiske, which, indeed, is very noble, and I much pleased with it, and so my Lady also. Here very pleasant my Lord was at dinner, and after dinner did look over his plate, which Burston hath brought him to-day, and is the last of the three that he will have made. After satisfied with that, he abroad, and I after much discourse with my Lady about Sir G. Carteret's son, of whom she hath some thoughts for a husband for my Lady Jemimah, we away home by coach again, and there sang a good while very pleasantly with Mr. Andrews and Hill. They gone; we to supper, and betimes to bed.

13th. Up betimes, this being the first morning of my promise upon a forfeite not to lie in bed a quarter of an hour after my first waking. Abroad to St. James's, and there much business, the King also being with us a great while. Thence to the 'Change, and thence with Captain Tayler and Sir W. Warren dined at a house hard by for discourse sake, and so I home, and there meeting a letter from Mrs. Martin desiring to speak with me, I (though against my promise of visiting her) did go, and there found her in her childbed dress desiring my favour to get her husband a place. I staid not long, but taking Sir W. Warren up at White Hall home, and among other discourse fell to a business which he says shall if accomplished bring me L100. He gone, I to supper and to bed. This day my wife begun to wear light-coloured locks, quite white almost, which, though it makes her look very pretty, yet not being natural, vexes me, that I will not have her wear them. This day I saw my Lord Castlemayne at St. James's, lately come from France.

14th. Up before six, to the office, where busy all the morning. At noon dined with Sir W. Batten and Sir J. Minnes, at the Tower, with Sir J. Robinson, at a farewell dinner which he gives Major Holmes at his going out of the Tower, where he hath for some time, since his coming from Guinny, been a prisoner, and, it seems, had presented the Lieutenant with fifty pieces yesterday. Here a great deale of good victuals and company. Thence home to my office, where very late, and home to supper and to bed weary of business.

15th. Up and by coach with Sir W. Batten to St. James's, where among other things before the Duke, Captain Taylor was called in, and, Sir J. Robinson his accuser not appearing, was acquitted quite from his charge, and declared that he should go to Harwich, which I was very well pleased at. Thence I to Mr. Coventry's chamber, and there privately an houre with him in discourse of the office, and did deliver to him many notes of things about which he is to get the Duke's command, before he goes, for the putting of business among us in better order. He did largely owne his dependance as to the office upon my care, and received very great expressions of love from him, and so parted with great satisfaction to myself. So home to the 'Change, and thence home to dinner, where my wife being gone down upon a sudden warning from my Lord Sandwich's daughters to the Hope with them to see "The Prince," I dined alone. After dinner to the office, and anon to Gresham College, where, among other good discourse, there was tried the great poyson of Maccassa upon a dogg,

["The experiment of trying to poison a dog with some of the Macassar powder in which a needle had been dipped was made, but without success."--Pepys himself made a communication at this meeting of the information he had received from the master of the Jersey ship, who had been in company of Major Holmes in the Guinea voyage, concerning the pendulum watches (Birch's "History," vol. ii., p. 23).]

but it had no effect all the time we sat there. We anon broke up and I home, where late at my office, my wife not coming home. I to bed, troubled, about 12 or past.

16th. Up and to the office, where we sat all the morning, my wife coming home from the water this morning, having lain with them on board "The Prince" all night. At noon home to dinner, where my wife told me the unpleasant journey she had yesterday among the children, whose fear upon the water and folly made it very unpleasing to her. A good dinner, and then to the office again. This afternoon Mr. Harris, the sayle-maker, sent me a noble present of two large silver candlesticks and snuffers, and a slice to keep them upon, which indeed is very handsome. At night come Mr. Andrews with L36, the further fruits of my Tangier contract, and so to bed late and weary with business, but in good content of mind, blessing God for these his benefits.

17th. Up and to my office, and then with Sir W. Batten to St. James's, where many come to take leave, as was expected, of the Duke, but he do not go till Monday. This night my Lady Wood died of the small-pox, and is much lamented among the great persons for a good-natured woman and a good wife, but for all that it was ever believed she was as others are. The Duke did give us some commands, and so broke up, not taking leave of him. But the best piece of newes is, that instead of a great many troublesome Lords, the whole business is to be left with the Duke of Albemarle to act as Admirall in his stead; which is a thing that do cheer my heart. For the other would have vexed us with attendance, and never done the business. Thence to the Committee of Tangier, where the Duke a little, and then left us and we staid. A very great Committee, the Lords Albemarle, Sandwich, Barkely, Fitzharding, Peterborough, Ashley, Sir Thos. Ingram, Sir G. Carteret and others. The whole business was the stating of Povy's accounts, of whom to say no more, never could man say worse himself nor have worse said of him than was by the company to his face; I mean, as to his folly and very reflecting words to his honesty. Broke up without anything but trouble and shame, only I got my businesses done to the signing of two bills for the Contractors and Captain Taylor, and so come away well pleased, and home, taking up my wife at the 'Change, to dinner. After dinner out again bringing my wife to her father's again at Charing Cross, and I to the Committee again, where a new meeting of trouble about Povy, who still makes his business worse and worse, and broke up with the most open shame again to him, and high words to him of disgrace that they would not trust him with any more money till he had given an account of this. So broke up. Then he took occasion to desire me to step aside, and he and I by water to London together. In the way, of his owne accord, he proposed to me that he would surrender his place of Treasurer' to me to have half the profit. The thing is new to me; but the more I think the more I like it, and do put him upon getting it done by the Duke. Whether it takes or no I care not, but I think at present it may have some convenience in it. Home, and there find my wife come home and gone to bed, of a cold got yesterday by water. At the office Bellamy come to me again, and I am in hopes something may be got by his business. So late home to supper and bed.

18th. Up and to the office, where all the morning. At noon to the 'Change, and took Mr. Hill along with me to Mr. Povy's, where we dined, and shewed him the house to his good content, and I expect when we meet we shall laugh at it. But I having business to stay, he went away, and Povy and Creed and I to do some business upon Povy's accounts all the afternoon till late at night, where, God help him! never man was so confounded, and all his people about him in this world as he and his are. After we had done something [to the] purpose we broke up, and Povy acquainted me before Creed (having said something of it also this morning at our office to me) what he had done in speaking to the Duke and others about his making me Treasurer, and has carried it a great way, so as I think it cannot well be set back. Creed, I perceive, envies me in it, but I think as that will do me no hurte, so if it did I am at a great losse to think whether it were not best for me to let it wholly alone, for it will much disquiett me and my business of the Navy, which in this warr will certainly be worth all my time to me. Home, continuing in this doubtfull condition what to think of it, but God Almighty do his will in it for the best. To my office, where late, and then home to supper and to bed.

19th (Lord's day). Mr. Povy sent his coach for me betimes, and I to him, and there to our great trouble do find that my Lord FitzHarding do appear for Mr. Brunkard

[Henry Brouncker, younger brother of William, Viscount Brouncker, President of the Royal Society. He was Groom of the Bedchamber to the Duke of York, and succeeded to the office of Cofferer on the death of William Ashburnham in 1671. His character was bad, and his conduct in the sea-fight of 1665 was impugned. He was expelled from the House of Commons, but succeeded to his brother's title in 1684. He died in January, 1687.]

to be Paymaster upon Povy's going out, by a former promise of the Duke's, and offering to give as much as any for it. This put us all into a great dumpe, and so we went to Creed's new lodging in the Mewes, and there we found Creed with his parrot upon his shoulder, which struck Mr. Povy coming by just by the eye, very deep, which, had it hit his eye, had put it out. This a while troubled us, but not proving very bad, we to our business consulting what to do; at last resolved, and I to Mr. Coventry, and there had his most friendly and ingenuous advice, advising me not to decline the thing, it being that that will bring me to be known to great persons, while now I am buried among three or four of us, says he, in the Navy; but do not make a declared opposition to my Lord FitzHarding. Thence I to Creed, and walked talking in the Park an hour with him, and then to my Lord Sandwich's to dinner, and after dinner to Mr. Povy's, who hath been with the Duke of Yorke, and, by the mediation of Mr. Coventry, the Duke told him that the business shall go on, and he will take off Brunkerd, and my Lord FitzHarding is quiett too. But to see the mischief, I hear that Sir G. Carteret did not seem pleased, but said nothing when he heard me proposed to come in

Povy's room, which may learn me to distinguish between that man that is a man's true and false friend. Being very glad of this news Mr. Povy and I in his coach to Hyde Parke, being the first day of the tour there. Where many brave ladies; among others, Castlemayne lay impudently upon her back in her coach asleep, with her mouth open. There was also my Lady Kerneguy,

[Daughter of William, Duke of Hamilton, wife of Lord Carnegy, who became Earl of Southesk on his father's death. She is frequently mentioned in the "Memoires de Grammont," and in the letters of the second Earl of Chesterfield.--B.]

once my Lady Anne Hambleton, that is said to have given the Duke a clap upon his first coming over. Here I saw Sir J. Lawson's daughter and husband, a fine couple, and also Mr. Southwell and his new lady, very pretty. Thence back, putting in at Dr. Whore's, where I saw his lady, a very fine woman. So home, and thither by my desire comes by and by Creed and lay with me, very merry and full of discourse, what to do to-morrow, and the conveniences that will attend my having of this place, and I do think they may be very great.

20th. Up, Creed and I, and had Mr. Povy's coach sent for us, and we to his house; where we did some business in order to the work of this day. Povy and I to my Lord Sandwich, who tells me that the Duke is not only a friend to the business, but to me, in terms of the greatest love and respect and value of me that can be thought, which overjoys me. Thence to St. James's, and there was in great doubt of Brunkerd, but at last I hear that Brunkerd desists. The Duke did direct Secretary Bennet, who was there, to declare his mind to the Tangier Committee, that he approves of me for Treasurer; and with a character of me to be a man whose industry and discretion he would trust soon as any man's in England: and did the like to my Lord Sandwich. So to White Hall to the Committee of Tangier, where there were present, my Lord of Albemarle, my Lord Peterborough, Sandwich, Barkeley, FitzHarding, Secretary Bennet, Sir Thomas Ingram, Sir John Lawson, Povy and I. Where, after other business, Povy did declare his business very handsomely; that he was sorry he had been so unhappy in his accounts, as not to give their Lordships the satisfaction he intended, and that he was sure his accounts are right, and continues to submit them to examination, and is ready to lay down in ready money the fault of his account; and that for the future, that the work might be better done and with more quiet to him, he desired, by approbation of the Duke, he might resign his place to Mr. Pepys. Whereupon, Secretary Bennet did deliver the Duke's command, which was received with great content and allowance beyond expectation; the Secretary repeating also the Duke's character of me. And I could discern my Lord FitzHarding was well pleased with me, and signified full satisfaction, and whispered something seriously of me to the Secretary. And there I received their constitution under all their hands presently; so that I am already confirmed their Treasurer, and put into a condition of striking of tallys;

[The practice of striking tallies at the Exchequer was a curious survival of an ancient method of keeping accounts. The method adopted is described in Hubert Hall's "Antiquities and Curiosities of the Exchequer," 1891. The following account of the use of tallies, so frequently alluded to in the Diary, was supplied by Lord Braybrooke. Formerly accounts were kept, and large sums of money paid and received, by the King's Exchequer, with little other form than the exchange or delivery of tallies, pieces of wood notched or scored, corresponding blocks being kept by the parties to the account; and from this usage one of the head officers of the Exchequer was called the tallier, or teller. These tallies were often negotiable; Adam Smith, in his "Wealth of Nations," book ii., ch. xi., says that "in 1696 tallies had been at forty, and fifty, and sixty per cent. discount, and bank-notes at twenty per cent." The system of tallies was discontinued in 1824; and the destruction of the old Houses of Parliament, in the night of October 16th, 1834, is thought to have been occasioned by the overheating of the flues, when the furnaces were employed to consume the tallies rendered useless by the alteration in the mode of keeping the Exchequer accounts.]

and all without one harsh word or word of dislike, but quite the contrary; which is a good fortune beyond all imagination. Here we rose, and Povy and Creed and I, all full of joy, thence to dinner, they setting me down at Sir J. Winter's, by promise, and dined with him; and a worthy fine man he seems to be, and of good discourse, our business was to discourse of supplying the King with iron for anchors, if it can be judged good enough, and a fine thing it is to see myself come to the condition of being received by persons of this rank, he being, and having long been, Secretary to the Queene-Mother. Thence to Povy's, and there sat and considered of business a little and then home, where late at it, W. Howe being with me about his business of accounts for his money laid out in the fleet, and he gone, I home to supper and to bed. Newes is this day come of Captain Allen's being come home from the Straights, as far as Portland, with eleven of the King's ships, and about twenty-two of merchantmen.

21st. Up, and my taylor coming to me, did consult all my wardrobe how to order my clothes against next summer. Then to the office, where busy all the morning. At noon to the 'Change, and brought home Mr. Andrews, and there with Mr. Sheply dined and very merry, and a good dinner. Thence to Mr. Povy's to discourse about settling our business of Treasurer, and I think all things will go very fayre between us and to my content, but the more I see the more silly the man seems to me. Thence by coach to the Mewes, but Creed was not there. In our way the coach drove through a lane by Drury Lane, where abundance of loose women stood at the doors, which, God forgive me, did put evil thoughts in me, but proceeded no further, blessed be God. So home, and late at my office, then home and there found a couple of state cups, very large, coming, I suppose, each to about L6 a piece, from Burrows the slopseller.

22nd. Up, and to Mr. Povy's about our business, and thence I to see Sir Ph. Warwicke, but could not meet with him. So to Mr. Coventry, whose profession of love and esteem for me to myself was so large and free that I never could expect or wish for more, nor could have it from any man in England, that I should value it more. Thence to Mr. Povy's, and with Creed to the 'Change and to my house, but, it being washing day, dined not at home, but took him (I being invited) to Mr. Hubland's, the merchant, where Sir William Petty, and abundance of most ingenious men, owners and freighters of "The Experiment," now going with her two bodies to sea. Most excellent discourse. Among others, Sir William Petty did tell me that in good earnest he hath in his will left such parts of his estate to him that could invent such and such things. As among others, that could discover truly the way of milk coming into the breasts of a woman; and he that could invent proper characters to express to another the mixture of relishes and tastes. And says, that to him that invents gold, he gives nothing for the philosopher's stone; for (says he) they that find out that, will be able to pay themselves. But, says he, by this means it is better than to give to a lecture; for here my executors, that must part with this, will be sure to be well convinced of the invention before they do part with their money. After dinner Mr. Hill took me with Mrs. Hubland, who is a fine gentlewoman, into another room, and there made her sing, which she do very well, to my great content. Then to Gresham College, and there did see a kitling killed almost quite, but that we could not quite kill her, with such a way; the ayre out of a receiver, wherein she was put, and then the ayre being let in upon her revives her immediately;

["Two experiments were made for the finding out a way to breathe under water, useful for divers." The first was on a bird and the second on "a kitling" (Birch's "History," vol. ii., p. 25).]

nay, and this ayre is to be made by putting together a liquor and some body that ferments, the steam of that do do the work. Thence home, and thence to White Hall, where the house full of the Duke's going to-morrow, and thence to St. James's, wherein these things fell out: (1) I saw the Duke, kissed his hand, and had his most kind expressions of his value and opinion of me, which comforted me above all things in the world, (2) the like from Mr. Coventry most heartily and affectionately. (3) Saw, among other fine ladies, Mrs. Middleton,

Jane, daughter to Sir Robert Needham, is frequently mentioned in the "Grammont Memoirs," and Evelyn calls her "that famous and indeed incomparable beauty" ("Diary," August 2nd, 1683). Her portrait is in the Royal Collection amongst the beauties of Charles II.'s Court. Sir Robert Needham was related to John Evelyn.]

a very great beauty I never knew or heard of before; (4) I saw Waller the poet, whom I never saw before. So, very late, by coach home with W. Pen, who was there. To supper and to bed, with my heart at rest, and my head very busy thinking of my several matters now on foot, the new comfort of my old navy business, and the new one of my employment on Tangier.

23rd. Up and to my Lord Sandwich, who follows the Duke this day by water down to the Hope, where "The Prince" lies. He received me, busy as he was, with mighty kindness and joy at my promotions; telling me most largely how the Duke hath expressed on all occasions his good opinion of my service and love for me. I paid my thanks and acknowledgement to him; and so back home, where at the office all the morning. At noon to the 'Change. Home, and Lewellin dined with me. Thence abroad, carried my wife to Westminster by coach, I to the Swan, Herbert's, and there had much of the good company of Sarah and to my wish, and then to see Mrs. Martin, who was very kind, three weeks of her month of lying in is over. So took up my wife and home, and at my office a while, and thence to supper and to bed. Great talk of noises of guns heard at Deale, but nothing particularly whether in earnest or not.

24th. Up betimes, and by agreement to the Globe taverne in Fleet Street to Mr. Clerke, my sollicitor, about the business of my uncle's accounts, and we went with one Jefferys to one of the Barons (Spelman), and there my accounts were declared and I sworn to the truth thereof to my knowledge, and so I shall after a few formalities be cleared of all. Thence to Povy's, and there delivered him his letters of greatest import to him that is possible, yet dropped by young Bland, just come from Tangier, upon the road by Sittingburne, taken up and sent to Mr. Pett, at Chatham. Thus everything done by Povy is done with a fatal folly and neglect. Then to our discourse with him, Creed, Mr. Viner, myself and Poyntz about the business of the Workehouse at Clerkenwell, and after dinner went thither and saw all the works there, and did also consult the Act concerning the business and other papers in order to our coming in to undertake it with Povy, the management of the House, but I do not think we can safely meddle with it, at least I, unless I had time to look after it myself, but the thing is very ingenious and laudable. Thence to my Lady Sandwich's, where my wife all this day, having kept Good Friday very strict with fasting. Here we supped, and talked very merry. My Lady alone with me, very earnest about Sir G. Carteret's son, with whom I perceive they do desire my Lady Jemimah may be matched. Thence home and to my office, and then to bed.

25th (Lady day). Up betimes and to my office, where all the morning. At noon dined alone with Sir W. Batten, where great discourse of Sir W. Pen, Sir W. Batten being, I perceive, quite out of love with him, thinking him too great and too high, and began to talk that the world do question his courage, upon which I told him plainly I have been told that he was articled against for it, and that Sir H. Vane was his great friend therein. This he was, I perceive, glad to hear. Thence to the office, and there very late, very busy, to my great content. This afternoon of a sudden is come home Sir W. Pen from the fleete, but upon what score I know not. Late home to supper and to bed.

26th (Lord's day and Easter day). Up (and with my wife, who has not been at church a month or two) to church. At noon home to dinner, my wife and I (Mercer staying to the Sacrament) alone. This is the day seven years which, by the blessing of God, I have survived of my being cut of the stone, and am now in very perfect good health and have long been; and though the last winter hath been as hard a winter as any have been these many years, yet I never was better in my life, nor have not, these ten years, gone colder in the summer than I have done all this winter, wearing only a doublet, and a waistcoate cut open on the back; abroad, a cloake and within doors a coate I slipped on. Now I am at a losse to know whether it be my hare's foot which is my preservative against wind, for I never had a fit of the collique since I wore it, and nothing but wind brings me pain, and the carrying away of wind takes away my pain, or my keeping my back cool; for when I do lie longer than ordinary upon my back in bed, my water the next morning is very hot, or whether it be my taking of a pill of turpentine every morning, which keeps me always loose, or all together, but this I know, with thanks to God Almighty, that I am now as well as ever I can wish or desire to be, having now and then little grudgings of wind, that brings me a little pain, but it is over presently, only I do find that my backe grows very weak, that I cannot stoop to write or tell money without sitting but I have pain for a good while after it. Yet a week or two ago I had one day's great pain; but it was upon my getting a bruise on one of my testicles, and then I did void two small stones, without pain though, and, upon my going to bed and bearing up of my testicles, I was well the next. But I did observe that my sitting with my back to the fire at the office did then, as it do at all times, make my back ake, and my water hot, and brings me some pain. I sent yesterday an invitation to Mrs. Turner and her family to come to keep this day with me, which she granted, but afterward sent me word that it being Sunday and Easter day she desired to choose another and put off this. Which I was willing enough to do; and so put it off as to this day, and will leave it to my own convenience when to choose another, and perhaps shall escape a feast by it. At my office all the afternoon drawing up my agreement with Mr. Povy for me to sign to him tomorrow morning. In the evening spent an hour in the garden walking with Sir J. Minnes, talking of the Chest business, wherein Sir W. Batten deals so unfairly, wherein the old man is very hot for the present, but that zeal will not last nor is to be trusted. So home to supper, prayers, and to bed.

27th. Up betimes to Mr. Povy's, and there did sign and seal my agreement with him about my place of being Treasurer for Tangier, it being the greatest part of it drawnout of a draught of his own drawing up, only I have added something here and there in favour of myself. Thence to the Duke of Albemarle, the first time that we officers of the Navy have waited upon him since the Duke of Yorke's going, who hath deputed him to be Admirall in his absence. And I find him a quiet heavy man, that will help business when he can, and hinder nothing, and am very well pleased with our attendance on him. I did afterwards alone give him thanks for his favour to me about my Tangier business, which he received kindly, and did speak much of his esteem of me. Thence, and did the same to Sir H. Bennet, who did the like to me very fully, and did give me all his letters lately come from hence for me to read, which I returned in the afternoon to him. Thence to Mrs. Martin, who, though her husband is gone away, as he writes, like a fool into France, yet is as simple and wanton as ever she was, with much I made myself merry and away. So to my Lord Peterborough's; where Povy, Creed, Williamson, Auditor Beale, and myself, and mighty merry to see how plainly my Lord and Povy did abuse one another about their accounts, each thinking the other a foole, and I thinking they were not either of them, in that point, much in the wrong, though in everything, and even in this manner of reproaching one another, very witty and pleasant. Among other things, we had here the genteelest dinner and the neatest house that I have seen many a day, and the latter beyond anything I ever saw in a nobleman's house. Thence visited my Lord Barkeley, and did sit discoursing with him in his chamber a good while, and [he] mighty friendly to me about the same business of Tangier. From that to other discourse of the times and the want of money, and he said that the Parliament must be called again soon, and more money raised, not by tax, for he said he believed the people could not pay it, but he would have either a general excise upon everything, or else that every city incorporate should pay a toll into the King's revenue, as he says it is in all the cities in the world; for here a citizen hath no more laid on them than their neighbours in the country, whereas, as a city, it ought to pay considerably to the King for their charter; but I fear this will breed ill blood. Thence to Povy, and after a little talk home to my office late. Then to supper and to bed.

28th. Up betimes and to the office, where we sat all the morning, and I did most of the business there, God wot. Then to the 'Change, and thence to the Coffee-house with Sir W. Warren, where much good discourse for us both till 9 o'clock with great pleasure and content, and then parted and I home to dinner, having eat nothing, and so to my office. At night supped with my wife at Sir W. Pen's, who is to go back for good and all to the fleete to-morrow. Took leave and to my office, where till 12 at night, and then home to bed.

29th. Up betimes and to Povy's, where a good while talking about our business; thence abroad into the City, but upon his tally could not get any money in Lumbard Streete, through the disrepute which he suffers, I perceive, upon his giving up his place, which people think was not choice, but necessity, as indeed it was. So back to his house, after we had been at my house to taste my wine, but my wife being abroad nobody could come at it, and so we were defeated. To his house, and before dinner he and I did discourse of the business of freight, wherein I am so much concerned, above L100 for myself, and in my over hasty making a bill out for the rest for him, but he resolves to move Creed in it. Which troubled me much, and Creed by and by comes, and after dinner he did, but in the most cunning ingenious manner, do his business with Creed by bringing it in by the by, that the most subtile man in the world could never have done it better, and I must say that he is a most witty, cunning man and one that I (am) most afeard of in my conversation, though in all serious matters of business the eeriest foole that ever I met with. The bill was produced and a copy given Creed, whereupon he wrote his Intratur upon the originall, and I hope it will pass, at least I am now put to it that I must stand by it and justify it, but I pray God it may never come to that test. Thence between vexed and joyed, not knowing what yet to make of it, home, calling for my Lord Cooke's 3 volumes at my bookseller's, and so home, where I found a new cook mayd, her name is----- that promises very little. So to my office, where late about drawing up a proposal for Captain Taylor, for him to deliver to the City about his building the new ship, which I have done well, and I hope will do the business, and so home to supper and to bed.

30th. Up, and to my Lord Ashly, but did nothing, and to Sir Ph. Warwicke and spoke with him about business, and so back to the office, where all the morning. At noon home to dinner, and thence to the Tangier Committee, where, Lord! to see how they did run into the giving of Sir J. Lawson (who is come to towne to-day to get this business done) L4000 about his Mole business, and were going to give him 4s. per yarde more, which arises in the whole Mole to L36,000, is a strange thing, but the latter by chance was stopped, the former was given. Thence to see Mrs. Martin, whose husband being it seems gone away, and as she is informed he hath another woman whom he uses, and has long done, as a wife, she is mighty reserved and resolved to keep herself so till the return of her husband, which a pleasant thing to think of her. Thence home, and to my office, where late, and to bed.

31st. Up betimes and walked to my Lord Ashly, and there with Creed after long waiting spoke with him, and was civilly used by him; thence to Sir Ph. Warwicke, and then to visit my Lord of Falmouth, who did also receive me pretty civilly, but not as I expected; he, I perceive, believing that I had undertaken to justify Povy's accounts, taking them upon myself, but I rectified him therein. So to my Lady Sandwich's to dinner, and up to her chamber after dinner, and there discoursed about Sir G. Carteret's son, in proposition between us two for my Lady Jemimah. So to Povy, and with him spent the afternoon very busy, till I was weary of following this and neglecting my navy business. So at night called my wife at my Lady's, and so home. To my office and there made up my month's account, which, God be praised! rose to L1300. Which I bless God for. So after 12 o'clock home to supper and to bed. I find Creed mightily transported by my Lord of Falmouth's kind words to him, and saying that he hath a place in his intention for him, which he believes will be considerable. A witty man he is in every respect, but of no good nature, nor a man ordinarily to be dealt with. My Lady Castlemayne is sicke again, people think, slipping her filly.

DIARY OF SAMUEL PEPYS.

APRIL 1665

April 1st. All the morning very busy at the office preparing a last half-year's account for my Lord Treasurer. At noon eat a bit and stepped to Sir Ph. Warwicke, by coach to my Lord Treasurer's, and after some private conference and examining of my papers with him I did return into the City and to Sir G. Carteret, whom I found with the Commissioners of Prizes dining at Captain Cocke's, in Broad Streete, very merry. Among other tricks, there did come a blind fiddler to the doore, and Sir G. Carteret did go to the doore and lead the blind fiddler by the hand in. Thence with Sir G. Carteret to my Lord Treasurer, and by and by come Sir W. Batten and Sir J. Minnes, and anon we come to my Lord, and there did lay open the expence for the six months past, and an estimate of the seven months to come, to November next: the first arising to above L500,000, and the latter will, as we judge, come to above L1,000,000. But to see how my Lord Treasurer did bless himself, crying he could do no more than he could, nor give more money than he had, if the occasion and expence were never so great, which is but a sad story. And then to hear how like a passionate and ignorant asse Sir G. Carteret did harangue upon the abuse of Tickets did make me mad almost and yet was fain to hold my tongue. Thence home, vexed mightily to see how simply our greatest ministers do content themselves to understand and do things, while the King's service in the meantime lies a-bleeding. At my office late writing letters till ready to drop down asleep with my late sitting up of late, and running up and down a-days. So to bed.

2nd (Lord's day). At my office all the morning, renewing my vowes in writing and then home to dinner. All the afternoon, Mr. Tasborough, one of Mr. Povy's clerks, with me about his master's accounts. In the evening Mr. Andrews and Hill sang, but supped not with me, then after supper to bed.

3rd. Up and to the Duke of Albemarle and White Hall, where much business. Thence home and to dinner, and then with Creed, my wife, and Mercer to a play at the Duke's, of my Lord Orrery's, called "Mustapha," which being not good, made Betterton's part and Ianthe's but ordinary too, so that we were not contented with it at all. Thence home and to the office a while, and then home to supper and to bed. All the pleasure of the play was, the King and my Lady Castlemayne were there; and pretty witty Nell,--[Nell Gwynne]--at the King's house, and the younger Marshall sat next us; which pleased me mightily.

4th. All the morning at the office busy, at noon to the 'Change, and then went up to the 'Change to buy a pair of cotton stockings, which I did at the husband's shop of the most pretty woman there, who did also invite me to buy some linnen of her, and I was glad of the occasion, and bespoke some bands of her, intending to make her my seamstress, she being one of the prettiest and most modest looked women that ever I did see. Dined at home and to the office, where very late till I was ready to fall down asleep, and did several times nod in the middle of my letters.

5th. This day was kept publiquely by the King's command, as a fast day against the Dutch warr, and I betimes with Mr. Tooker, whom I have brought into the Navy to serve us as a husband to see goods timely shipped off from hence to the Fleete and other places, and took him with me to Woolwich and Deptford, where by business I have been hindered a great while of going, did a very great deale of business, and home, and there by promise find Creed, and he and my wife, Mercer and I by coach to take the ayre; and, where we had formerly been, at Hackney, did there eat some pullets we carried with us, and some things of the house; and after a game or two at shuffle-board, home, and Creed lay with me; but, being sleepy, he had no mind to talk about business, which indeed I intended, by inviting him to lie with me, but I would not force it on him, and so to bed, he and I, and to sleep, being the first time I have been so much at my ease and taken so much fresh ayre these many weeks or months.

6th. At the office sat all the morning, where, in the absence of Sir W. Batten, Sir G. Carteret being angry about the business of tickets, spoke of Sir W. Batten for speaking some words about the signing of tickets, and called Sir W. Batten in his discourse at the table to us (the clerks being withdrawn) "shitten foole," which vexed me. At noon to the 'Change, and there set my business of lighters' buying for the King, to Sir W. Warren, and I think he will do it for me to very great advantage, at which I am mightily rejoiced. Home and after a mouthfull of dinner to the office, where till 6 o'clock, and then to White Hall, and there with Sir G. Carteret and my Lord Brunkerd attended the Duke of Albemarle about the business of money. I also went to Jervas's, my barber, for my periwigg that was mending there, and there do hear that Jane is quite undone, taking the idle fellow for her husband yet not married, and lay with him several weeks that had another wife and child, and she is now going into Ireland. So called my wife at the 'Change and home, and at my office writing letters till one o'clock in the morning, that I was ready to fall down asleep again. Great talke of a new Comett; and it is certain one do now appear as bright as the late one at the best; but I have not seen it myself.

7th. Up betimes to the Duke of Albemarle about money to be got for the Navy, or else we must shut up shop. Thence to Westminster Hall and up and down, doing not much; then to London, but to prevent Povy's dining with me (who I see is at the 'Change) I went back again and to Herbert's at Westminster, there sent for a bit of meat and dined, and then to my Lord Treasurer's, and there with Sir Philip Warwicke, and thence to White Hall in my Lord Treasurer's chamber with Sir Philip Warwicke till dark night, about fower hours talking of the business of the Navy Charge, and how Sir G. Carteret do order business, keeping us in ignorance what he do with his money, and also Sir Philip did shew me nakedly the King's condition for money for the Navy; and he do assure me, unless the King can get some noblemen or rich money-gentlemen to lend him money, or to get the City to do it, it is impossible to find money: we having already, as he says, spent one year's share of the three-years' tax, which comes to

L2,500,000. Being very glad of this day's discourse in all but that I fear I shall quite lose Sir G. Carteret, who knows that I have been privately here all this day with Sir Ph. Warwicke. However, I will order it so as to give him as little offence as I can. So home to my office, and then to supper and to bed.

8th. Up, and all the morning full of business at the office. At noon dined with Mr. Povy, and then to the getting some business looked over of his, and then I to my Lord Chancellor's, where to have spoke with the Duke of Albemarle, but the King and Council busy, I could not; then to the Old Exchange and there of my new pretty seamstress bought four bands, and so home, where I found my house mighty neat and clean. Then to my office late, till past 12, and so home to bed. The French Embassadors

[The French ambassadors were Henri de Bourbon, Duc de Verneuil, natural son of Henry IV. and brother of Henrietta Maria, and M. de Courtin.--B.]

are come incognito before their train, which will hereafter be very pompous. It is thought they come to get our King to joyne with the King of France in helping him against Flanders, and they to do the like to us against Holland. We have laine a good while with a good fleete at Harwich. The Dutch not said yet to be out. We, as high as we make our shew, I am sure, are unable to set out another small fleete, if this should be worsted. Wherefore, God send us peace! I cry.

9th (Lord's day). To church with my wife in the morning, in her new light-coloured silk gowne, which is, with her new point, very noble. Dined at home, and in the afternoon to Fanchurch, the little church in the middle of Fanchurch Streete, where a very few people and few of any rank. Thence, after sermon, home, and in the evening walking in the garden, my Lady Pen and her daughter walked with my wife and I, and so to my house to eat with us, and very merry, and so broke up and to bed.

10th. Up, and to the Duke of Albemarle's, and thence to White Hall to a Committee for Tangier, where new disorder about Mr. Povy's accounts, that I think I shall never be settled in my business of Treasurer for him. Here Captain Cooke met me, and did seem discontented about my boy Tom's having no time to mind his singing nor lute, which I answered him fully in, that he desired me that I would baste his coate. So home and to the 'Change, and thence to the "Old James" to dine with Sir W. Rider, Cutler, and Mr. Deering, upon the business of hemp, and so hence to White Hall to have attended the King and Lord Chancellor about the debts of the navy and to get some money, but the meeting failed. So my Lord Brunkard took me and Sir Thomas Harvy in his coach to the Parke, which is very troublesome with the dust; and ne'er a great beauty there to-day but Mrs. Middleton, and so home to my office, where Mr. Warren proposed my getting of L100 to get him a protection for a ship to go out, which I think I shall do. So home to supper and to bed.

11th. Up and betimes to Alderman Cheverton to treat with him about hempe, and so back to the office. At noon dined at the Sun, behind the 'Change, with Sir Edward Deering and his brother and Commissioner Pett, we having made a contract with Sir Edward this day about timber. Thence to the office, where late very busy, but with some trouble have also some hopes of profit too. So home to supper and to bed.

12th. Up, and to White Hall to a Committee of Tangier, where, contrary to all expectation, my Lord Ashly, being vexed with Povy's accounts, did propose it as necessary that Povy should be still continued Treasurer of Tangier till he had made up his accounts; and with such arguments as, I confess, I was not prepared to answer, but by putting off of the discourse, and so, I think, brought it right again; but it troubled me so all the day after, and night too, that I was not quiet, though I think it doubtfull whether I shall be much the worse for it or no, if it should come to be so. Dined at home and thence to White Hall again (where I lose most of my time now-a-days to my great trouble, charge, and loss of time and benefit), and there, after the Council rose, Sir G. Carteret, my Lord Brunkard, Sir Thomas Harvy, and myself, down to my Lord Treasurer's chamber to him and the Chancellor, and the Duke of Albemarle; and there I did give them a large account of the charge of the Navy, and want of money. But strange to see how they held up their hands crying, "What shall we do?" Says my Lord Treasurer, "Why, what means all this, Mr. Pepys? This is true, you say; but what would you have me to do? I have given all I can for my life. Why will not people lend their money? Why will they not trust the King as well as Oliver? Why do our prizes come to nothing, that yielded so much heretofore?" And this was all we could get, and went away without other answer, which is one of the saddest things that, at such a time as this, with the greatest action on foot that ever was in England, nothing should be minded, but let things go on of themselves do as well as they can. So home, vexed, and going to my Lady Batten's, there found a great many women with her, in her chamber merry, my Lady Pen and her daughter, among others; where my Lady Pen flung me down upon the bed, and herself and others, one after another, upon me, and very merry we were, and thence I home and called my wife with my Lady Pen to supper, and very merry as I could be, being vexed as I was. So home to bed.

13th. Lay long in bed, troubled a little with wind, but not much. So to the office, and there all the morning. At noon to Sheriff Waterman's to dinner, all of us men of the office in towne, and our wives, my Lady Carteret and daughters, and Ladies Batten, Pen, and my wife, &c., and very good cheer we had and merry; musique at and after dinner, and a fellow danced a jigg; but when the company begun to dance, I came away lest I should be taken out; and God knows how my wife carried herself, but I left her to try her fortune. So home, and late at the office, and then home to supper and to bed.

14th. Up, and betimes to Mr. Povy, being desirous to have an end of my trouble of mind touching my Tangier business, whether he hath any desire of accepting what my Lord Ashly offered, of his becoming Treasurer again; and there I did, with a seeming most generous spirit, offer him to take it back again upon his owne terms; but he did answer to me that he would not above all things in the world, at which I was for the present satisfied; but, going away thence and speaking with Creed, he puts me in doubt that the very nature of the thing will require that he be put in again; and did give me the reasons of the auditors, which, I confess, are so plain, that I know not how to withstand them. But he did give me most ingenious advice what to do in it, and anon, my Lord Barkeley and some of the Commissioners coming together, though not in a meeting, I did procure that they should order Povy's payment of his remain of accounts to me; which order if it do pass will put a good stop to the fastening of the thing upon me. At noon Creed and I to a cook's shop at Charing Cross, and there dined and had much discourse, and his very good upon my business, and upon other things, among the rest upon Will Howe's dissembling with us, we discovering one to another his carriage to us, present and absent, being a very false fellow. Thence to White Hall again, and there spent the afternoon, and then home to fetch a letter for the Council, and so back to White Hall, where walked an hour with Mr. Wren, of my Lord Chancellor's, and Mr. Ager, and then to Unthanke's and called my wife, and with her through the city to Mile-End Greene, and eat some creame and cakes and so back home, and I a little at the office, and so home to supper and to bed. This morning I was saluted with newes that the fleetes, ours and the Dutch, were engaged, and that the guns were heard at Walthamstow to play all yesterday, and that Captain Teddiman's legs were shot off in the Royall Katherine. But before night I hear the contrary, both by letters of my owne and messengers thence, that they were all well of our side and no enemy appears yet, and that the Royall Katherine is come to the fleete, and likely to prove as good a ship as any the King hath, of which I am heartily glad, both for Christopher Pett's sake and Captain Teddiman that is in her.

15th. Up, and to White Hall about several businesses, but chiefly to see the proposals of my warrants about Tangier under Creed, but to my trouble found them not finished. So back to the office, where all the morning, busy, then home to dinner, and then all the afternoon till very late at my office, and then home to supper and to bed, weary.

16th (Lord's day). Lay long in bed, then up and to my chamber and my office, looking over some plates which I find necessary for me to understand pretty well, because of the Dutch warr. Then home to dinner, where Creed dined with us, and so after dinner he and I walked to the Rolls' Chappell, expecting to hear the great Stillingfleete preach, but he did not; but a very sorry fellow, which vexed me. The sermon done, we parted, and I home, where I find Mr. Andrews, and by and by comes Captain Taylor, my old acquaintance at Westminster, that understands musique very well and composes mighty bravely; he brought us some things of two parts to sing, very hard; but that that is the worst, he is very conceited of them, and that though they are good makes them troublesome to one, to see him every note commend and admire them. He supped with me, and a good understanding man he is and a good scholler, and, among other things, a great antiquary, and among other things he can, as he says, show the very originall Charter to Worcester, of King Edgar's, wherein he stiles himself, Rex Marium Brittanniae, &c.; which is the great text that Mr. Selden and others do quote, but imperfectly and upon trust. But he hath the very originall, which he says he will shew me. He gone we to bed. This night I am told that newes is come of our taking of three Dutch men-of-warr, with the loss of one of our Captains.

17th. Up and to the Duke of Albemarle's, where he shewed me Mr. Coventry's letters, how three Dutch privateers are taken, in one whereof Everson's' son is captaine. But they have killed poor Captaine Golding in The Diamond. Two of them, one of 32 and the other of 20 odd guns, did stand stoutly up against her, which hath 46, and the Yarmouth that hath 52 guns, and as many more men as they. So that they did more than we could expect, not yielding till many of their men were killed. And Everson, when he was brought before the Duke of Yorke, and was observed to be shot through the hat, answered, that he wished it had gone through his head, rather than been taken. One thing more is written: that two of our ships the other day appearing upon the coast of Holland, they presently fired their beacons round the country to give notice. And newes is brought the King, that the Dutch Smyrna fleete is seen upon the back of Scotland; and thereupon the King hath wrote to the Duke, that he do appoint a fleete to go to the Northward to try to meet them coming home round: which God send! Thence to White Hall; where the King seeing me, did come to me, and calling me by name, did discourse with me about the ships in the River: and this is the first time that ever I knew the King did know me personally; so that hereafter I must not go thither, but with expectation to be questioned, and to be ready to give good answers. So home, and thence with Creed, who come to dine with me, to the Old James, where we dined with Sir W. Rider and Cutler, and, by and by, being called by my wife, we all to a play, "The Ghosts," at the Duke's house, but a very simple play. Thence up and down, with my wife with me, to look [for] Sir Ph. Warwicke (Mr. Creed going from me), but missed of him and so home, and late and busy at my office. So home to supper and to bed. This day was left at my house a very neat silver watch, by one Briggs, a scrivener and sollicitor, at which I was angry with my wife for receiving, or, at least, for opening the box wherein it was, and so far witnessing our receipt of it, as to give the messenger 5s. for bringing it; but it can't be helped, and I will endeavour to do the man a kindnesse, he being a friend of my uncle Wight's.

18th. Up and to Sir Philip Warwicke, and walked with him an houre with great delight in the Parke about Sir G. Carteret's accounts, and the endeavours that he hath made to bring Sir G. Carteret to show his accounts and let the world see what he receives and what he pays. Thence home to the office, where I find Sir J. Minnes come home from Chatham, and Sir W. Batten both this morning from Harwich, where they have been these 7 or 8 days. At noon with my wife and Mr. Moore by water to Chelsey about my Privy Seale for Tangier, but my Lord Privy Seale was gone abroad, and so we, without going out of the boat, forced to return, and found him not at White Hall. So I to Sir Philip Warwicke and with him to my Lord Treasurer, who signed my commission for

Tangier-Treasurer and the docquet of my Privy Seale, for the monies to be paid to me. Thence to White Hall to Mr. Moore again, and not finding my Lord I home, taking my wife and woman up at Unthanke's. Late at my office, then to supper and to bed.

19th. Up by five o'clock, and by water to White Hall; and there took coach, and with Mr. Moore to Chelsy; where, after all my fears what doubts and difficulties my Lord Privy Seale would make at my Tangier Privy Seale, he did pass it at first reading, without my speaking with him. And then called me in, and was very civil to me. I passed my time in contemplating (before I was called in) the picture of my Lord's son's lady, a most beautiful woman, and most like to Mrs. Butler. Thence very much joyed to London back again, and found out Mr. Povy; told him this; and then went and left my Privy Seale at my Lord Treasurer's; and so to the 'Change, and thence to Trinity-House; where a great dinner of Captain Crisp, who is made an Elder Brother. And so, being very pleasant at dinner, away home, Creed with me; and there met Povy; and we to Gresham College, where we saw some experiments upon a hen, a dogg, and a cat, of the Florence poyson.

["Sir Robert Moray presented the Society from the King with a phial of Florentine poison sent for by his Majesty from Florence, on purpose to have those experiments related of the efficacy thereof, tried by the Society." The poison had little effect upon the kitten (Birch's "History;" vol. ii., p. 31).]

The first it made for a time drunk, but it come to itself again quickly; the second it made vomitt mightily, but no other hurt. The third I did not stay to see the effect of it, being taken out by Povy. He and I walked below together, he giving me most exceeding discouragements in the getting of money (whether by design or no I know not, for I am now come to think him a most cunning fellow in most things he do, but his accounts), and made it plain to me that money will be hard to get, and that it is to be feared Backewell hath a design in it to get the thing forced upon himself. This put me into a cruel melancholy to think I may lose what I have had so near my hand; but yet something may be hoped for which to-morrow will shew. He gone, Creed and I together a great while consulting what to do in this case, and after all I left him to do what he thought fit in his discourse to-morrow with my Lord Ashly. So home, and in my way met with Mr. Warren, from whom my hopes I fear will fail of what I hoped for, by my getting him a protection. But all these troubles will if not be over, yet we shall see the worst of there in a day or two. So to my office, and thence to supper, and my head akeing, betimes, that is by 10 or 11 o'clock, to bed.

20th. Up, and all the morning busy at the office. At noon dined, and Mr. Povy by agreement with me (where his boldness with Mercer, poor innocent wench, did make both her and me blush, to think how he were able to debauch a poor girl if he had opportunity) at a dish or two of plain meat of his own choice. After dinner comes Creed and then Andrews, where want of money to

Andrews the main discourse, and at last in confidence of Creed's judgement I am resolved to spare him 4 or L500 of what lies by me upon the security of some Tallys. This went against my heart to begin, but when obtaining Mr. Creed to joyne with me we do resolve to assist Mr. Andrews. Then anon we parted, and I to my office, where late, and then home to supper and to bed. This night I am told the first play is played in White Hall noon-hall, which is now turned to a house of playing. I had a great mind, but could not go to see it.

21st. Up and to my office about business. Anon comes Creed and Povy, and we treat about the business of our lending money, Creed and I, upon a tally for the satisfying of Andrews, and did conclude it as in papers is expressed, and as I am glad to have an opportunity of having 10 per cent. for my money, so I am as glad that the sum I begin this trade with is no more than L350. We all dined at Andrews' charge at the Sun behind the 'Change, a good dinner the worst dressed that ever I eat any, then home, and there found Kate Joyce and Harman come to see us. With them, after long talk, abroad by coach, a tour in the fields, and drunk at Islington, it being very pleasant, the dust being laid by a little rain, and so home very well pleased with this day's work. So after a while at my office to supper and to bed. This day we hear that the Duke and the fleete are sailed yesterday. Pray God go along with them, that they have good speed in the beginning of their worke.

22nd. Up, and Mr. Caesar, my boy's lute-master, being come betimes to teach him, I did speak with him seriously about the boy, what my mind was, if he did not look after his lute and singing that I would turn him away; which I hope will do some good upon the boy. All the morning busy at the office. At noon dined at home, and then to the office again very busy till very late, and so home to supper and to bed. My wife making great preparation to go to Court to Chappell to-morrow. This day I have newes from Mr. Coventry that the fleete is sailed yesterday from Harwich to the coast of Holland to see what the Dutch will do. God go along with them!

23rd (Lord's day). Mr. Povy, according to promise, sent his coach betimes, and I carried my wife and her woman to White Hall Chappell and set them in the Organ Loft, and I having left to untruss went to the Harp and Ball and there drank also, and entertained myself in talke with the mayde of the house, a pretty mayde and very modest. Thence to the Chappell and heard the famous young Stillingfleete, whom I knew at Cambridge, and is now newly admitted one of the King's chaplains; and was presented, they say, to my Lord Treasurer for St. Andrew's, Holborne, where he is now minister, with these words: that they (the Bishops of Canterbury, London, and another) believed he is the ablest young man to preach the Gospel of any since the Apostles. He did make the most plain, honest, good, grave sermon, in the most unconcerned and easy yet substantial manner, that ever I heard in my life, upon the words of Samuell to the people, "Fear the Lord in truth with all your heart, and remember the great things that he hath done for you." It being proper to this day, the day of the King's Coronation. Thence to Mr. Povy's, where mightily treated, and Creed with us. But Lord! to see how Povy overdoes every thing in commending it, do make it nauseous to me, and was not (by reason of my large praise of his house) over acceptable to my wife. Thence after dinner Creed and we by coach took the ayre in the fields beyond St. Pancras, it raining now and then, which it seems is most welcome weather, and then all to my house, where comes Mr. Hill, Andrews, and Captain Taylor, and good musique, but at supper to hear the arguments we had against Taylor concerning a Corant, he saying that the law of a dancing Corant is to have every barr to end in a pricked crochet and quaver, which I did deny, was very strange. It proceeded till I vexed him, but all parted friends, for Creed and I to laugh at when he was gone. After supper, Creed and I together to bed, in Mercer's bed, and so to sleep.

24th. Up and with Creed in Sir W. Batten's coach to White Hall. Sir W. Batten and I to the Duke of Albemarle, where very busy. Then I to Creed's chamber, where I received with much ado my two orders about receiving Povy's monies and answering his credits, and it is strange how he will preserve his constant humour of delaying all business that comes before him. Thence he and I to London to my office, and back again to my Lady Sandwich's to dinner, where my wife by agreement. After dinner alone, my Lady told me, with the prettiest kind of doubtfullnesse, whether it would be fit for her with respect to Creed to do it, that is, in the world, that Creed had broke his desire to her of being a servant to Mrs. Betty Pickering, and placed it upon encouragement which he had from some discourse of her ladyship, commending of her virtues to him, which, poor lady, she meant most innocently. She did give him a cold answer, but not so severe as it ought to have been; and, it seems, as the lady since to my Lady confesses, he had wrote a letter to her, which she answered slightly, and was resolved to contemn any motion of his therein. My Lady takes the thing very ill, as it is fit she should; but I advise her to stop all future occasions of the world's taking notice of his coming thither so often as of late he hath done. But to think that he should have this devilish presumption to aime at a lady so near to my Lord is strange, both for his modesty and discretion. Thence to the Cockepitt, and there walked an houre with my Lord Duke of Albemarle alone in his garden, where he expressed in great words his opinion of me; that I was the right hand of the Navy here, nobody but I taking any care of any thing therein; so that he should not know what could be done without me. At which I was (from him) not a little proud. Thence to a Committee of Tangier, where because not a quorum little was done, and so away to my wife (Creed with me) at Mrs. Pierce's, who continues very pretty and is now great with child. I had not seen her a great while. Thence by coach to my Lord Treasurer's, but could not speak with Sir Ph. Warwicke. So by coach with my wife and Mercer to the Parke; but the King being there, and I now-a-days being doubtfull of being seen in any pleasure, did part from the tour, and away out of the Parke to Knightsbridge, and there eat and drank in the coach, and so home, and after a while at my office, home to supper and to bed, having got a great cold I think by my pulling off my periwigg so often.

25th. At the office all the morning, and the like after dinner, at home all the afternoon till very late, and then to bed, being very hoarse with a cold I did lately get with leaving off my periwigg. This afternoon W. Pen, lately come from his father in the fleete, did give me an account how the fleete did sayle, about 103 in all, besides small catches, they being in sight of six or seven Dutch scouts, and sent ships in chase of them.

26th. Up very betimes, my cold continuing and my stomach sick with the buttered ale that I did drink the last night in bed, which did lie upon me till I did this morning vomitt it up. So walked to Povy's, where Creed met me, and there I did receive the first parcel of money as Treasurer of Tangier, and did give him my receipt for it, which was about L2,800 value in Tallys; we did also examine and settle several other things, and then I away to White Hall, talking, with Povy alone, about my opinion of Creed's indiscretion in looking after Mrs. Pickering, desiring him to make no more a sport of it, but to correct him, if he finds that he continues to owne any such thing. This I did by my Lady's desire, and do intend to pursue the stop of it. So to the Carrier's by Cripplegate, to see whether my mother be come to towne or no, I expecting her to-day, but she is not come. So to dinner to my Lady Sandwich's, and there after dinner above in the diningroom did spend an houre or two with her talking again about Creed's folly; but strange it is that he should dare to propose this business himself of Mrs. Pickering to my Lady, and to tell my Lady that he did it for her virtue sake, not minding her money, for he could have a wife with more, but, for that, he did intend to depend upon her Ladyshipp to get as much of her father and mother for her as she could; and that, what he did, was by encouragement from discourse of her Ladyshipp's: he also had wrote to Mrs. Pickering, but she did give him a slighting answer back again. But I do very much fear that Mrs. Pickering's honour, if the world comes to take notice of it, may be wronged by it. Thence home, and all the afternoon till night at my office, then home to supper and to bed.

27th. Up, and to my office, where all the morning, at noon Creed dined with me; and, after dinner, walked in the garden, he telling me that my Lord Treasurer now begins to be scrupulous, and will know what becomes of the L26,000 saved by my Lord Peterborough, before he parts with any more money, which puts us into new doubts, and me into a great fear, that all my cake will be doe still.

[An obsolete proverb, signifying to lose one's hopes, a cake coming out of the oven in a state of dough being considered spoiled.

"My cake is dough; but I'll in among the rest;
Out of hope of all, but my share in the feast."
Shakespeare, Taming of the Shrew, act v., sc. i.-M. B.]

But I am well prepared for it to bear it, being not clear whether it will be more for my profit to have it, or go without it, as my profits of the Navy are likely now to be. All the afternoon till late hard at the office. Then to supper and to bed. This night William Hewer is returned from Harwich, where he hath been paying off of some ships this fortnight, and went to sea a good way with the fleete, which was 96 in company then, men of warr, besides some come in, and following them since, which makes now above 100, whom God bless!

28th. Up by 5 o'clock, and by appointment with Creed by 6 at his chamber, expecting Povy, who come not. Thence he and I out to Sir Philip Warwicke's, but being not up we took a turn in the garden hard by, and thither comes Povy to us. After some discourse of the reason of the difficulty that Sir Philip Warwicke makes in issuing a warrant for my striking of tallys, namely, the having a clear account of the L26,000 saved by my Lord of Peterborough, we parted, and I to Sir P. Warwicke, who did give me an account of his demurr, which I applied myself to remove by taking Creed with me to my Lord Ashly, from whom, contrary to all expectation, I received a very kind answer, just as we could have wished it, that he would satisfy my Lord Treasurer. Thence very well satisfied I home, and down the River to visit the victualling-ships, where I find all out of order. And come home to dinner, and then to write a letter to the Duke of Albemarle about the victualling-ships, and carried it myself to the Council-chamber, where it was read; and when they rose, my Lord Chancellor passing by stroked me on the head, and told me that the Board had read my letter, and taken order for the punishing of the watermen for not appearing on board the ships.

> [Among the State Papers are lists of watermen impressed and put on board the victualling ships. Attached to one of these is a "note of their unfitness and refractory conduct; also that many go ashore to sleep, and are discontent that they, as masters of families, are pressed, while single men are excused on giving money to the pressmen" ("Calendar," Domestic, 1664-65, p. 323).]

And so did the King afterwards, who do now know me so well, that he never sees me but he speaks to me about our Navy business. Thence got my Lord Ashly to my Lord Treasurer below in his chamber, and there removed the scruple, and by and by brought Mr. Sherwin to Sir Philip Warwicke and did the like, and so home, and after a while at my office, to bed.

29th. All the morning busy at the office. In the afternoon to my Lord Treasurer's, and there got my Lord Treasurer to sign the warrant for my striking of tallys, and so doing many jobbs in my way home, and there late writeing letters, being troubled in my mind to hear that Sir W. Batten and Sir J. Minnes do take notice that I am now-a-days much from the office upon no office business, which vexes me, and will make me mind my business the better, I hope in God; but what troubles me more is, that I do omit to write, as I should do, to Mr. Coventry, which I must not do, though this night I minded it so little as to sleep in the middle of my letter to him, and committed forty blotts and blurrs in my letter to him, but of this I hope never more to be guilty, if I have not already given him sufficient offence. So, late home, and to bed.

30th (Lord's day). Up and to my office alone all the morning, making up my monthly accounts, which though it hath been very intricate, and very great disbursements and receipts and odd reckonings, yet I differed not from the truth; viz.: between my first computing what my profit ought to be and then what my cash and debts do really make me worth, not above 10s., which is very much, and I do much value myself upon the account, and herein I with great joy find myself to have gained this month above L100 clear, and in the whole to be worth above L1400, the greatest sum I ever yet was worth. Thence home to dinner, and there find poor Mr. Spong walking at my door, where he had knocked, and being told I was at the office staid modestly there walking because of disturbing me, which methinks was one of the most modest acts (of a man that hath no need of being so to me) that ever I knew in my life. He dined with me, and then after dinner to my closet, where abundance of mighty pretty discourse, wherein, in a word, I find him the man of the world that hath of his own ingenuity obtained the most in most things, being withall no scholler. He gone, I took boat and down to Woolwich and Deptford, and made it late home, and so to supper and to bed. Thus I end this month in great content as to my estate and gettings: in much trouble as to the pains I have taken, and the rubs I expect yet to meet with, about the business of Tangier. The fleete, with about 106 ships upon the coast of Holland, in sight of the Dutch, within the Texel. Great fears of the sickenesse here in the City, it being said that two or three houses are already shut up. God preserve as all!

THE DIARY OF SAMUEL PEPYS M.A. F.R.S.
CLERK OF THE ACTS AND SECRETARY TO THE ADMIRALTY
TRANSCRIBED FROM THE SHORTHAND MANUSCRIPT IN THE
PEPYSIAN LIBRARY
MAGDALENE COLLEGE CAMBRIDGE BY THE REV. MYNORS
BRIGHT M.A. LATE FELLOW
AND PRESIDENT OF THE COLLEGE
(Unabridged)
WITH LORD BRAYBROOKE'S NOTES
EDITED WITH ADDITIONS BY
HENRY B. WHEATLEY F.S.A.

DIARY OF SAMUEL PEPYS.

MAY & JUNE 1665

May 1st. Up and to Mr. Povy's, and by his bedside talked a good while. Among other things he do much insist I perceive upon the difficulty of getting of money, and would fain have me to concur in the thinking of some other way of disposing of the place of Treasurer to one Mr. Bell, but I did seem slight of it, and resolved to try to do the best or to give it up. Thence to the Duke of Albemarle, where I was sorry to find myself to come a little late, and so home, and at noon going to the 'Change I met my Lord Brunkard, Sir Robert Murry, Deane Wilkins, and Mr. Hooke, going by coach to Colonell Blunts to dinner. So they stopped and took me with them. Landed at the Tower-wharf, and thence by water to Greenwich; and there coaches met us; and to his house, a very stately sight for situation and brave plantations; and among others, a vineyard, the first that ever I did see. No extraordinary dinner, nor any other entertainment good; but only after dinner to the tryall of some experiments about making of coaches easy. And several we tried; but one did prove mighty easy (not here for me to describe, but the whole body of the coach lies upon one long spring), and we all, one after another, rid in it; and it is very fine and likely to take. These experiments were the intent of their coming, and pretty they are. Thence back by coach to Greenwich, and in his pleasure boat to Deptford, and there stopped and in to Mr. Evelyn's,--[Sayes Court, the well-known residence of John Evelyn.]--which is a most beautiful place; but it being dark and late, I staid not; but Deane Wilkins and Mr. Hooke and I walked to Redriffe; and noble discourse all day long did please me, and it being late did take them to my house to drink, and did give them some sweetmeats, and thence sent them with a lanthorn home, two worthy persons as are in England, I think, or the world. So to my Lady Batten, where my wife is tonight, and so after some merry talk home and to bed.

2nd. Up and to the office all day, where sat late, and then to the office again, and by and by Sir W. Batten and my Lady and my wife and I by appointment yesterday (my Lady Pen failed us, who ought to have been with us) to the Rhenish winehouse at the Steelyard, and there eat a couple of lobsters and some prawns, and pretty merry, especially to see us four together, while my wife and my Lady did never intend ever to be together again after a year's distance between one another. Hither by and by come Sir Richard Ford and also Mrs. Esther, that lived formerly with my Lady Batten, now well married to a priest, come to see my Lady. Thence toward evening home, and to my office, where late, and then home to supper and to bed.

3rd. Up betimes and walked to Sir Ph. Warwicke's, where a long time with him in his chamber alone talking of Sir G. Carteret's business, and the abuses he puts on the nation by his bad payments to both our vexations, but no hope of remedy for ought I see. Thence to my Lord Ashly to a Committee of Tangier for my Lord Rutherford's accounts, and that done we to my Lord Treasurer's, where I did receive my Lord's warrant to Sir R. Long for drawing a warrant for my striking of tallys. So to the Inne again by Cripplegate, expecting my mother's coming to towne, but she is not come this weeke neither, the coach being too full. So to the 'Change and thence home to dinner, and so out to Gresham College, and saw a cat killed with the Duke of Florence's poyson, and saw it proved that the oyle of tobacco

> ["Mr. Daniel Coxe read an account of the effects of tobacco-oil distilled in a retort, by one drop of which given at the mouth he had killed a lusty cat, which being opened, smelled strongly of the oil, and the blood of the heart more strongly than the rest .... One drop of the Florentine 'oglio di tobacco' being again given to a dog, it proved stupefying and vomitive, as before" (Birch's "History of the Royal Society," vol, ii., pp. 42, 43).]

drawn by one of the Society do the same effect, and is judged to be the same thing with the poyson both in colour and smell, and effect. I saw also an abortive child preserved fresh in spirits of salt. Thence parted, and to White Hall to the Councilchamber about an order touching the Navy (our being empowered to commit seamen or Masters that do not, being hired or pressed, follow their worke), but they could give us none. So a little vexed at that, because I put in the memorial to the Duke of Albemarle alone under my own hand, home, and after some time at the office home to bed. My Lord Chief Justice Hide did die suddenly this week, a day or two ago, of an apoplexy.

4th. Up, and to the office, where we sat busy all the morning. At noon home to dinner, and then to the office again all day till almost midnight, and then, weary, home to supper and to bed.

5th. Up betimes, and by water to Westminster, there to speak the first time with Sir Robert Long, to give him my Privy Seal and my Lord Treasurer's order for Tangier Tallys; he received me kindly enough. Thence home by water, and presently down to Woolwich and back to Blackewall, and there, viewed the Breach, in order to a Mast Docke, and so to Deptford to the Globe, where my Lord Brunkard, Sir J. Minnes, Sir W. Batten, and Commissioner Pett were at dinner, having been at the Breach also, but they find it will be too great charge to make use of it. After dinner to Mr. Evelyn's; he being abroad, we walked in his garden, and a lovely noble ground he hath indeed. And among other rarities, a hive of bees, so as being hived in glass, you may see the bees making their honey and combs mighty pleasantly. Thence home, and I by and by to Mr. Povy's to see him, who is yet in his chamber not well, and thence by his advice to one Lovett's, a varnisher, to see his manner of new varnish, but found not him at home, but his wife, a very beautiful woman, who shewed me much variety of admirable work, and is in order to my having of some papers fitted with his lines for my use for tables and the like. I know not whether I was more pleased with the thing, or that I was shewed it by her, but resolved I am to have some made. So home to my office late, and then to supper and to bed. My wife tells me that she hears that my poor aunt James hath had her breast cut off here in town, her breast having long been out of order. This day, after I had suffered my owne hayre to grow long, in order to wearing it, I find the convenience of periwiggs is so great, that I have cut off all short again, and will keep to periwiggs.

6th. Up, and all day at the office, but a little at dinner, and there late till past 12. So home to bed, pleased as I always am after I have rid a great deal of work, it being very satisfactory to me.

7th (Lord's day). Up, and to church with my wife. Home and dined. After dinner come Mr. Andrews and spent the afternoon with me, about our Tangier business of the victuals, and then parted, and after sermon comes Mr. Hill and a gentleman, a friend of his, one Mr. Scott, that sings well also, and then comes Mr. Andrews, and we all sung and supped, and then to sing again and passed the Sunday very pleasantly and soberly, and so I to my office a little, and then home to prayers and to bed. Yesterday begun my wife to learn to, limn of one Browne,

> [Alexander Browne, a printseller, who taught drawing, and practised it with success. He published in 1669, "Ars Pictoria, or an Academy treating of Drawing, Painting, Limning and Etching."]

which Mr. Hill helps her to, and, by her beginning upon some eyes, I think she will [do] very fine things, and I shall take great delight in it.

8th. Up very betimes, and did much business before I went out with several persons, among others Captain Taylor, who would leave the management of most of his business now he is going to Harwich, upon me, and if I can get money by it, which I believe it will, I shall take some of it upon me. Thence with Sir W. Batten to the Duke of Albemarle's and there did much business, and then to the 'Change, and thence off with Sir W. Warren to an ordinary, where we dined and sat talking of most usefull discourse till 5 in the afternoon, and then home, and very busy till late, and so home and to bed.

9th. Up betimes, and to my business at the office, where all the morning. At noon comes Mrs. The. Turner, and dines with us, and my wife's painting-master staid and dined; and I take great pleasure in thinking that my wife will really come to something in that business. Here dined also Luellin. So after dinner to my office, and there very busy till almost midnight, and so home to supper and to bed. This day we have newes of eight ships being taken by some of ours going into the Texel, their two men of warr, that convoyed them, running in. They come from about Ireland, round to the north.

10th. Up betimes, and abroad to the Cocke-Pitt, where the Duke [of Albemarle] did give Sir W. Batten and me an account of the late taking of eight ships, and of his intent to come back to the Gunfleete--[The Gunfleet Sand off the Essex coast.]--with the fleete presently; which creates us much work and haste therein, against the fleete comes. So to Mr. Povy, and after discourse with him home, and thence to the Guard in Southwarke, there to get some soldiers, by the Duke's order, to go keep pressmen on board our ships. So to the 'Change and did much business, and then home to dinner, and there find my poor mother come out of the country today in good health, and I am glad to see her, but my business, which I am sorry for, keeps me from paying the respect I ought to her at her first coming, she being grown very weak in her judgement, and doating again in her discourse, through age and some trouble in her family. I left her and my wife to go abroad to buy something, and then I to my office. In the evening by appointment to Sir W. Warren and Mr. Deering at a taverne hard by with intent to do some good upon their agreement in a great bargain of planks. So home to my office again, and then to supper and to bed, my mother being in bed already.

11th. Up betimes, and at the office all the morning. At home dined, and then to the office all day till late at night, and then home to supper, weary with business, and to bed.

12th. Up betimes, and find myself disappointed in my receiving presently of my L50 I hoped for sure of Mr. Warren upon the benefit of my press warrant, but he promises to make it good. So by water to the Exchequer, and there up and down through all the offices to strike my tallys for L17,500, which methinks is so great a testimony of the goodness of God to me, that I, from a mean clerke there, should come to strike tallys myself for that sum, and in the authority that I do now, is a very stupendous mercy to me. I shall have them struck to-morrow. But to see how every little fellow looks after his fees, and to get what he can for everything, is a strange consideration; the King's fees that he must pay himself for this L17,500 coming to above L100. Thence called my wife at Unthanke's to the New Exchange and elsewhere to buy a lace band for me, but we did not buy, but I find it so necessary to have some handsome clothes that I cannot but lay out some money thereupon. To the 'Change and thence to my watchmaker, where he has put it [i.e. the watch] in order, and a good and brave piece it is, and he tells me worth L14 which is a greater present than I valued it. So home to dinner, and after dinner comes several people, among others my cozen, Thomas Pepys, of Hatcham,

[Thomas Pepys, of Hatcham Barnes, Surrey, Master of the Jewel House to Charles II. and James II.]

to receive some money, of my Lord Sandwich's, and there I paid him what was due to him upon my uncle's score, but, contrary to my expectation, did get him to sign and seale to my sale of lands for payment of debts. So that now I reckon myself in better condition by L100 in my content than I was before, when I was liable to be called to an account and others after me by my uncle Thomas or his children for every foot of land we had sold before. This I reckon a great good fortune in the getting of this done. He gone, come Mr. Povy, Dr. Twisden, and Mr. Lawson about settling my security in the paying of the L4000 ordered to Sir J. Lawson. So a little abroad and then home, and late at my office and closet settling this day's disordering of my papers, then to supper and to bed.

13th. Up, and all day in some little gruntings of pain, as I used to have from winde, arising I think from my fasting so long, and want of exercise, and I think going so hot in clothes, the weather being hot, and the same clothes I wore all winter. To the 'Change after office, and received my watch from the watchmaker, and a very fine [one] it is, given me by Briggs, the Scrivener. Home to dinner, and then I abroad to the Atturney Generall, about advice upon the Act for Land Carriage, which he desired not to give me before I had received the King's and Council's order therein; going home bespoke the King's works, will cost me 50s., I believe. So home and late at my office. But, Lord! to see how much of my old folly and childishnesse hangs upon me still that I cannot forbear carrying my watch in my hand in the coach all this afternoon, and seeing what o'clock it is one hundred times; and am apt to think with myself, how could I be so long without one; though I remember since, I had one, and found it a trouble, and resolved to carry one no more about me while I lived. So home to supper and to bed, being troubled at a letter from Mr. Gholmly from Tangier, wherein he do advise me how people are at worke to overthrow our Victualling business, by which I shall lose L300 per annum, I am much obliged to him for this, secret kindnesse, and concerned to repay it him in his own concernments and look after this.

14th (Lord's day). Up, and with my wife to church, it being Whitsunday; my wife very fine in a new yellow bird's-eye hood, as the fashion is now. We had a most sorry sermon; so home to dinner, my mother having her new suit brought home, which makes her very fine. After dinner my wife and she and Mercer to Thomas Pepys's wife's christening of his first child, and I took a coach, and to Wanstead, the house where Sir H. Mildmay died, and now Sir Robert Brookes lives, having bought it of the Duke of Yorke, it being forfeited to him. A fine seat, but an old-fashioned house; and being not full of people looks desolately. Thence to Walthamstow, where (failing at the old place) Sir W. Batten by and by come home, I walking up and down the house and garden with my Lady very pleasantly, then to supper very merry, and then back by coach by dark night. I all the afternoon in the coach reading the treasonous book of the Court of King James, printed a great while ago, and worth reading, though ill intended. As soon as I come home, upon a letter from the Duke of Albemarle, I took boat at about 12 at night, and down the River in a gally, my boy and I, down to the Hope and so up again, sleeping and waking, with great pleasure, my business to call upon every one of

15th. Our victualling ships to set them agoing, and so home, and after dinner to the King's playhouse, all alone, and saw "Love's Maistresse." Some pretty things and good variety in it, but no or little fancy in it. Thence to the Duke of Albemarle to give him account of my day's works, where he shewed me letters from Sir G. Downing, of four days' date, that the Dutch are come out and joyned, well-manned, and resolved to board our best ships, and fight for certain they will. Thence to the Swan at Herbert's, and there the company of Sarah a little while, and so away and called at the Harp and Ball, where the mayde, Mary, is very 'formosa'--[handsome]--; but, Lord! to see in what readiness I am, upon the expiring of my vowes this day, to begin to run into all my pleasures and neglect of business. Thence home, and being sleepy to bed.

16th. Up betimes, and to the Duke of Albemarle with an account of my yesterday's actions in writing. So back to the office, where all the morning very busy. After dinner by coach to see and speak with Mr. Povy, and after little discourse back again home, where busy upon letters till past 12 at night, and so home to supper and to bed, weary.

17th. Up, and by appointment to a meeting of Sir John Lawson and Mr. Cholmly's atturney and Mr. Povy at the Swan taverne at Westminster to settle their business about my being secured in the payment of money to Sir J. Lawson in the other's absence. Thence at Langford's, where I never was since my brother died there. I find my wife and Mercer, having with him agreed upon two rich silk suits for me, which is fit for me to have, but yet the money is too much, I doubt, to lay out altogether; but it is done, and so let it be, it being the expense of the world that I can the best bear with and the worst spare. Thence home, and after dinner to the office, where late, and so home to supper and to bed. Sir J. Minnes and I had an angry bout this afternoon with Commissioner Pett about his neglecting his duty and absenting himself, unknown to us, from his place at Chatham, but a most false man I every day find him more and more, and in this very full of equivocation. The fleete we doubt not come to Harwich by this time. Sir W. Batten is gone down this day thither, and the Duchesse of Yorke went down yesterday to meet the Duke.

18th. Up, and with Sir J. Minnes to the Duke of Albemarle, where we did much business, and I with good content to myself; among other things we did examine Nixon and Stanesby, about their late running from two Dutchmen;

[Captain Edward Nixon, of the "Elizabeth," and Captain John Stanesby, of the "Eagle." John Lanyon wrote to the Navy Commissioners from Plymouth, May 16th: "Understands from the seamen that the conduct of Captains Nixon and Stanesby in their late engagement with two Dutch capers was very foul; the night they left the Dutch, no lights were put out as formerly, and though in sight of them in the morning, they still kept on their way; the Eagle lay by some time, and both the enemy's ships plied on her, but finding the Elizabeth nearly out of sight she also made sail; it is true the wind and sea were high, but there were no sufficient reasons for such endeavours to get from them." ("Calendar of State Papers," Domestic, 1664-65, p. 367). Both captains were tried; Nixon was condemned to be shot but Stanesby was cleared, and Charnock asserts that he was commander the "Happy Return" in 1672.]

for which they are committed to a vessel to carry them to the fleete to be tried. A most fowle unhandsome thing as ever was heard, for plain cowardice on Nixon's part. Thence with the Duke of Albemarle in his coach to my Lord Treasurer, and there was before the King (who ever now calls me by my name) and Lord Chancellor, and many other great Lords, discoursing about insuring of some of the King's goods, wherein the King accepted of my motion that we should; and so away, well pleased. To the office, and dined, and then to the office again, and abroad to speak with Sir G. Carteret; but, Lord! to see how fraile a man I am, subject to my vanities, that can hardly forbear, though pressed with never so much business, my pursuing of pleasure, but home I got, and there very busy very late. Among other things consulting with Mr. Andrews about our Tangier business, wherein we are like to meet with some trouble, and my Lord Bellasses's endeavour to supplant us, which vexes my mind; but, however, our undertaking is so honourable that we shall stand a tug for it I think. So home to supper and to bed.

19th. Up, and to White Hall, where the Committee for Tangier met, and there, though the case as to the merit of it was most plain and most of the company favourable to our business, yet it was with much ado that I got the business not carried fully against us, but put off to another day, my Lord Arlington being the great man in it, and I was sorry to be found arguing so greatly against him. The business I believe will in the end be carried against us, and the whole business fall; I must therefore endeavour the most I can to get money another way. It vexed me to see Creed so hot against it, but I cannot much blame him, having never declared to him my being concerned in it. But that that troubles me most is my Lord Arlington calls to me privately and asks me whether I had ever said to any body that I desired to leave this employment, having not time to look after it. I told him, No, for that the thing being settled it will not require much time to look after it. He told me then he would do me right to the King, for he had been told so, which I desired him to do, and by and by he called me to him again and asked me whether I had no friend about the Duke, asking me (I making a stand) whether Mr. Coventry was not my friend. I told him I had received many friendships from him. He then advised me to procure that the Duke would in his next letter write to him to continue me in my place and remove any obstruction; which I told him I would, and thanked him. So parted, vexed at the first and amazed at this business of my Lord Arlington's. Thence to the Exchequer, and there got my tallys for L17,500, the first payment I ever had out of the Exchequer, and at the Legg spent 14s. upon my old acquaintance, some of them the clerks, and away home with my tallys in a coach, fearful every step of having one of them fall out, or snatched from me. Being come home, I much troubled out again by coach (for company taking Sir W. Warren with me), intending to have spoke to my Lord Arlington to have known the bottom of it, but missed him, and afterwards discoursing the thing as a confidant to Sir W. Warren, he did give me several good hints and principles not to do anything suddenly, but consult my pillow upon that and every great thing of my life, before I resolve anything in it. Away back home, and not being fit for business I took my wife and Mercer down by water to Greenwich at 8 at night, it being very fine and cool and moonshine afterward. Mighty pleasant passage it was; there eat a cake or two, and so home by 10 or 11 at night, and then to bed, my mind not settled what to think.

20th. Up, and to my office, where busy all the morning. At noon dined at home, and to my office, very busy.

21st. Till past one, Lord's day, in the morning writing letters to the fleete and elsewhere, and my mind eased of much business, home to bed and slept till 8. So up, and this day is brought home one of my new silk suits, the plain one, but very rich camelott and noble. I tried it and it pleases me, but did not wear it, being I would not go out today to church. So laid it by, and my mind changed, thinking to go see my Lady Sandwich, and I did go a little way, but stopped and returned home to dinner, after dinner up to my chamber to settle my Tangier accounts, and then to my office, there to do the like with other papers. In the evening home to supper and to bed.

22nd. Up, and down to the ships, which now are hindered from going down to the fleete (to our great sorrow and shame) with their provisions, the wind being against them. So to the Duke of Albemarle, and thence down by water to Deptford, it being Trinity Monday, and so the day of choosing the Master of Trinity House for the next yeare, where, to my great content, I find that, contrary to the practice and design of Sir W. Batten, to breake the rule and custom of the Company in choosing their Masters by succession, he would have brought in Sir W. Rider or Sir W. Pen, over the head of Hurleston (who is a knave too besides, I believe), the younger brothers did all oppose it against the elder, and with great heat did carry it for Hurleston, which I know will vex him to the heart. Thence, the election being over, to church, where an idle sermon from that conceited fellow, Dr. Britton, saving that his advice to unity, and laying aside all envy and enmity among them was very apposite. Thence walked to Redriffe, and so to the Trinity House, and a great dinner, as is usual, and so to my office, where busy all the afternoon till late, and then home to bed, being much troubled in mind for several things, first, for the condition of the fleete for lacke of provisions, the blame this office lies under and the shame that they deserve to have brought upon them for the ships not being gone out of the River, and then for my business of Tangier which is not settled, and lastly for fear that I am not observed to have attended the office business of late as much as I ought to do, though there has been nothing but my attendance on Tangier that has occasioned my absence, and that of late not much.

23rd. Up, and at the office busy all the morning. At noon dined alone, my wife and mother being gone by invitation to dine with my mother's old servant Mr. Cordery, who made them very welcome. So to Mr. Povy's, where after a little discourse about his business I home again, and late at the office busy. Late comes Sir Arthur Ingram to my office, to tell me that, by letters from Amsterdam of the 28th of this month (their style),

> [The new style was adopted by most of the countries of Europe long before it was legalized in England, although Russia still retains the old style.]

the Dutch fleete, being about 100 men-of-war, besides fire-ships, &c., did set out upon the 23rd and 24th inst. Being divided into seven squadrons; viz., 1. Generall Opdam. 2. Cottenar, of Rotterdam. 3. Trump. 4. Schram, of Horne. 5. Stillingworth, of Freezland. 6. Everson. 7. One other, not named, of Zealand.

24th. Up, and by 4 o'clock in the morning, and with W. Hewer, there till 12 without intermission putting some papers in order. Thence to the Coffee-house with Creed, where I have not been a great while, where all the newes is of the Dutch being gone out, and of the plague growing upon us in this towne; and of remedies against it: some saying one thing, some another. So home to dinner, and after dinner Creed and I to Colvill's, thinking to shew him all the respect we could by obliging him in carrying him 5 tallys of L5000 to secure him for so much credit he has formerly given Povy to Tangier, but he, like an impertinent fool, cavills at it, but most ignorantly that ever I heard man in my life. At last Mr. Viner by chance comes, who I find a very moderate man, but could not persuade the fool to reason, but brought away the tallys again, and so vexed to my office, where late, and then home to my supper and to bed.

25th. Up, and to the office, where all the morning. At noon dined at home, and then to the office all the afternoon, busy till almost 12 at night, and then home to supper and to bed.

26th. Up at 4 o'clock, and all the morning in my office with W. Hewer finishing my papers that were so long out of order, and at noon to my bookseller's, and there bespoke a book or two, and so home to dinner, where Creed dined with me, and he and I afterwards to Alderman Backewell's to try him about supplying us with money, which he denied at first and last also, saving that he spoke a little fairer at the end than before. But the truth is I do fear I shall have a great deale of trouble in getting of money. Thence home, and in the evening by water to the Duke of Albemarle, whom I found mightily off the hooks, that the ships are not gone out of the River; which vexed me to see, insomuch that I am afeard that we must expect some change or addition of new officers brought upon us, so that I must from this time forward resolve to make myself appear eminently serviceable in attending at my office duly and no where else, which makes me wish with all my heart that I had never anything to do with this business of Tangier. After a while at my office, home to supper vexed, and to bed.

27th. Up, and to the office, where all the morning; at noon dined at home, and then to my office again,, where late, and so to bed, with my mind full of fears for the business of this office and troubled with that of Tangier, concerning which Mr. Povy was with me, but do give me little help, but more reason of being troubled. So that were it not for our Plymouth business I would be glad to be rid of it.

28th (Lord's day). By water to the Duke of Albemarle, where I hear that Nixon is condemned to be shot to death, for his cowardice, by a Council of War. Went to chapel and heard a little musique, and there met with Creed, and with him a little while walking, and to Wilkinson's for me to drink, being troubled with winde, and at noon to Sir Philip Warwicke's to dinner, where abundance of company come in unexpectedly; and here I saw one pretty piece of household stuff, as the company increaseth, to put a larger leaf upon an oval table. After dinner much good discourse with Sir Philip, who I find, I think, a most pious, good man, and a professor of a philosophical manner of life and principles like Epictetus, whom he cites in many things. Thence to my Lady Sandwich's, where, to my shame, I had not been a great while before. Here, upon my telling her a story of my Lord Rochester's running away on Friday night last with Mrs. Mallett, the great beauty and fortune of the North, who had supped at White Hall with Mrs. Stewart, and was going home to her lodgings with her grandfather, my Lord Haly, by coach; and was at Charing Cross seized on by both horse and foot men, and forcibly taken from him, and put into a coach with six horses, and two women provided to receive her, and carried away. Upon immediate pursuit, my Lord of Rochester (for whom the King had spoke to the lady often, but with no successe) was taken at Uxbridge; but the lady is not yet heard of, and the King mighty angry, and the Lord sent to the Tower. Hereupon my Lady did confess to me, as a great secret, her being concerned in this story. For if this match breaks between my Lord Rochester and her, then, by the consent of all her friends, my Lord Hinchingbroke stands fair, and is invited for her. She is worth, and will be at her mother's death (who keeps but a little from her), L2500 per annum. Pray God give a good success to it! But my poor Lady, who is afeard of the sickness, and resolved to be gone into the country, is forced to stay in towne a day or two, or three about it, to see the event of it. Thence home and to see my Lady Pen, where my wife and I were shown a fine rarity: of fishes kept in a glass of water, that will live so for ever; and finely marked they are, being foreign.--[Gold-fish introduced from China.]--So to supper at home and to bed, after many people being with me about business, among others the two Bellamys about their old debt due to them from the King for their victualling business, out of which I hope to get some money.

29th. Lay long in bed, being in some little pain of the wind collique, then up and to the Duke of Albemarle, and so to the Swan, and there drank at Herbert's, and so by coach home, it being kept a great holiday through the City, for the birth and restoration of the King. To my office, where I stood by and saw Symson the joyner do several things, little jobbs, to the rendering of my closet handsome and the setting up of some neat plates that Burston has for my money made me, and so home to dinner, and then with my wife, mother, and Mercer in one boat, and I in another, down to Woolwich. I walking from Greenwich, the others going to and fro upon the water till my coming back, having done but little business. So home and to supper, and, weary, to bed. We have every where taken some prizes. Our merchants have good luck to come home safe: Colliers from the North, and some Streights men just now. And our Hambrough ships, of whom we were so much afeard, are safe in Hambrough. Our fleete resolved to sail out again from Harwich in a day or two.

30th. Lay long, and very busy all the morning, at noon to the 'Change, and thence to dinner to Sir G. Carteret's, to talk upon the business of insuring our goods upon the Hambrough [ships]. Here a very fine, neat French dinner, without much cost, we being all alone with my Lady and one of the house with her; thence home and wrote letters, and then in the evening, by coach, with my wife and mother and Mercer, our usual tour by coach, and eat at the old house at Islington; but, Lord! to see how my mother found herself talk upon every object to think of old stories. Here I met with one that tells me that Jack Cole, my old schoolefellow, is dead and buried lately of a consumption, who was a great crony of mine. So back again home, and there to my closet to write letters. Hear to my great trouble that our Hambrough ships,

> [On May 29th Sir William Coventry wrote to Lord Arlington: "Capt. Langhorne has arrived with seven ships, and reports the taking of the Hamburg fleet with the man of war their convoy; mistaking the Dutch fleet for the English, he fell into it" ("Calendar of State Papers," Domestic, 1664-65, p. 393)]

valued of the King's goods and the merchants' (though but little of the former) to L200,000 [are lost]. By and by, about 11 at night, called into the garden by my Lady Pen and daughter, and there walked with them and my wife till almost twelve, and so in and closed my letters, and home to bed.

31st. Up, and to my office, and to Westminster, doing business till noon, and then to the 'Change, where great the noise and trouble of having our Hambrough ships lost; and that very much placed upon Mr. Coventry's forgetting to give notice to them of the going away of our fleete from the coast of Holland. But all without reason, for he did; but the merchants not being ready, staid longer than the time ordered for the convoy to stay, which was ten days. Thence home with Creed and Mr. Moore to dinner. Anon we broke up, and Creed and I to discourse about our Tangier matters of money, which vex me. So to Gresham College, staid a very little while, and away and I home busy, and busy late, at the end of the month, about my month's accounts, but by the addition of Tangier it is rendered more intricate, and so (which I have not done these 12 months, nor would willingly have done now) failed of having it done, but I will do it as soon as I can. So weary and sleepy to bed. I endeavoured but missed of seeing Sir Thomas Ingram at Westminster, so went to Houseman's the

Painter, who I intend shall draw my wife, but he was not within, but I saw several very good pictures.

DIARY OF SAMUEL PEPYS.

JUNE 1665

June 1st. Up and to the office, where sat all the morning, at noon to the 'Change, and there did some business, and home to dinner, whither Creed comes, and after dinner I put on my new silke camelott sute; the best that ever I wore in my life, the sute costing me above L24. In this I went with Creed to Goldsmiths' Hall, to the burial of Sir Thomas Viner; which Hall, and Haberdashers also, was so full of people, that we were fain for ease and coolness to go forth to Pater Noster Row, to choose a silke to make me a plain ordinary suit. That done, we walked to Cornehill, and there at Mr. Cade's' stood in the balcon and saw all the funeral, which was with the blue-coat boys and old men, all the Aldermen, and Lord Mayor, &c., and the number of the company very great; the greatest I ever did see for a taverne. Hither come up to us Dr. Allen, and then Mr. Povy and Mr. Fox. The show being over, and my discourse with Mr. Povy, I took coach and to Westminster Hall, where I took the fairest flower, and by coach to Tothill Fields for the ayre till it was dark. I 'light, and in with the fairest flower to eat a cake, and there did do as much as was safe with my flower, and that was enough on my part. Broke up, and away without any notice, and, after delivering the rose where it should be, I to the Temple and 'light, and come to the middle door, and there took another coach, and so home to write letters, but very few, God knows, being by my pleasure made to forget everything that is. The coachman that carried [us] cannot know me again, nor the people at the house where we were. Home to bed, certain news being come that our fleete is in sight of the Dutch ships.

2nd. Lay troubled in mind abed a good while, thinking of my Tangier and victualling business, which I doubt will fall. Up and to the Duke of Albemarle, but missed him. Thence to the Harp and Ball and to Westminster Hall, where I visited "the flowers" in each place, and so met with Mr. Creed, and he and I to Mrs. Croft's to drink and did, but saw not her daughter Borroughes. I away home, and there dined and did business. In the afternoon went with my tallys, made a fair end with Colvill and Viner, delivering them L5000 tallys to each and very quietly had credit given me upon other tallys of Mr. Colvill for L2000 and good words for more, and of Mr. Viner too. Thence to visit the Duke of Albemarle, and thence my Lady Sandwich and Lord Crew. Thence home, and there met an expresse from Sir W. Batten at Harwich, that the fleete is all sailed from Solebay, having spied the Dutch fleete at sea, and that, if the calmes hinder not, they must needs now be engaged with them. Another letter also come to me from Mr. Hater, committed by the Council this afternoon to the Gate House, upon the misfortune of having his name used by one, without his knowledge or privity, for the receiving of some powder that he had bought. Up to Court about these two, and for the former was led up to my Lady Castlemayne's lodgings, where the King and she and others were at supper, and there I read the letter and returned; and then to Sir G. Carteret about Hater, and shall have him released to-morrow, upon my giving bail for his appearance, which I have promised to do. Sir G. Carteret did go on purpose to the King to ask this, and it was granted. So home at past 12, almost one o'clock in the morning. To my office till past two, and then home to supper and to bed.

3rd. Up and to White Hall, where Sir G. Carteret did go with me to Secretary Morris, and prevailed with him to let Mr. Hater be released upon bail for his appearance. So I at a loss how to get another besides myself, and got Mr. Hunt, who did patiently stay with me all the morning at Secretary Morris's chamber, Mr. Hater being sent for with his keeper, and at noon comes in the Secretary, and upon entering [into] recognizances, he for L200, and Mr. Hunt and I for L100 each for his appearance upon demand, he was released, it costing him, I think, above L3. I thence home, vexed to be kept from the office all the morning, which I had not been in many months before, if not some years. At home to dinner, and all the afternoon at the office, where late at night, and much business done, then home to supper and to bed. All this day by all people upon the River, and almost every where else hereabout were heard the guns, our two fleets for certain being engaged; which was confirmed by letters from Harwich, but nothing particular: and all our hearts full of concernment for the Duke, and I particularly for my Lord Sandwich and Mr. Coventry after his Royall Highnesse.

4th (Sunday). Up and at my chamber all the forenoon, at evening my accounts, which I could not do sooner, for the last month, and, blessed be God! am worth L1400 odd money, something more than ever I was yet in the world. Dined very well at noon, and then to my office, and there and in the garden discoursed with several people about business, among others Mr. Howell, the turner, who did give me so good a discourse about the practices of the Paymaster J. Fenn that I thought fit to recollect all when he was gone, and have entered it down to be for ever remembered. Thence to my chamber again to settle my Tangier accounts against tomorrow and some other things, and with great joy ended them, and so to supper, where a good fowl and tansy, and so to bed. Newes being come that our fleete is pursuing the Dutch, who, either by cunning, or by being worsted, do give ground, but nothing more for certain. Late to bed upon my papers being quite finished.

5th. Up very betimes to look some other papers, and then to White Hall to a Committee of Tangier, where I offered my accounts with great acceptation, and so had some good words and honour by it, and one or two things done to my content in my business of Treasurer, but I do clearly see that we shall lose our business of victualling, Sir Thomas Ingram undertaking that it shall be done by persons there as cheap as we do it, and give the seamen their full allowance and themselves give good security here for performance of contract, upon which terms there is no opposing it. This would trouble me, but that I hope when that fails to spend my time to some good advantage other ways, and so shall permit it all to God Almighty's pleasure. Thence home to dinner, after 'Change, where great talke of the Dutch being fled and we in pursuit of them, and that our ship Charity

[Sir William Coventry and Sir William Penn to the Navy Commissioners, June 4th: "Engaged yesterday with the Dutch; they began to stand away at 3 p.m. Chased them all the rest of the day and night; 20 considerable ships are destroyed and taken; we have only lost the Great Charity. The Earl of Marlborough, Rear-Admiral Sansum, and Captain Kirby are slain, and Sir John Lawson wounded" ("Calendar of State Papers," Domestic, 1664-65, p. 406).]

is lost upon our Captain's, Wilkinson, and Lieutenant's yielding, but of this there is no certainty, save the report of some of the sicke men of the Charity, turned adrift in a boat out of the Charity and taken up and brought on shore yesterday to Sole Bay, and the newes hereof brought by Sir Henry Felton. Home to dinner, and Creed with me. Then he and I down to Deptford, did some business, and back again at night. He home, and I to my office, and so to supper and to bed. This morning I had great discourse with my Lord Barkeley about Mr. Hater, towards whom from a great passion reproaching him with being a fanatique and dangerous for me to keepe, I did bring him to be mighty calme and to ask me pardons for what he had thought of him and to desire me to ask his pardon of Hater himself for the ill words he did give him the other day alone at White Hall (which was, that he had always thought him a man that was no good friend to the King, but did never think it would breake out in a thing of this nature), and did advise him to declare his innocence to the Council and pray for his examination and vindication. Of which I shall consider and say no more, but remember one compliment that in great kindness to me he did give me, extolling my care and diligence, that he did love me heartily for my owne sake, and more that he did will me whatsoever I thought for Mr. Coventry's sake, for though the world did think them enemies, and to have an ill aspect, one to another, yet he did love him with all his heart, which was a strange manner of noble compliment, confessing his owning me as a confidant and favourite of Mr. Coventry's.

6th. Waked in the morning before 4 o'clock with great pain to piss, and great pain in pissing by having, I think, drank too great a draught of cold drink before going to bed. But by and by to sleep again, and then rose and to the office, where very busy all the morning, and at noon to dinner with Sir G. Carteret to his house with all our Board, where a good pasty and brave discourse. But our great fear was some fresh news of the fleete, but not from the fleete, all being said to be well and beaten the Dutch, but I do not give much belief to it, and indeed the news come from Sir W. Batten at Harwich, and writ so simply that we all made good mirth of it. Thence to the office, where upon Sir G. Carteret's accounts, to my great vexation there being nothing done by the Controller to right the King therein. I thence to my office and wrote letters all the afternoon, and in the evening by coach to Sir Ph. Warwicke's about my Tangier business to get money, and so to my Lady Sandwich's, who, poor lady, expects every hour to hear of my Lord; but in the best temper, neither confident nor troubled with fear, that I ever did see in my life. She tells me my Lord Rochester is now declaredly out of hopes of Mrs. Mallett, and now she is to receive notice in a day or two how the King stands inclined to the giving leave for my Lord Hinchingbroke to look after her, and that being done to bring it to an end shortly. Thence by coach home, and to my office a little, and so before 12 o'clock home and to bed.

7th. This morning my wife and mother rose about two o'clock; and with Mercer, Mary, the boy, and W. Hewer, as they had designed, took boat and down to refresh themselves on the water to Gravesend. Lay till 7 o'clock, then up and to the office upon Sir G. Carteret's accounts again, where very busy; thence abroad and to the 'Change, no news of certainty being yet come from the fleete. Thence to the Dolphin Taverne, where Sir J. Minnes, Lord Brunkard, Sir Thomas Harvy, and myself dined, upon Sir G. Carteret's charge, and very merry we were, Sir Thomas Harvy being a very drolle. Thence to the office, and meeting Creed away with him to my Lord Treasurer's, there thinking to have met the goldsmiths, at White Hall, but did not, and so appointed another time for my Lord to speak to them to advance us some money. Thence, it being the hottest day that ever I felt in my life, and it is confessed so by all other people the hottest they ever knew in England in the beginning of June, we to the New Exchange, and there drunk whey, with much entreaty getting it for our money, and [they] would not be entreated to let us have one glasse more. So took water and to Fox-Hall, to the Spring garden, and there walked an houre or two with great pleasure, saving our minds ill at ease concerning the fleete and my Lord Sandwich, that we have no newes of them, and ill reports run up and down of his being killed, but without ground. Here staid pleasantly walking and spending but 6d. till nine at night, and then by water to White Hall, and there I stopped to hear news of the fleete, but none come, which is strange, and so by water home, where, weary with walking and with the mighty heat of the weather, and for my wife's not coming home, I staying walking in the garden till twelve at night, when it begun to lighten exceedingly, through the greatness of the heat. Then despairing of her coming home, I to bed. This day, much against my will, I did in Drury Lane see two or three houses marked with a red cross upon the doors, and "Lord have mercy upon us" writ there; which was a sad sight to me, being the first of the kind that, to my remembrance, I ever saw. It put me into an ill conception of myself and my smell, so that I was forced to buy some roll-tobacco to smell to and chaw, which took away the apprehension.

8th. About five o'clock my wife come home, it having lightened all night hard, and one great shower of rain. She come and lay upon the bed; I up and to the office, where all the morning. Alone at home to dinner, my wife, mother, and Mercer dining at W. Joyce's; I giving her a caution to go round by the Half Moone to his house, because of the plague. I to my Lord Treasurer's by appointment of Sir Thomas Ingram's, to meet the Goldsmiths; where I met with the great news at last newly come, brought by Bab May' from the Duke of Yorke, that we have totally routed the Dutch; that the Duke himself, the Prince, my Lord Sandwich, and Mr. Coventry are all well: which did put me into such joy, that I forgot almost all other thoughts. The particulars I shall set down by and by. By and by comes Alderman Maynell and Mr. Viner, and there my Lord Treasurer did intreat them to furnish me with money upon my tallys, Sir Philip Warwicke before my Lord declaring the King's changing of the hand from Mr. Povy to me, whom he called a very sober person, and one whom the Lord Treasurer would owne in all things that I should concern myself with them in the business of money. They did at present declare they could not part with money at present. My Lord did press them very hard, and I hope upon their considering we shall get some of them. Thence with great joy to the Cocke-pitt; where the Duke of Albemarle, like a man out of himself with content, new-told me all; and by and by comes a letter from Mr. Coventry's own hand to him, which he never opened (which was a strange thing), but did give it me to open and read, and consider what was fit for our office to do in it, and leave the letter with Sir W. Clerke; which upon such a time and occasion was a strange piece of indifference, hardly pardonable. I copied out the letter, and did also take minutes out of Sir W. Clerke's other letters; and the sum of the newes is:

VICTORY OVER THE DUTCH, JUNE 3RD, 1665.

This day they engaged; the Dutch neglecting greatly the opportunity of the wind they had of us, by which they lost the benefit of their fire-ships. The Earl of Falmouth, Muskerry, and Mr. Richard Boyle killed on board the Duke's ship, the Royall Charles, with one shot: their blood and brains flying in the Duke's face; and the head of Mr. Boyle striking down the Duke, as some say. Earle of Marlborough, Portland, Rear-Admirall Sansum (to Prince Rupert) killed, and Capt. Kirby and Ableson. Sir John Lawson wounded on the knee; hath had some bones taken out, and is likely to be well again. Upon receiving the hurt, he sent to the Duke for another to command the Royall Oake. The Duke sent Jordan

[Afterwards Sir Joseph Jordan, commander of the "Royal Sovereign," and Vice-Admiral of the Red, 1672. He was knighted on July 1st, 1665.--B.]

out of the St. George, who did brave things in her. Capt. Jer. Smith of the Mary was second to the Duke, and stepped between him and Captain Seaton of the Urania (76 guns and 400 men), who had sworn to board the Duke; killed him, 200 men, and took the ship; himself losing 99 men, and never an officer saved but himself and lieutenant. His master indeed is saved, with his leg cut off: Admirall Opdam blown up, Trump killed, and said by Holmes; all the rest of their admiralls, as they say, but Everson (whom they dare not trust for his affection to the Prince of Orange), are killed: we having taken and sunk, as is believed, about 24 of their best ships; killed and taken near 8 or 10,000 men, and lost, we think, not above 700. A great[er] victory never known in the world. They are all fled, some 43 got into the Texell, and others elsewhere, and we in pursuit of the rest. Thence, with my heart full of joy; home, and to my office a little; then to my Lady Pen's, where they are all joyed and not a little puffed up at the good successe of their father;

[In the royal charter granted by Charles II. in 1680 to William Penn for the government of his American province, to be styled Pennsylvania, special reference is made to "the memory and merits of Sir William Penn in divers services, and particularly his conduct, courage, and discretion under our dearest brother, James, Duke of York, in that signal battle and victory fought and obtained against the Dutch fleet commanded by Heer van Opdam in 1665" ("Penn's Memorials of Sir W. Penn," vol. ii., p. 359).]

and good service indeed is said to have been done by him. Had a great bonefire at the gate; and I with my Lady Pen's people and others to Mrs. Turner's great room, and then down into the streete. I did give the boys 4s. among them, and mighty merry. So home to bed, with my heart at great rest and quiett, saving that the consideration of the victory is too great for me presently to comprehend.

[Mrs. Ady (Julia Cartwright), in her fascinating life of Henrietta, Duchess of Orleans, gives an account of the receipt of the news of the great sea-fight in Paris, and quotes a letter of Charles II. to his sister, dated, "Whitehall, June 8th, 1665" The first report that reached Paris was that "the Duke of York's ship had been blown up, and he himself had been drowned." "The shock was too much for Madame . . . she was seized with convulsions, and became so dangerously ill that Lord Hollis wrote to the king, 'If things had gone ill at sea I really believe Madame would have died.'" Charles wrote: "I thanke God we have now the certayne newes of a very considerable victory over the Duch; you will see most of the particulars by the relation my Lord Hopis will shew you, though I have had as great a losse as 'tis possible in a good frinde, poore C. Barckely. It troubles me so much, as I hope you will excuse the shortnesse of this letter, haveing receaved the newes of it but two houres agoe" ("Madame," 1894, pp. 215, 216).]

9th. Lay long in bed, my head akeing with too much thoughts I think last night. Up and to White Hall, and my Lord Treasurer's to Sir Ph. Warwicke, about Tangier business, and in my way met with Mr. Moore, who eases me in one point wherein I was troubled; which was, that I heard of nothing said or done by my Lord Sandwich: but he tells me that Mr. Cowling, my Lord Chamberlain's secretary, did hear the King say that my Lord Sandwich had done nobly and worthily. The King, it seems, is much troubled at the fall of my Lord of Falmouth; but I do not meet with any man else that so much as wishes him alive again, the world conceiving him a man of too much pleasure to do the

King any good, or offer any good office to him. But I hear of all hands he is confessed to have been a man of great honour, that did show it in this his going with the Duke, the most that ever any man did. Home, where my people busy to make ready a supper against night for some guests, in lieu of my stonefeast. At noon eat a small dinner at home, and so abroad to buy several things, and among others with my taylor to buy a silke suit, which though I had one lately, yet I do, for joy of the good newes we have lately had of our victory over the Dutch, which makes me willing to spare myself something extraordinary in clothes; and after long resolution of having nothing but black, I did buy a coloured silk ferrandin. So to the Old Exchange, and there at my pretty seamstresses bought a pair of stockings of her husband, and so home, where by and by comes Mr. Honiwood and Mrs. Wilde, and Roger Pepys and, after long time spent, Mrs. Turner, The. and Joyce. We had a very good venison pasty, this being instead of my stone-feast the last March, and very merry we were, and the more I know the more I like Mr. Honiwood's conversation. So after a good supper they parted, walking to the 'Change for a coach, and I with them to see them there. So home and to bed, glad it was over.

10th. Lay long in bed, and then up and at the office all the morning. At noon dined at home, and then to the office busy all the afternoon. In the evening home to supper; and there, to my great trouble, hear that the plague is come into the City (though it hath these three or four weeks since its beginning been wholly out of the City); but where should it begin but in my good friend and neighbour's, Dr. Burnett, in Fanchurch Street: which in both points troubles me mightily. To the office to finish my letters and then home to bed, being troubled at the sicknesse, and my head filled also with other business enough, and particularly how to put my things and estate in order, in case it should please God to call me away, which God dispose of to his glory!

11th (Lord's day). Up, and expected long a new suit; but, coming not, dressed myself in my late new black silke camelott suit; and, when fully ready, comes my new one of coloured ferrandin, which my wife puts me out of love with, which vexes me, but I think it is only my not being used to wear colours which makes it look a little unusual upon me. To my chamber and there spent the morning reading. At noon, by invitation, comes my two cozen Joyces and their wives, my aunt James and he-cozen Harman, his wife being ill. I had a good dinner for them, and as merry as I could be in such company. They being gone, I out of doors a little, to shew, forsooth, my new suit, and back again, and in going I saw poor Dr. Burnett's door shut; but he hath, I hear, gained great goodwill among his neighbours; for he discovered it himself first, and caused himself to be shut up of his own accord: which was very handsome. In the evening comes Mr. Andrews and his wife and Mr. Hill, and staid and played, and sung and supped, most excellent pretty company, so pleasant, ingenious, and harmless, I cannot desire better. They gone we to bed, my mind in great present ease.

12th. Up, and in my yesterday's new suit to the Duke of Albemarle, and after a turne in White Hall, and then in Westminster Hall, returned, and with my taylor bought some gold lace for my sleeve hands in Pater Noster Row. So home to dinner, and then to the office, and down the River to Deptford, and then back again and to my Lord Treasurer's, and up and down to look after my Tangier business, and so home to my office, then to supper and to bed. The Duke of Yorke is sent for last night and expected to be here to-morrow.

13th. Up and to the office, where all the morning doing business. At noon with Sir G. Carteret to my Lord Mayor's to dinner, where much company in a little room, and though a good, yet no extraordinary table. His name, Sir John Lawrence, whose father, a very ordinary old man, sat there at table, but it seems a very rich man. Here were at table three Sir Richard Brownes, viz.: he of the Councill, a clerk, and the Alderman, and his son; and there was a little grandson also Richard, who will hereafter be Sir Richard Browne. The Alderman did here openly tell in boasting how he had, only upon suspicion of disturbances, if there had been any bad newes from sea, clapped up several persons that he was afeard of; and that he had several times done the like and would do, and take no bail where he saw it unsafe for the King. But by and by he said that he was now sued in the Exchequer by a man for false imprisonment, that he had, upon the same score, imprisoned while he was Mayor four years ago, and asked advice upon it. I told him I believed there was none, and told my story of Field, at which he was troubled, and said that it was then unsafe for any man to serve the King, and, I believed, knows not what to do therein; but that Sir Richard Browne, of the Councill, advised him to speak with my Lord Chancellor about it. My Lord Mayor very respectfull to me; and so I after dinner away and found Sir J. Minnes ready with his coach and four horses at our office gate, for him and me to go out of towne to meet the Duke of Yorke coming from Harwich to-night, and so as far as Ilford, and there 'light. By and by comes to us Sir John Shaw and Mr. Neale, that married the rich widow Gold, upon the same errand. After eating a dish of creame, we took coach again, hearing nothing of the Duke, and away home, a most pleasant evening and road. And so to my office, where, after my letters wrote, to supper and to bed. All our discourse in our way was Sir J. Minnes's telling me passages of the late King's and his father's, which I was mightily pleased to hear for information, though the pride of some persons and vice of most was but a sad story to tell how that brought the whole kingdom and King to ruine.

14th. Up, and to Sir Ph. Warwicke's and other places, about Tangier business, but to little purpose. Among others to my Lord Treasurer's, there to speak with him, and waited in the lobby three long hours for to speake with him, to the trial of my utmost patience, but missed him at last, and forced to go home without it, which may teach me how I make others wait. Home to dinner and staid Mr. Hater with me, and after dinner drew up a petition for Mr. Hater to present to the Councill about his troublesome business of powder, desiring a trial that his absence may be vindicated, and so to White Hall, but it was not proper to present it to-day. Here I met with Mr. Cowling, who observed to me how he finds every body silent in the praise of my Lord Sandwich, to set up the

Duke and the Prince; but that the Duke did both to the King and my Lord Chancellor write abundantly of my Lord's courage and service.

> [Charles II.'s letter of thanks to Lord Sandwich, dated "Whitehall, June 9th, 1665," written entirely in the king's hand, is printed in Ellis's "Original Letters," 1st series, vol. iii., p. 327.]

And I this day met with a letter of Captain Ferrers, wherein he tells [us] my Lord was with his ship in all the heat of the day, and did most worthily. Met with Creed, and he and I to Westminster; and there saw my Lord Marlborough

> [Of the four distinguished men who died after the late action with the Dutch and were buried in Westminster Abbey, the Earl of Marlborough was interred on June 14th, Viscount Muskerry on the 19th, the Earl of Falmouth on the 22nd, and Sir Edward Broughton on the 26th. After the entries in the Abbey Registers is this note: "These four last Honble Persons dyed in his Majy's service against the Dutch, excepting only that ST Ed Br received his death's wound at sea, but dyed here at home" (Chester's "Westminster Abbey Registers," p. 162).]

brought to be buried, several Lords of the Council carrying him, and with the herald in some state. Thence, vexed in my mind to think that I do so little in my Tangier business, and so home, and after supper to bed.

15th. Up, and put on my new stuff suit with close knees, which becomes me most nobly, as my wife says. At the office all day. At noon, put on my first laced band, all lace; and to Kate Joyce's to dinner, where my mother, wife, and abundance of their friends, and good usage. Thence, wife and Mercer and I to the Old Exchange, and there bought two lace bands more, one of my semstresse, whom my wife concurs with me to be a pretty woman. So down to Deptford and Woolwich, my boy and I. At Woolwich, discoursed with Mr. Sheldon about my bringing my wife down for a month or two to his house, which he approves of, and, I think, will be very convenient. So late back, and to the office, wrote letters, and so home to supper and to bed. This day the Newes book upon Mr. Moore's showing L'Estrange

> ["The Public Intelligencer," published by Roger L'Estrange, the predecessor of the "London Gazette."]

(Captain Ferrers's letter) did do my Lord Sandwich great right as to the late victory. The Duke of Yorke not yet come to towne. The towne grows very sickly, and people to be afeard of it; there dying this last week of the plague 112, from 43 the week before, whereof but [one] in Fanchurch-streete, and one in Broad-streete, by the Treasurer's office.

16th. Up and to the office, where I set hard to business, but was informed that the Duke of Yorke is come, and hath appointed us to attend him this afternoon. So after dinner, and doing some business at the office, I to White Hall, where the Court is full of the Duke and his courtiers returned from sea. All fat and lusty, and ruddy by being in the sun. I kissed his hands, and we waited all the afternoon. By and by saw Mr. Coventry, which rejoiced my very heart. Anon he and I, from all the rest of the company, walked into the Matted Gallery; where after many expressions of love, we fell to talk of business. Among other things, how my Lord Sandwich, both in his counsells and personal service, hath done most honourably and serviceably. Sir J. Lawson is come to Greenwich; but his wound in his knee yet very bad. Jonas Poole, in the Vantguard, did basely, so as to be, or will be, turned out of his ship. Captain Holmes

[Captain Robert Holmes (afterwards knighted). Sir William Coventry, in a letter to Lord Arlington (dated from "The Royal Charles," Southwold Bay, June 13th), writes: "Capt. Holmes asked to be rear admiral of the white squadron in place of Sansum who was killed, but the Duke gave the place to Captain Harman, on which he delivered up his commission, which the Duke received, and put Captain Langhorne in his stead" ("Calendar of State Papers," Domestic, 1664-65, p. 423).]

expecting upon Sansum's death to be made Rear-admirall to the Prince (but Harman is

[John Harman, afterwards knighted. He had served with great reputation in several naval fights, and was desperately wounded in 1673, while]

put in) hath delivered up to the Duke his commission, which the Duke took and tore. He, it seems, had bid the Prince, who first told him of Holmes's intention, that he should dissuade him from it; for that he was resolved to take it if he offered it. Yet Holmes would do it, like a rash, proud coxcombe. But he is rich, and hath, it seems, sought an occasion of leaving the service. Several of our captains have done ill. The great ships are the ships do the business, they quite deadening the enemy. They run away upon sight of "The Prince."

["The Prince" was Lord Sandwich's ship; the captain was Roger Cuttance. It was put up at Chatham for repair at this date.]

It is strange to see how people do already slight Sir William Barkeley,

[Sir William Berkeley, see note, vol. iii., p. 334. His behaviour after the death of his brother, Lord Falmouth, is severely commented on in "Poems on State Affairs," vol. i., p. 29

"Berkeley had heard it soon, and thought not good

To venture more of royal Harding's blood;
To be immortal he was not of age,
And did e'en now the Indian Prize presage;
And judged it safe and decent, cost what cost,
To lose the day, since his dear brother's lost.
With his whole squadron straight away he bore,
And, like good boy, promised to fight no more."--B.]

my Lord FitzHarding's brother, who, three months since, was the delight of the Court. Captain Smith of "The Mary" the Duke talks mightily of; and some great thing will be done for him. Strange to hear how the Dutch do relate, as the Duke says, that they are the conquerors; and bonefires are made in Dunkirke in their behalf; though a clearer victory can never be expected. Mr. Coventry thinks they cannot have lost less than 6000 men, and we not dead above 200, and wounded about 400; in all about 600. Thence home and to my office till past twelve, and then home to supper and to bed, my wife and mother not being yet come home from W. Hewer's chamber, who treats my mother tonight. Captain Grovel the Duke told us this day, hath done the basest thing at Lowestoffe, in hearing of the guns, and could not (as others) be got out, but staid there; for which he will be tried; and is reckoned a prating coxcombe, and of no courage.

17th. My wife come to bed about one in the morning. I up and abroad about Tangier business, then back to the office, where we sat, and at noon home to dinner, and then abroad to Mr. Povy's, after I and Mr. Andrews had been with Mr. Ball and one Major Strange, who looks after the getting of money for tallys and is helping Mr. Andrews. I had much discourse with Ball, and it may be he may prove a necessary man for our turns. With Mr. Povy I spoke very freely my indifference as to my place of Treasurer, being so much troubled in it, which he took with much seeming trouble, that I should think of letting go so lightly the place, but if the place can't be held I will. So hearing that my Lord Treasurer was gone out of town with his family because of the sicknesse, I returned home without staying there, and at the office find Sir W. Pen come home, who looks very well; and I am gladder to see him than otherwise I should be because of my hearing so well of him for his serviceablenesse in this late great action. To the office late, and then home to bed. It struck me very deep this afternoon going with a hackney coach from my Lord Treasurer's down Holborne, the coachman I found to drive easily and easily, at last stood still, and come down hardly able to stand, and told me that he was suddenly struck very sicke, and almost blind, he could not see; so I 'light and went into another coach, with a sad heart for the poor man and trouble for myself, lest he should have been struck with the plague, being at the end of the towne that I took him up; but God have mercy upon us all! Sir John Lawson, I hear, is worse than yesterday: the King went to see him to-day most kindly. It seems his wound is not very bad; but he hath a fever, a thrush, and a hickup, all three together, which are, it seems, very bad symptoms.

18th (Lord's day). Up, and to church, where Sir W. Pen was the first time [since he] come from sea, after the battle. Mr. Mills made a sorry sermon to prove that there was a world to come after this. Home and dined and then to my chamber, where all the afternoon. Anon comes Mr. Andrews to see and sing with me, but Mr. Hill not coming, and having business, we soon parted, there coming Mr. Povy and Creed to discourse about our Tangier business of money. They gone, I hear Sir W. Batten and my Lady are returned from Harwich. I went to see them, and it is pretty to see how we appear kind one to another, though neither of us care 2d. one for another. Home to supper, and there coming a hasty letter from Commissioner Pett for pressing of some calkers (as I would ever on his Majesty's service), with all speed, I made a warrant presently and issued it. So to my office a little, and then home to bed.

19th. Up, and to White Hall with Sir W. Batten (calling at my Lord Ashly's, but to no purpose, by the way, he being not up), and there had our usual meeting before the Duke with the officers of the Ordnance with us, which in some respects I think will be the better for us, for despatch sake. Thence home to the 'Change and dined alone (my wife gone to her mother's), after dinner to my little new goldsmith's,

[John Colvill of Lombard Street, see ante, May 24th. He lost L85,832 17s. 2d. by the closing of the Exchequer in 1672, and he died between 1672 and 1677 (Price's "Handbook of London Bankers ").]

whose wife indeed is one of the prettiest, modest black women that ever I saw. I paid for a dozen of silver salts L6 14s. 6d. Thence with Sir W. Pen from the office down to Greenwich to see Sir J. Lawson, who is better, but continues ill; his hickupp not being yet gone, could have little discourse with him. So thence home and to supper, a while to the office, my head and mind mightily vexed to see the multitude of papers and business before [me] and so little time to do it in. So to bed.

20th. Thankes-giving-day for victory over ye Dutch. Up, and to the office, where very busy alone all the morning till church time, and there heard a mean sorry sermon of Mr. Mills. Then to the Dolphin Taverne, where all we officers of the Navy met with the Commissioners of the Ordnance by agreement, and dined: where good musique at my direction. Our club--[share]

["Next these a sort of Sots there are,
Who crave more wine than they can bear,
Yet hate, when drunk, to pay or spend
Their equal Club or Dividend,
But wrangle, when the Bill is brought,
And think they're cheated when they're not."

The Delights of the Bottle, or the Compleat Vintner, 3rd ed., 1721, p. 29.]

--come to 34s. a man, nine of us. Thence after dinner, to White Hall with Sir W. Berkely in his coach, and so walked to Herbert's and there spent a little time . . . . Thence by water to Fox-hall, and there walked an hour alone, observing the several humours of the citizens that were there this holyday, pulling of cherries,--[The game of bob-cherry]--and God knows what, and so home to my office, where late, my wife not being come home with my mother, who have been this day all abroad upon the water, my mother being to go out of town speedily. So I home and to supper and to bed, my wife come home when I come from the office. This day I informed myself that there died four or five at Westminster of the plague in one alley in several houses upon Sunday last, Bell Alley, over against the Palace-gate; yet people do think that the number will be fewer in the towne than it was the last weeke! The Dutch are come out again with 20 sail under Bankert; supposed gone to the Northward to meete their East India fleete.

21st. Up, and very busy all the morning. At noon with Creed to the Excise Office, where I find our tallys will not be money in less than sixteen months, which is a sad thing for the King to pay all that interest for every penny he spends; and, which is strange, the goldsmiths with whom I spoke, do declare that they will not be moved to part with money upon the increase of their consideration of ten per cent. which they have, and therefore desire I would not move in it, and indeed the consequence would be very ill to the King, and have its ill consequences follow us through all the King's revenue. Home, and my uncle Wight and aunt James dined with me, my mother being to go away to-morrow. So to White Hall, and there before and after Council discoursed with Sir Thomas Ingram about our ill case as to Tangier for money. He hath got the King to appoint a meeting on Friday, which I hope will put an end one way or other to my pain. So homewards and to the Cross Keys at Cripplegate, where I find all the towne almost going out of towne, the coaches and waggons being all full of people going into the country. Here I had some of the company of the tapster's wife a while, and so home to my office, and then home to supper and to bed.

22nd. Up pretty betimes, and in great pain whether to send my another into the country to-day or no, I hearing, by my people, that she, poor wretch, hath a mind to stay a little longer, and I cannot blame her, considering what a life she will through her own folly lead when she comes home again, unlike the pleasure and liberty she hath had here. At last I resolved to put it to her, and she agreed to go, so I would not oppose it, because of the sicknesse in the towne, and my intentions of removing my wife. So I did give her money and took a kind leave of her, she, poor wretch, desiring that I would forgive my brother John, but I refused it to her, which troubled her, poor soul, but I did it in kind words and so let the discourse go off, she leaving me though in a great deal of sorrow. So I to my office and left my wife and people to see her out of town, and I at the office all the morning. At noon my wife tells me that she is with much ado gone, and I pray God bless her, but it seems she was to the last unwilling to go, but would not say so, but put it off till she lost her place in the coach, and was fain to ride in the waggon part. After dinner to the office again till night, very busy, and so home not very late to supper and to bed.

23rd. Up and to White Hall to a Committee for Tangier, where his Royal Highness was. Our great design was to state to them the true condition of this Committee for want of money, the want whereof was so great as to need some sudden help, and it was with some content resolved to see it supplied and means proposed towards the doing of it. At this Committee, unknown to me, comes my Lord of Sandwich, who, it seems, come to towne last night. After the Committee was up, my Lord Sandwich did take me aside, and we walked an hour alone together in the robe-chamber, the door shut, telling me how much the Duke and Mr. Coventry did, both in the fleete and here, make of him, and that in some opposition to the Prince; and as a more private message, he told me that he hath been with them both when they have made sport of the Prince and laughed at him: yet that all the discourse of the towne, and the printed relation, should not give him one word of honour my Lord thinks mighty strange; he assuring me, that though by accident the Prince was in the van the beginning of the fight for the first pass, yet all the rest of the day my Lord was in the van, and continued so. That notwithstanding all this noise of the Prince, he had hardly a shot in his side nor a man killed, whereas he hath above 30 in her hull, and not one mast whole nor yard; but the most battered ship of the fleet, and lost most men, saving Captain Smith of "The Mary." That the most the Duke did was almost out of gun-shot; but that, indeed, the Duke did come up to my Lord's rescue after he had a great while fought with four of them. How poorly Sir John Lawson performed, notwithstanding all that was said of him; and how his ship turned out of the way, while Sir J. Lawson himself was upon the deck, to the endangering of the whole fleete. It therefore troubles my Lord that Mr. Coventry should not mention a word of him in his relation. I did, in answer, offer that I was sure the relation was not compiled by Mr. Coventry, but by L'Estrange, out of several letters, as I could witness; and that Mr. Coventry's letter that he did give the Duke of Albemarle did give him as much right as the Prince, for I myself read it first and then copied it out, which I promised to show my Lord, with which he was somewhat satisfied. From that discourse my Lord did begin to tell me how much he was concerned to dispose of his children, and would have my advice and help; and propounded to match my Lady Jemimah to Sir G. Carteret's eldest son, which I approved of, and did undertake the speaking with him about it as from myself, which my Lord liked. So parted, with my head full of care about this business. Thence home to the 'Change, and so to dinner, and thence by coach to Mr. Povy's. Thence by appointment with him and Creed to one Mr. Finch; one of the Commissioners for the Excise, to be informed about some things of the Excise, in order to our settling matters therein better for us for our Tangier business. I find him a very discreet, grave person. Thence well satisfied I and Creed to Mr. Fox at White Hall to speak with him about the same matter, and having some pretty satisfaction from him also, he and I took boat and to Fox Hall, where we spent two or three hours talking of several matters very soberly and contentfully to me, which, with the ayre and pleasure of the garden, was a great refreshment to me, and, 'methinks, that which we ought to joy ourselves in. Thence back to White Hall, where we parted, and I to find my Lord to receive his farther direction about his proposal this morning. Wherein I did that I should first by another hand break my intentions to Sir G. Carteret. I pitched upon Dr. Clerke, which my Lord liked, and so I endeavoured but in vain to find him out to-night. So home by hackney-coach, which is become a very dangerous passage now-a-days, the sickness increasing mightily, and to bed.

24th (Midsummer-day). Up very betimes, by six, and at Dr. Clerke's at Westminster by 7 of the clock, having over night by a note acquainted him with my intention of coming, and there I, in the best manner I could, broke my errand about a match between Sir G. Carteret's eldest son and my Lord Sandwich's eldest daughter, which he (as I knew he would) took with great content: and we both agreed that my Lord and he, being both men relating to the sea, under a kind aspect of His Majesty, already good friends, and both virtuous and good familys, their allyance might be of good use to us; and he did undertake to find out Sir George this morning, and put the business in execution. So being both well pleased with the proposition, I saw his niece there and made her sing me two or three songs very prettily, and so home to the office, where to my great trouble I found Mr. Coventry and the board met before I come. I excused my late coming by having been on the River about office business. So to business all the morning. At noon Captain Ferrers and Mr. Moore dined with me, the former of them the first time I saw him since his corning from sea, who do give me the best conversation in general, and as good an account of the particular service of the Prince and my Lord of Sandwich in the late sea-fight that I could desire. After dinner they parted. So I to White Hall, where I with Creed and Povy attended my Lord Treasurer, and did prevail with him to let us have an assignment for 15 or L20,000, which, I hope, will do our business for Tangier. So to Dr. Clerke, and there found that he had broke the business to Sir G. Carteret, and that he takes the thing mighty well. Thence I to Sir G. Carteret at his chamber, and in the best manner I could, and most obligingly, moved the business: he received it with great respect and content, and thanks to me, and promised that he would do what he could possibly for his son, to render him fit for my Lord's daughter, and shewed great kindness to me, and sense of my kindness to him herein. Sir William Pen told me this day that Mr. Coventry is to be sworn a Privy Counsellor, at which my soul is glad. So home and to my letters by the post, and so home to supper and bed.

25th (Lord's day). Up, and several people about business come to me by appointment relating to the office. Thence I to my closet about my Tangier papers. At noon dined, and then I abroad by water, it raining hard, thinking to have gone down to Woolwich, but I did not, but back through bridge to White Hall, where, after I had again visited Sir G. Carteret, and received his (and now his Lady's) full content in my proposal, I went to my Lord Sandwich, and having told him how Sir G. Carteret received it, he did direct me to return to Sir G.

Carteret, and give him thanks for his kind reception of this offer, and that he would the next day be willing to enter discourse with him about the business. Which message I did presently do, and so left the business with great joy to both sides. My Lord, I perceive, intends to give L5000 with her, and expects about L800 per annum joynture. So by water home and to supper and bed, being weary with long walking at Court, but had a Psalm or two with my boy and Mercer before bed, which pleased me mightily. This night Sir G. Carteret told me with great kindnesse that the order of the Council did run for the making of Hater and Whitfield incapable of any serving the King again, but that he had stopped the entry of it, which he told me with great kindnesse, but the thing troubles me. After dinner, before I went to White Hall, I went down to Greenwich by water, thinking to have visited Sir J. Lawson, where, when I come, I find that he is dead, and died this morning, at which I was much surprized; and indeed the nation hath a great loss; though I cannot, without dissembling, say that I am sorry for it, for he was a man never kind to me at all. Being at White Hall, I visited Mr. Coventry, who, among other talk, entered about the great question now in the House about the Duke's going to sea again; about which the whole House is divided. He did concur with me that, for the Duke's honour and safety, it were best, after so great a service and victory and danger, not to go again; and, above all, that the life of the Duke cannot but be a security to the Crowne; if he were away, it being more easy to attempt anything upon the King; but how the fleete will be governed without him, the Prince--[Rupert]--being a man of no government and severe in council, that no ordinary man can offer any advice against his; saying truly that it had been better he had gone to Guinny, and that were he away, it were easy to say how matters might be ordered, my Lord Sandwich being a man of temper and judgment as much as any man he ever knew, and that upon good observation he said this, and that his temper must correct the Prince's. But I perceive he is much troubled what will be the event of the question. And so I left him.

26th. Up and to White Hall with Sir J. Minnes, and to the Committee of Tangier, where my Lord Treasurer was, the first and only time he ever was there, and did promise us L15,000 for Tangier and no more, which will be short. But if I can pay Mr. Andrews all his money I care for no more, and the bills of Exchange. Thence with Mr. Povy and Creed below to a new chamber of Mr. Povy's, very pretty, and there discourse about his business, not to his content, but with the most advantage I could to him, and Creed also did the like. Thence with Creed to the King's Head, and there dined with him at the ordinary, and good sport with one Mr. Nicholls, a prating coxcombe, that would be thought a poet, but would not be got to repeat any of his verses. Thence I home, and there find my wife's brother and his wife, a pretty little modest woman, where they dined with my wife. He did come to desire my assistance for a living, and, upon his good promises of care, and that it should be no burden to me, I did say and promise I would think of finding something for him, and the rather because his wife seems a pretty discreet young thing, and humble, and he, above all things, desirous to do something to maintain her, telling me sad stories of what she endured with him in Holland, and I hope it will not be burdensome. So down by water to Woolwich, walking to and again from Greenwich thither and back again, my business being to speak again with Sheldon, who desires and expects my wife coming thither to spend the summer, and upon second thoughts I do agree that it will be a good place for her and me too. So, weary, home, and to my office a while, till almost midnight, and so to bed. The plague encreases mightily, I this day seeing a house, at a bitt-maker's over against St. Clement's Church, in the open street, shut up; which is a sad sight.

27th. Up and to the office, where all the morning. At noon dined by chance at my Lady Batten's, and they sent for my wife, and there was my Lady Pen and Pegg. Very merry, and so I to my office again, where till 12 o'clock at night, and so home to supper and to bed.

28th. Sir J. Minnes carried me and my wife to White Hall, and thence his coach along with my wife where she would. There after attending the Duke to discourse of the navy. We did not kiss his hand, nor do I think, for all their pretence, of going away to-morrow. Yet I believe they will not go for good and all, but I did take my leave of Sir William Coventry, who, it seems, was knighted and sworn a Privy-Counsellor two days since; who with his old kindness treated me, and I believe I shall ever find [him] a noble friend. Thence by water to Blackfriars, and so to Paul's churchyard and bespoke severall books, and so home and there dined, my man William giving me a lobster sent him by my old maid Sarah. This morning I met with Sir G. Carteret, who tells me how all things proceed between my Lord Sandwich and himself to full content, and both sides depend upon having the match finished presently, and professed great kindnesse to me, and said that now we were something akin. I am mightily, both with respect to myself and much more of my Lord's family, glad of this alliance. After dinner to White Hall, thinking to speak with my Lord Ashly, but failed, and I whiled away some time in Westminster Hall against he did come, in my way observing several plague houses in King's Street and [near] the Palace. Here I hear Mrs. Martin is gone out of town, and that her husband, an idle fellow, is since come out of France, as he pretends, but I believe not that he hath been. I was fearful of going to any house, but I did to the Swan, and thence to White Hall, giving the waterman a shilling, because a young fellow and belonging to the Plymouth. Thence by coach to several places, and so home, and all the evening with Sir J. Minnes and all the women of the house (excepting my Lady Batten) late in the garden chatting. At 12 o'clock home to supper and to bed. My Lord Sandwich is gone towards the sea to-day, it being a sudden resolution, I having taken no leave of him.

29th. Up and by water to White Hall, where the Court full of waggons and people ready to go out of towne. To the Harp and Ball, and there drank and talked with Mary, she telling me in discourse that she lived lately at my neighbour's, Mr. Knightly, which made me forbear further discourse. This end of the towne every day grows very bad of the plague. The Mortality Bill is come to 267;

[According to the Bills of Mortality, the total number of deaths in London for the week ending June 27th was 684, of which number 267 were deaths from the plague. The number of deaths rose week by week until September 19th, when the total was 8,297, and the deaths from the plague 7,165. On September 26th the total had fallen to 6,460, and deaths from the plague to 5,533 The number fell gradually, week by week, till October 31st, when the total was 1,388, and deaths from the plague 1,031. On November 7th there was a rise to 1,787 and 1,414 respectively. On November 14th the numbers had gone down to 1,359 and 1,050 respectively. On December 12th the total had fallen to 442, and deaths from the plague to 243. On December 19th there was a rise to 525 and 281 respectively. The total of burials in 1665 was 97,506, of which number the plague claimed 68,596 victims.]

which is about ninety more than the last: and of these but four in the City, which is a great blessing to us. Thence to Creed, and with him up and down about Tangier business, to no purpose. Took leave again of Mr. Coventry; though I hope the Duke has not gone to stay, and so do others too. So home, calling at Somersett House, where all are packing up too: the Queene-Mother setting out for France this day to drink Bourbon waters this year, she being in a consumption; and intends not to come till winter come twelvemonths.

[The Queen-Mother never came to England again. She retired to her chateau at Colombes, near Paris, where she died in August, 1669, after a long illness; the immediate cause of her death being an opiate ordered by her physicians. She was buried, September 12th, in the church of St. Denis. Her funeral sermon was preached by Bossuet. Sir John Reresby speaks of Queen Henrietta Maria in high terms. He says that in the winter, 1659-60, although the Court of France was very splendid, there was a greater resort to the Palais Royal, "the good humour and wit of our Queen Mother, and the beauty of the Princess [Henrietta] her daughter, giving greater invitation than the more particular humour of the French Queen, being a Spaniard." In another place he says: "Her majesty had a great affection for England, notwithstanding the severe usage she and hers had received from it. Her discourse was much with the great men and ladies of France in praise of the people and of the country; of their courage, generosity, good nature; and would excuse all their miscarriages in relation to unfortunate effects of the late war, as if it were a convulsion of some desperate and infatuated persons, rather than from the genius and temper of the kingdom" ("Memoirs of Sir John Reresby," ed. Cartwright, pp. 43, 45).]

So by coach home, where at the office all the morning, and at noon Mrs. Hunt dined with us. Very merry, and she a very good woman. To the office, where busy a while putting some things in my office in order, and then to letters till night. About 10 a'clock home, the days being sensibly shorter before I have once kept a summer's day by shutting up office by daylight; but my life hath been still as it was in winter almost. But I will for a month try what I can do by daylight. So home to supper and to bed.

30th. Up and to White Hall, to the Duke of Albemarle, who I find at Secretary Bennet's, there being now no other great Statesman, I think, but my Lord Chancellor, in towne. I received several commands from them; among others, to provide some bread and cheese for the garrison at Guernsey, which they promised to see me paid for. So to the 'Change, and home to dinner. In the afternoon I down to Woolwich and after me my wife and Mercer, whom I led to Mr. Sheldon's to see his house, and I find it a very pretty place for them to be at. So I back again, walking both forward and backward, and left my wife to come by water. I straight to White Hall, late, to Secretary Bennet's to give him an account of the business I received from him to-day, and there staid weary and sleepy till past 12 at night. Then writ my mind to him, and so back by water and in the dark and against tide shot the bridge, groping with their pole for the way, which troubled me before I got through. So home, about one or two o'clock in the morning, my family at a great losse what was become of me. To supper, and to bed. Thus this book of two years ends. Myself and family in good health, consisting of myself and wife, Mercer, her woman, Mary, Alice, and Susan our maids, and Tom my boy. In a sickly time of the plague growing on. Having upon my hands the troublesome care of the Treasury of Tangier, with great sums drawn upon me, and nothing to pay them with: also the business of the office great. Consideration of removing my wife to Woolwich; she lately busy in learning to paint, with great pleasure and successe. All other things well; especially a new interest I am making, by a match in hand between the eldest son of Sir G. Carteret, and my Lady Jemimah Montage. The Duke of Yorke gone down to the fleete, but all suppose not with intent to stay there, as it is not fit, all men conceive, he should.

THE DIARY OF SAMUEL PEPYS M.A. F.R.S.
CLERK OF THE ACTS AND SECRETARY TO THE ADMIRALTY
TRANSCRIBED FROM THE SHORTHAND MANUSCRIPT IN THE
PEPYSIAN LIBRARY
MAGDALENE COLLEGE CAMBRIDGE BY THE REV. MYNORS
BRIGHT M.A. LATE FELLOW
AND PRESIDENT OF THE COLLEGE
(Unabridged)
WITH LORD BRAYBROOKE'S NOTES
EDITED WITH ADDITIONS BY
HENRY B. WHEATLEY F.S.A.

DIARY OF SAMUEL PEPYS.

JULY 1665

July 1st, 1665. Called up betimes, though weary and sleepy, by appointment by Mr. Povy and Colonell Norwood to discourse about some payments of Tangier. They gone, I to the office and there sat all the morning. At noon dined at home, and then to the Duke of Albemarle's, by appointment, to give him an account of some disorder in the Yarde at Portsmouth, by workmen's going away of their owne accord, for lacke of money, to get work of hay-making, or any thing else to earne themselves bread.

> [There are several letters among the State Papers from Commissioner Thomas Middleton relating to the want of workmen at Portsmouth Dockyard. On June 29th Middleton wrote to Pepys, "The ropemakers have discharged themselves for want of money, and gone into the country to make hay." The blockmakers, the joiners, and the sawyers all refused to work longer without money ("Calendar," 1664-65, p. 453).]

Thence to Westminster, where I hear the sicknesse encreases greatly, and to the Harp and Ball with Mary talking, who tells me simply her losing of her first love in the country in Wales, and coming up hither unknown to her friends, and it seems Dr. Williams do pretend love to her, and I have found him there several times. Thence by coach and late at the office, and so to bed. Sad at the newes that seven or eight houses in Bazing Hall street, are shut up of the plague.

2nd (Sunday). Up, and all the morning dressing my closet at the office with my plates, very neatly, and a fine place now it is, and will be a pleasure to sit in, though I thank God I needed none before. At noon dined at home, and after dinner to my accounts and cast them up, and find that though I have spent above L90 this month yet I have saved L17, and am worth in all above L1450, for which the Lord be praised! In the evening my Lady Pen and daughter come to see, and supped with us, then a messenger about business of the office from

Sir G. Carteret at Chatham, and by word of mouth did send me word that the business between my Lord and him is fully agreed on,

[The arrangements for the marriage of Lady Jemimah Montagu to Philip Carteret were soon settled, for the wedding took place on July 31st]

and is mightily liked of by the King and the Duke of Yorke, and that he sent me this word with great joy; they gone, we to bed. I hear this night that Sir J. Lawson was buried late last night at St. Dunstan's by us, without any company at all, and that the condition of his family is but very poor, which I could be contented to be sorry for, though he never was the man that ever obliged me by word or deed.

3rd. Up and by water with Sir W. Batten and Sir J. Minnes to White Hall to the Duke of Albemarle, where, after a little business, we parted, and I to the Harp and Ball, and there staid a while talking to Mary, and so home to dinner. After dinner to the Duke of Albemarle's again, and so to the Swan, and there 'demeurais un peu'de temps con la fille', and so to the Harp and Ball, and alone 'demeurais un peu de temps baisant la', and so away home and late at the office about letters, and so home, resolving from this night forwards to close all my letters, if possible, and end all my business at the office by daylight, and I shall go near to do it and put all my affairs in the world in good order, the season growing so sickly, that it is much to be feared how a man can escape having a share with others in it, for which the good Lord God bless me, or to be fitted to receive it. So after supper to bed, and mightily troubled in my sleep all night with dreams of Jacke Cole, my old schoolfellow, lately dead, who was born at the same time with me, and we reckoned our fortunes pretty equal. God fit me for his condition!

4th. Up, and sat at the office all the morning. At noon to the 'Change and thence to the Dolphin, where a good dinner at the cost of one Mr. Osbaston, who lost a wager to Sir W. Batten, Sir W. Rider, and Sir R. Ford, a good while since and now it is spent. The wager was that ten of our ships should not have a fight with ten of the enemy's before Michaelmas. Here was other very good company, and merry, and at last in come Mr. Buckeworth, a very fine gentleman, and proves to be a Huntingdonshire man. Thence to my office and there all the afternoon till night, and so home to settle some accounts of Tangier and other papers. I hear this day the Duke and Prince Rupert are both come back from sea, and neither of them go back again. The latter I much wonder at, but it seems the towne reports so, and I am very glad of it. This morning I did a good piece of work with Sir W. Warren, ending the business of the lotterys, wherein honestly I think I shall get above L100. Bankert, it seems, is come home with the little fleete he hath been abroad with, without doing any thing, so that there is nobody of an enemy at sea. We are in great hopes of meeting with the Dutch East India fleete, which is mighty rich, or with De Ruyter, who is so also. Sir

Richard Ford told me this day, at table, a fine account, how the Dutch were like to have been mastered by the present Prince of Orange

> [The period alluded to is 1650, when the States-General disbanded part of the forces which the Prince of Orange (William) wished to retain. The prince attempted, but unsuccessfully, to possess himself of Amsterdam. In the same year he died, at the early age of twenty-four; some say of the small-pox; others, with Sir Richard Ford, say of poison.--B.]

his father to be besieged in Amsterdam, having drawn an army of foot into the towne, and horse near to the towne by night, within three miles of the towne, and they never knew of it; but by chance the Hamburgh post in the night fell among the horse, and heard their design, and knowing the way, it being very dark and rainy, better than they, went from them, and did give notice to the towne before the others could reach the towne, and so were saved. It seems this De Witt and another family, the Beckarts, were among the chief of the familys that were enemys to the Prince, and were afterwards suppressed by the Prince, and continued so till he was, as they say, poysoned; and then they turned all again, as it was, against the young Prince, and have so carried it to this day, it being about 12 and 14 years, and De Witt in the head of them.

5th. Up, and advised about sending of my wife's bedding and things to Woolwich, in order to her removal thither. So to the office, where all the morning till noon, and so to the 'Change, and thence home to dinner. In the afternoon I abroad to St. James's, and there with Mr. Coventry a good while, and understand how matters are ordered in the fleete: that is, my Lord Sandwich goes Admiral; under him Sir G. Ascue, and Sir T. Teddiman; Vice-Admiral, Sir W. Pen; and under him Sir W. Barkeley, and Sir Jos. Jordan: Reere-Admiral, Sir Thomas Allen; and under him Sir Christopher Mings,

> [The son of a shoemaker, bred to the sea-service; he rose to the rank of an admiral, and was killed in the fight with the Dutch, June, 1666.--B. See post, June 10th, 1666.]

and Captain Harman. We talked in general of business of the Navy, among others how he had lately spoken to Sir G. Carteret, and professed great resolution of friendship with him and reconciliation, and resolves to make it good as well as he can, though it troubles him, he tells me, that something will come before him wherein he must give him offence, but I do find upon the whole that Mr. Coventry do not listen to these complaints of money with the readiness and resolvedness to remedy that he used to do, and I think if he begins to draw in it is high time for me to do so too. From thence walked round to White Hall, the Parke being quite locked up; and I observed a house shut up this day in the Pell Mell, where heretofore in Cromwell's time we young men used to keep our weekly clubs. And so to White Hall to Sir G. Carteret, who is come this day from Chatham, and mighty glad he is to see me, and begun to talk of our great business of the match, which goes on as fast as possible, but for convenience we took water and over to his coach to Lambeth, by which we went to Deptford, all the way talking, first, how matters are quite concluded with all possible content between my Lord and him and signed and sealed, so that my Lady Sandwich is to come thither to-morrow or next day, and the young lady is sent for, and all likely to be ended between them in a very little while, with mighty joy on both sides, and the King, Duke, Lord Chancellor, and all mightily pleased. Thence to newes, wherein I find that Sir G. Carteret do now take all my Lord Sandwich's business to heart, and makes it the same with his owne. He tells me how at Chatham it was proposed to my Lord Sandwich to be joined with the Prince in the command of the fleete, which he was most willing to; but when it come to the Prince, he was quite against it; saying, there could be no government, but that it would be better to have two fleetes, and neither under the command of the other, which he would not agree to. So the King was not pleased; but, without any unkindnesse, did order the fleete to be ordered as above, as to the Admirals and commands: so the Prince is come up; and Sir G. Carteret, I remember, had this word thence, that, says he, by this means, though the King told him that it would be but for this expedition, yet I believe we shall keepe him out for altogether. He tells me how my Lord was much troubled at Sir W. Pen's being ordered forth (as it seems he is, to go to Solebay, and with the best fleete he can, to go forth), and no notice taken of my Lord Sandwich going after him, and having the command over him. But after some discourse Mr. Coventry did satisfy, as he says, my Lord, so as they parted friends both in that point and upon the other wherein I know my Lord was troubled, and which Mr. Coventry did speak to him of first thinking that my Lord might justly take offence at, his not being mentioned in the relation of the fight in the news book, and did clear all to my Lord how little he was concerned in it, and therewith my Lord also satisfied, which I am mightily glad of, because I should take it a very great misfortune to me to have them two to differ above all the persons in the world. Being come to Deptford, my Lady not being within, we parted, and I by water to Woolwich, where I found my wife come, and her two mayds, and very prettily accommodated they will be; and I left them going to supper, grieved in my heart to part with my wife, being worse by much without her, though some trouble there is in having the care of a family at home in this plague time, and so took leave, and I in one boat and W. Hewer in another home very late, first against tide, we having walked in the dark to Greenwich. Late home and to bed, very lonely.

6th. Up and forth to give order to my pretty grocer's wife's house, who, her husband tells me, is going this day for the summer into the country. I bespoke some sugar, &c., for my father, and so home to the office, where all the morning. At noon dined at home, and then by water to White Hall to Sir G. Carteret about money for the office, a sad thought, for in a little while all must go to wracke, winter coming on apace, when a great sum must be ready to pay part of the fleete, and so far we are from it that we have not enough to stop the mouths of poor people and their hands from falling about our eares here almost in the office. God give a good end to it! Sir G. Carteret told me one considerable thing: Alderman Backewell is ordered abroad upon some private score with a great sum of money; wherein I was instrumental the other day in shipping him away. It seems some of his creditors have taken notice of it, and he was like to be broke yesterday in his absence; Sir G. Carteret telling me that the King and the kingdom must as good as fall with that man at this time; and that he was forced to get L4000 himself to answer Backewell's people's occasions, or he must have broke; but committed this to me as a great secret and which I am heartily sorry to hear. Thence, after a little merry discourse of our marrying business, I parted, and by coach to several places, among others to see my Lord Brunkerd, who is not well, but was at rest when I come. I could not see him, nor had much mind, one of the great houses within two doors of him being shut up: and, Lord! the number of houses visited, which this day I observed through the town quite round in my way by Long Lane and London Wall. So home to the office, and thence to Sir W. Batten, and spent the evening at supper; and, among other discourse, the rashness of Sir John Lawson, for breeding up his daughter so high and proud, refusing a man of great interest, Sir W. Barkeley, to match her with a melancholy fellow, Colonell Norton's' son, of no interest nor good nature nor generosity at all, giving her L6000, when the other would have taken her with two; when he himself knew that he was not worth the money himself in all the world, he did give her that portion, and is since dead, and left his wife and two daughters beggars, and the other gone away with L6000, and no content in it, through the ill qualities of her father-in-law and husband, who, it seems, though a pretty woman, contracted for her as if he had been buying a horse; and, worst of all, is now of no use to serve the mother and two little sisters in any stead at Court, whereas the other might have done what he would for her: so here is an end of this family's pride, which, with good care, might have been what they would, and done well. Thence, weary of this discourse, as the act of the greatest rashness that ever I heard of in all my little conversation, we parted, and I home to bed. Sir W. Pen, it seems, sailed last night from Solebay with, about sixty sail of ship, and my Lord Sandwich in "The Prince" and some others, it seems, going after them to overtake them, for I am sure my Lord Sandwich will do all possible to overtake them, and will be troubled to the heart if he do it not.

7th. Up, and having set my neighbour, Mr. Hudson, wine coopers, at work drawing out a tierce of wine for the sending of some of it to my wife, I abroad, only taking notice to what a condition it hath pleased God to bring me that at this time I have two tierces of Claret, two quarter casks of Canary, and a smaller vessel of Sack; a vessel of Tent, another of Malaga, and another of white wine, all in my wine cellar together; which, I believe, none of my friends of my name now alive ever had of his owne at one time. To Westminster, and there with Mr. Povy and Creed talking of our Tangier business, and by and by I drew Creed aside and acquainted him with what Sir G. Carteret did tell me about Backewell the other day, because he hath money of his in his hands. So home, taking some new books, L5 worth, home to my great content. At home all the day after busy. Some excellent discourse and advice of Sir W. Warren's in the afternoon, at night home to look over my new books, and so late to bed.

8th. All day very diligent at the office, ended my letters by 9 at night, and then fitted myself to go down to Woolwich to my wife, which I did, calling at Sir G. Carteret's at Deptford, and there hear that my Lady Sandwich is come, but not very well. By 12 o'clock to Woolwich, found my wife asleep in bed, but strange to think what a fine night I had down, but before I had been one minute on shore, the mightiest storm come of wind and rain that almost could be for a quarter of an houre and so left. I to bed, being the first time I come to her lodgings, and there lodged well.

9th (Lord's day). Very pleasant with her and among my people, while she made her ready, and, about 10 o'clock, by water to Sir G. Carteret, and there find my Lady [Sandwich] in her chamber, not very well, but looks the worst almost that ever I did see her in my life. It seems her drinking of the water at Tunbridge did almost kill her before she could with most violent physique get it out of her body again. We are received with most extraordinary kindnesse by my Lady Carteret and her children, and dined most nobly. Sir G. Carteret went to Court this morning. After dinner I took occasion to have much discourse with Mr. Ph. Carteret, and find him a very modest man; and I think verily of mighty good nature, and pretty understanding. He did give me a good account of the fight with the Dutch. My Lady Sandwich dined in her chamber. About three o'clock I, leaving my wife there, took boat and home, and there shifted myself into my black silke suit, and having promised Harman yesterday, I to his house, which I find very mean, and mean company. His wife very ill; I could not see her. Here I, with her father and Kate Joyce, who was also very ill, were godfathers and godmother to his boy, and was christened Will. Mr. Meriton christened him. The most observable thing I found there to my content, was to hear him and his clerk tell me that in this parish of Michell's, Cornhill, one of the middlemost parishes and a great one of the towne, there hath, notwithstanding this sickliness, been buried of any disease, man, woman, or child, not one for thirteen months last past; which [is] very strange. And the like in a good degree in most other parishes, I hear, saving only of the plague in them, but in this neither the plague nor any other disease. So back again home and reshifted myself, and so down to my Lady Carteret's, where mighty merry and great pleasantnesse between my Lady Sandwich and the young ladies and me, and all of us mighty merry, there never having been in the world sure a greater business of general content than this match proposed between Mr. Carteret and my Lady Jemimah. But withal it is mighty pretty to think how my poor Lady Sandwich, between her and me, is doubtfull whether her daughter will like of it or no, and how troubled she is for fear of it, which I do not fear at all, and desire her not to do it, but her fear is the most discreet and pretty that ever I did see. Late here, and then my wife and I, with most hearty kindnesse from my Lady Carteret by boat to Woolwich, come thither about 12 at night, and so to bed.

10th. Up, and with great pleasure looking over a nest of puppies of Mr. Shelden's, with which my wife is most extraordinary pleased, and one of them is promised her. Anon I took my leave, and away by water to the Duke of Albemarle's, where he tells me that I must be at Hampton Court anon. So I home to look over my Tangier papers, and having a coach of Mr. Povy's attending me, by appointment, in order to my coming to dine at his country house at Brainford, where he and his family is, I went and Mr. Tasbrough with me therein, it being a pretty chariot, but most inconvenient as to the horses throwing dust and dirt into one's eyes and upon one's clothes. There I staid a quarter of an houre, Creed being there, and being able to do little business (but the less the better). Creed rode before, and Mr. Povy and I after him in the chariot; and I was set down by him at the Parke pale, where one of his saddle horses was ready for me, he himself not daring to come into the house or be seen, because that a servant of his, out of his horse, happened to be sicke, but is not yet dead, but was never suffered to come into his house after he was ill. But this opportunity was taken to injure Povy, and most horribly he is abused by some persons hereupon, and his fortune, I believe, quite broke; but that he hath a good heart to bear, or a cunning one to conceal his evil. There I met with Sir W. Coventry, and by and by was heard by my Lord Chancellor and Treasurer about our Tangier money, and my Lord Treasurer had ordered me to forbear meddling with the L15,000 he offered me the other day, but, upon opening the case to them, they did offer it again, and so I think I shall have it, but my Lord General must give his consent in it, this money having been promised to him, and he very angry at the proposal. Here though I have not been in many years, yet I lacke time to stay, besides that it is, I perceive, an unpleasing thing to be at Court, everybody being fearful one of another, and all so sad, enquiring after the plague, so that I stole away by my horse to Kingston, and there with trouble was forced, to press two sturdy rogues to carry me to London, and met at the waterside with Mr. Charnocke, Sir Philip Warwicke's clerke, who had been in company and was quite foxed. I took him with me in my boat, and so away to Richmond, and there, by night, walked with him to Moreclacke, a very pretty walk, and there staid a good while, now and then talking and sporting with Nan the servant, who says she is a seaman's wife, and at last bade good night.

11th. And so all night down by water, a most pleasant passage, and come thither by two o'clock, and so walked from the Old Swan home, and there to bed to my Will, being very weary, and he lodging at my desire in my house. At 6 o'clock up and to Westminster (where and all the towne besides, I hear, the plague encreases), and, it being too soon to go to the Duke of Albemarle, I to the Harp and Ball, and there made a bargain with Mary to go forth with me in the afternoon, which she with much ado consented to. So I to the Duke of Albemarle's, and there with much ado did get his consent in part to my having the money promised for Tangier, and the other part did not concur. So being displeased with this, I back to the office and there sat alone a while doing business, and then by a solemn invitation to the Trinity House, where a great dinner and company, Captain Dobbin's feast for Elder Brother. But I broke up before the dinner half over and by water to the Harp and Ball, and thence had Mary meet me at the New Exchange, and there took coach and I with great pleasure took the ayre to Highgate, and thence to Hampstead, much pleased with her company, pretty and innocent, and had what pleasure almost I would with her, and so at night, weary and sweaty, it being very hot beyond bearing, we back again, and I set her down in St. Martin's Lane, and so I to the evening 'Change, and there hear all the towne full that Ostend is delivered to us, and that Alderman Backewell

> [Among the State Papers is a letter from the king to the Lord General (dated August 8th, 1665): "Alderman Backwell being in great straits for the second payment he has to make for the service in Flanders, as much tin is to be transmitted to him as will raise the sum. Has authorized him and Sir George Carteret to treat with the tin farmers for 500 tons of tin to be speedily transported under good convoy; but if, on consulting with Alderman Backwell, this plan of the tin seems insufficient, then without further difficulty he is to dispose for that purpose of the L10,000 assigned for pay of the Guards, not doubting that before that comes due, other ways will be found for supplying it; the payment in Flanders is of such importance that some means must be found of providing for it" ("Calendar," Domestic, 1664-65, pp. 508, 509)]

did go with L50,000 to that purpose. But the truth of it I do not know, but something I believe there is extraordinary in his going. So to the office, where I did what I could as to letters, and so away to bed, shifting myself, and taking some Venice treakle, feeling myself out of order, and thence to bed to sleep.

12th. After doing what business I could in the morning, it being a solemn fast-day

> ["A form of Common Prayer; together with an order for fasting for the averting of God's heavy visitation upon many places of this realm. The fast to be observed within the cities of London and Westminster and places adjacent, on Wednesday the twelfth of this instant July, and both there and in all parts of this realm on the first Wednesday in every month during the visitation" ("Calendar of State Papers," Domestic, 1664-65, p. 466).]

for the plague growing upon us, I took boat and down to Deptford, where I stood with great pleasure an houre or two by my Lady Sandwich's bedside, talking to her (she lying prettily in bed) of my Lady Jemimah's being from my Lady Pickering's when our letters come to that place; she being at my Lord Montagu's, at Boughton. The truth is, I had received letters of it two days ago, but had dropped them, and was in a very extraordinary straite what to do for them, or what account to give my Lady, but sent to every place; I sent to

Moreclacke, where I had been the night before, and there they were found, which with mighty joy come safe to me; but all ending with satisfaction to my Lady and me, though I find my Lady Carteret not much pleased with this delay, and principally because of the plague, which renders it unsafe to stay long at Deptford. I eat a bit (my Lady Carteret being the most kind lady in the world), and so took boat, and a fresh boat at the Tower, and so up the river, against tide all the way, I having lost it by staying prating to and with my Lady, and, from before one, made it seven ere we got to Hampton Court; and when I come there all business was over, saving my finding Mr. Coventry at his chamber, and with him a good while about several businesses at his chamber, and so took leave, and away to my boat, and all night upon the water, staying a while with Nan at Moreclacke, very much pleased and merry with her, and so on homeward, and come home by two o'clock, shooting the bridge at that time of night, and so to bed, where I find Will is not, he staying at Woolwich to come with my wife to dinner tomorrow to my Lady Carteret's. Heard Mr. Williamson repeat at Hampton Court to-day how the King of France hath lately set out a most high arrest against the Pope, which is reckoned very lofty and high.

[Arret. The rupture between Alexander VII. and Louis XIV. was healed in 1664, by the treaty signed at Pisa, on February 12th. On August 9th, the pope's nephew, Cardinal Chigi, made his entry into Paris, as legate, to give the king satisfaction for the insult offered at Rome by the Corsican guard to the Duc de Crequi, the French ambassador; (see January 25th, 1662-63). Cardinal Imperiali, Governor of Rome, asked pardon of the king in person, and all the hard conditions of the treaty were fulfilled. But no arret against the pope was set forth in 1665. On the contrary, Alexander, now wishing to please the king, issued a constitution on February 2nd, 1665, ordering all the clergy of France, without any exception, to sign a formulary condemning the famous five propositions extracted from the works of Jansenius; and on April 29th, the king in person ordered the parliament to register the bull. The Jansenist party, of course, demurred to this proceeding; the Bishops of Alais, Angers, Beauvais, and Pamiers, issuing mandates calling upon their clergy to refuse. It was against these mandates, as being contrary to the king's declaration and the pope's intentions, that the arret was directed.--B.]

13th. Lay long, being sleepy, and then up to the office, my Lord Brunker (after his sickness) being come to the office, and did what business there was, and so I by water, at night late, to Sir G. Carteret's, but there being no oars to carry me, I was fain to call a skuller that had a gentleman already in it, and he proved a man of love to musique, and he and I sung together the way down with great pleasure, and an incident extraordinary to be met with. There come to dinner, they haveing dined, but my Lady caused something to be brought for me, and I dined well and mighty merry, especially my Lady Slaning and I about eating of creame and brown bread, which she loves as much as I. Thence after long discourse with them and my Lady alone, I and [my] wife, who by agreement met here, took leave, and I saw my wife a little way down (it troubling me that this absence makes us a little strange instead of more fond), and so parted, and I home to some letters, and then home to bed. Above 700 died of the plague this week.

14th. Up, and all the morning at the Exchequer endeavouring to strike tallys for money for Tangier, and mightily vexed to see how people attend there, some out of towne, and others drowsy, and to others it was late, so that the King's business suffers ten times more than all their service is worth. So I am put off to to-morrow. Thence to the Old Exchange, by water, and there bespoke two fine shirts of my pretty seamstress, who, she tells me, serves Jacke Fenn. Upon the 'Change all the news is that guns have been heard and that news is come by a Dane that my Lord was in view of De Ruyter, and that since his parting from my Lord of Sandwich he hath heard guns, but little of it do I think true. So home to dinner, where Povy by agreement, and after dinner we to talk of our Tangier matters, about keeping our profit at the pay and victualling of the garrison, if the present undertakers should leave it, wherein I did [not] nor will do any thing unworthy me and any just man, but they being resolved to quit it, it is fit I should suffer Mr. Povy to do what he can with Mr. Gauden about it to our profit. Thence to the discoursing of putting some sums of money in order and tallys, which we did pretty well. So he in the evening gone, I by water to Sir G. Carteret's, and there find my Lady Sandwich and her buying things for my Lady Jem.'s wedding; and my Lady Jem. is beyond expectation come to Dagenhams, where Mr. Carteret is to go to visit her to-morrow; and my proposal of waiting on him, he being to go alone to all persons strangers to him, was well accepted, and so I go with him. But, Lord! to see how kind my Lady Carteret is to her! Sends her most rich jewells, and provides bedding and things of all sorts most richly for her, which makes my Lady and me out of our wits almost to see the kindnesse she treats us all with, as if they would buy the young lady. Thence away home and, foreseeing my being abroad two days, did sit up late making of letters ready against tomorrow, and other things, and so to bed, to be up betimes by the helpe of a larum watch, which by chance I borrowed of my watchmaker to-day, while my owne is mending.

15th. Up, and after all business done, though late, I to Deptford, but before I went out of the office saw there young Bagwell's wife returned, but could not stay to speak to her, though I had a great mind to it, and also another great lady, as to fine clothes, did attend there to have a ticket signed; which I did do, taking her through the garden to my office, where I signed it and had a salute--[kiss]-- of her, and so I away by boat to Redriffe, and thence walked, and after dinner, at Sir G. Carteret's, where they stayed till almost three o'clock for me, and anon took boat, Mr. Carteret and I to the ferry-place at Greenwich, and there staid an hour crossing the water to and again to get our coach and horses over; and by and by set out, and so toward Dagenhams. But, Lord! what silly discourse we had by the way as to love-matters, he being the most awkerd man I ever met with in my life as to that business. Thither we come, by that time it begun to be dark, and were kindly received by Lady Wright and my Lord Crew. And to discourse they went, my Lord discoursing with him, asking of him questions of travell, which he answered well enough in a few words; but nothing to the lady from him at all. To supper, and after supper to talk again, he yet taking no notice of the lady. My Lord would have had me have consented to leaving the young people together to-night, to begin their amours, his staying being but to be little. But I advised against it, lest the lady might be too much surprised. So they led him up to his chamber, where I staid a little, to know how he liked the lady, which he told me he did mightily; but, Lord! in the dullest insipid manner that ever lover did. So I bid him good night, and down to prayers with my Lord Crew's family, and after prayers, my Lord, and Lady Wright, and I, to consult what to do; and it was agreed at last to have them go to church together, as the family used to do, though his lameness was a great objection against it. But at last my Lady Jem. sent me word by my Lady Wright that it would be better to do just as they used to do before his coming; and therefore she desired to go to church, which was yielded then to.

16th (Lord's day). I up, having lain with Mr. Moore in the chaplin's chamber. And having trimmed myself, down to Mr. Carteret; and he being ready we down and walked in the gallery an hour or two, it being a most noble and pretty house that ever, for the bigness, I saw. Here I taught him what to do: to take the lady always by the hand to lead her, and telling him that I would find opportunity to leave them two together, he should make these and these compliments, and also take a time to do the like to Lord Crew and Lady Wright. After I had instructed him, which he thanked me for, owning that he needed my teaching him, my Lord Crew come down and family, the young lady among the rest; and so by coaches to church four miles off; where a pretty good sermon, and a declaration of penitence of a man that had undergone the Churches censure for his wicked life. Thence back again by coach, Mr. Carteret having not had the confidence to take his lady once by the hand, coming or going, which I told him of when we come home, and he will hereafter do it. So to dinner. My Lord excellent discourse. Then to walk in the gallery, and to sit down. By and by my Lady Wright and I go out (and then my Lord Crew, he not by design), and lastly my Lady Crew come out, and left the young people together. And a little pretty daughter of my Lady Wright's most innocently come out afterward, and shut the door to, as if she had done it, poor child, by inspiration; which made us without, have good sport to laugh at. They together an hour, and by and by church-time, whither he led her into the coach and into the church, and so at church all the afternoon, several handsome ladies at church. But it was most extraordinary hot that ever I knew it. So home again and to walk in the gardens, where we left the young couple a second time; and my Lady Wright and I to walk together, who to my trouble tells me that my Lady Jem. must have something done to her body by Scott before she can be married, and therefore care must be had to send him, also that some more new clothes must of necessity be made her, which and other things I took care of. Anon to supper, and excellent discourse and dispute between my Lord Crew and the chaplin, who is a good scholler, but a nonconformist. Here this evening I spoke with Mrs. Carter, my old acquaintance, that hath lived with my Lady these twelve or thirteen years, the sum of all whose discourse and others for her, is, that I would get her a good husband; which I have promised, but know not when I shall perform. After Mr. Carteret was carried to his chamber, we to prayers again and then to bed.

17th. Up all of us, and to billiards; my Lady Wright, Mr. Carteret, myself, and every body. By and by the young couple left together. Anon to dinner; and after dinner Mr. Carteret took my advice about giving to the servants, and I led him to give L10 among them, which he did, by leaving it to the chief man-servant, Mr. Medows, to do for him. Before we went, I took my Lady Jem. apart, and would know how she liked this gentleman, and whether she was under any difficulty concerning him. She blushed, and hid her face awhile; but at last I forced her to tell me. She answered that she could readily obey what her father and mother had done; which was all she could say, or I expect. So anon I took leave, and for London. But, Lord! to see, among other things, how all these great people here are afeard of London, being doubtfull of anything that comes from thence, or that hath lately been there, that I was forced to say that I lived wholly at Woolwich. In our way Mr. Carteret did give me mighty thanks for my care and pains for him, and is mightily pleased, though the truth is, my Lady Jem. hath carried herself with mighty discretion and gravity, not being forward at all in any degree, but mighty serious in her answers to him, as by what he says and I observed, I collect. To London to my office, and there took letters from the office, where all well, and so to the Bridge, and there he and I took boat and to Deptford, where mighty welcome, and brought the good newes of all being pleased to them. Mighty mirth at my giving them an account of all; but the young man could not be got to say one word before me or my Lady Sandwich of his adventures, but, by what he afterwards related to his father and mother and sisters, he gives an account that pleases them mightily. Here Sir G. Carteret would have me lie all night, which I did most nobly, better than ever I did in my life, Sir G. Carteret being mighty kind to me, leading me to my chamber; and all their care now is, to have the business ended, and they have reason, because the sicknesse puts all out of order, and they cannot safely stay where they are.

18th. Up and to the office, where all the morning, and so to my house and eat a bit of victuals, and so to the 'Change, where a little business and a very thin Exchange; and so walked through London to the Temple, where I took water for Westminster to the Duke of Albemarle, to wait on him, and so to Westminster Hall, and there paid for my newes-books, and did give Mrs. Michell, who is going out of towne because of the sicknesse, and her husband, a pint of wine, and so Sir W. Warren coming to me by appointment we away by water home, by the way discoursing about the project I have of getting some money and doing the King good service too about the mast docke at Woolwich, which I fear will never be done if I do not go about it. After dispatching letters at the office, I by water down to Deptford, where I staid a little while, and by water to my wife, whom I have not seen 6 or 5 days, and there supped with her, and mighty pleasant, and saw with content her drawings, and so to bed mighty merry. I was much troubled this day to hear at Westminster how the officers do bury the dead in the open Tuttle-fields, pretending want of room elsewhere; whereas the New Chappell churchyard was walled-in at the publick charge in the last plague time, merely for want of room and now none, but such as are able to pay dear for it, can be buried there.

19th. Up and to the office, and thence presently to the Exchequer, and there with much trouble got my tallys, and afterwards took Mr. Falconer, Spicer, and another or two to the Leg and there give them a dinner, and so with my tallys and about 30 dozen of bags, which it seems are my due, having paid the fees as if I had received the money I away home, and after a little stay down by water to Deptford, where I find all full of joy, and preparing to go to Dagenhams to-morrow. To supper, and after supper to talk without end. Very late I went away, it raining, but I had a design 'pour aller a la femme de Bagwell' and did so . . . . So away about 12, and it raining hard I back to Sir G. Carteret and there called up the page, and to bed there, being all in a most violent sweat.

20th. Up, in a boat among other people to the Tower, and there to the office, where we sat all the morning. So down to Deptford and there dined, and after dinner saw my Lady Sandwich and Mr. Carteret and his two sisters over the water, going to Dagenhams, and my Lady Carteret towards Cranburne.

[The royal lodge of that name in Windsor Forest, occupied by Sir George Carteret as Vice-Chamberlain to the King.--B.]

So all the company broke up in most extraordinary joy, wherein I am mighty contented that I have had the good fortune to be so instrumental, and I think it will be of good use to me. So walked to Redriffe, where I hear the sickness is, and indeed is scattered almost every where, there dying 1089 of the plague this week. My Lady Carteret did this day give me a bottle of plague-water home with me. So home to write letters late, and then home to bed, where I have not lain these 3 or 4 nights. I received yesterday a letter from my Lord Sandwich, giving me thanks for my care about their marriage business, and desiring it to be dispatched, that no disappointment may happen therein, which I will help on all I can. This afternoon I waited on the Duke of Albemarle, and so to Mrs. Croft's, where I found and saluted Mrs. Burrows, who is a very pretty woman for a mother of so many children. But, Lord! to see how the plague spreads. It being now all over King's Streete, at the Axe, and next door to it, and in other places.

21st. Up and abroad to the goldsmiths, to see what money I could get upon my present tallys upon the advance of the Excise, and I hope I shall get L10,000. I went also and had them entered at the Excise Office. Alderman Backewell is at sea. Sir R. Viner come to towne but this morning. So Colvill was the only man I could yet speak withal to get any money of. Met with Mr. Povy, and I with him and dined at the Custom House Taverne, there to talk of our Tangier business, and Stockedale and Hewet with us. So abroad to several places, among others to Anthony Joyce's, and there broke to him my desire to have Pall married to

Harman, whose wife, poor woman, is lately dead, to my trouble, I loving her very much, and he will consider it. So home and late at my chamber, setting some papers in order; the plague growing very raging, and my apprehensions of it great. So very late to bed.

22nd. As soon as up I among my goldsmiths, Sir Robert Viner and Colvill, and there got L10,000 of my new tallys accepted, and so I made it my work to find out Mr. Mervin and sent for others to come with their bills of Exchange, as Captain Hewett, &c., and sent for Mr. Jackson, but he was not in town. So all the morning at the office, and after dinner, which was very late, I to Sir R. Viner's, by his invitation in the morning, and got near L5000 more accepted, and so from this day the whole, or near, L15,000, lies upon interest. Thence I by water to Westminster, and the Duke of Albemarle being gone to dinner to my Lord of Canterbury's, I thither, and there walked and viewed the new hall, a new old-fashion hall as much as possible. Begun, and means left for the ending of it, by Bishop Juxon. Not coming proper to speak with him, I to Fox-hall, where to the Spring garden; but I do not see one guest there, the town being so empty of any body to come thither. Only, while I was there, a poor woman come to scold with the master of the house that a kinswoman, I think, of hers, that was newly dead of the plague, might be buried in the church-yard; for, for her part, she should not be buried in the commons, as they said she should. Back to White Hall, and by and by comes the Duke of Albemarle, and there, after a little discourse, I by coach home, not meeting with but two coaches, and but two carts from White Hall to my own house, that I could observe; and the streets mighty thin of people. I met this noon with Dr. Burnett, who told me, and I find in the newsbook this week that he posted upon the 'Change, that whoever did spread the report that, instead of the plague, his servant was by him killed, it was forgery, and shewed me the acknowledgment of the master of the pest-house, that his servant died of a bubo on his right groine, and two spots on his right thigh, which is the plague. To my office, where late writing letters, and getting myself prepared with business for Hampton Court to-morrow, and so having caused a good pullet to be got for my supper, all alone, I very late to bed. All the news is great: that we must of necessity fall out with France, for He will side with the Dutch against us. That Alderman Backewell is gone over (which indeed he is) with money, and that Ostend is in our present possession. But it is strange to see how poor Alderman Backewell is like to be put to it in his absence, Mr. Shaw his right hand being ill. And the Alderman's absence gives doubts to people, and I perceive they are in great straits for money, besides what Sir G. Carteret told me about fourteen days ago. Our fleet under my Lord Sandwich being about the latitude 55 (which is a great secret) to the Northward of the Texell. So to bed very late. In my way I called upon Sir W. Turner, and at Mr. Shelcrosse's (but he was not at home, having left his bill with Sir W. Turner), that so I may prove I did what I could as soon as I had money to answer all bills.

23rd (Lord's day). Up very betimes, called by Mr. Cutler, by appointment, and with him in his coach and four horses over London Bridge to Kingston, a very pleasant journey, and at Hampton Court by nine o'clock, and in our way very good and various discourse, as he is a man, that though I think he be a knave, as the world thinks him, yet a man of great experience and worthy to be heard discourse. When we come there, we to Sir W. Coventry's chamber, and there discoursed long with him, he and I alone, the others being gone away, and so walked together through the garden to the house, where we parted, I observing with a little trouble that he is too great now to expect too much familiarity with, and I find he do not mind me as he used to do, but when I reflect upon him and his business I cannot think much of it, for I do not observe anything but the same great kindness from him. I followed the King to chappell, and there hear a good sermon; and after sermon with my Lord Arlington, Sir Thomas Ingram and others, spoke to the Duke about Tangier, but not to much purpose. I was not invited any whither to dinner, though a stranger, which did also trouble me; but yet I must remember it is a Court, and indeed where most are strangers; but, however, Cutler carried me to Mr. Marriott's the house-keeper, and there we had a very good dinner and good company, among others Lilly, the painter. Thence to the councill-chamber, where in a back room I sat all the afternoon, but the councill begun late to sit, and spent most of the time upon Morisco's Tarr businesse. They sat long, and I forced to follow Sir Thomas Ingram, the Duke, and others, so that when I got free and come to look for Cutler, he was gone with his coach, without leaving any word with any body to tell me so; so that I was forced with great trouble to walk up and down looking of him, and at last forced to get a boat to carry me to Kingston, and there, after eating a bit at a neat inne, which pleased me well, I took boat, and slept all the way, without intermission, from thence to Queenhive, where, it being about two o'clock, too late and too soon to go home to bed, I lay and slept till about four,

24th. And then up and home, and there dressed myself, and by appointment to Deptford, to Sir G. Carteret's, between six and seven o'clock, where I found him and my Lady almost ready, and by and by went over to the ferry, and took coach and six horses nobly for Dagenhams, himself and lady and their little daughter, Louisonne, and myself in the coach; where, when we come, we were bravely entertained and spent the day most pleasantly with the young ladies, and I so merry as never more. Only for want of sleep, and drinking of strong beer had a rheum in one of my eyes, which troubled me much. Here with great content all the day, as I think I ever passed a day in my life, because of the contentfulnesse of our errand, and the noblenesse of the company and our manner of going. But I find Mr. Carteret yet as backward almost in his caresses, as he was the first day. At night, about seven o'clock, took coach again; but, Lord! to see in what a pleasant humour Sir G. Carteret hath been both coming and going; so light, so fond, so merry, so boyish (so much content he takes in this business), it is one of the greatest wonders I ever saw in my mind. But once in serious discourse he did say that, if he knew his son to be a debauchee, as many and, most are now-a-days about the Court, he would tell it, and my Lady Jem. should not have him; and so enlarged both he and she about the baseness and looseness of the Court, and told several stories of the Duke of Monmouth, and Richmond, and some great person, my Lord of Ormond's second son, married to a lady of extraordinary quality (fit and that might have been made a wife for the King himself), about six months since, that this great person hath given the pox to------; and discoursed how much this would oblige the Kingdom if the King would banish some of these great persons publiquely from the Court, and wished it with all their hearts. We set out so late that it grew dark, so as we doubted the losing of our way; and a long time it was, or seemed, before we could get to the water-side, and that about eleven at night, where, when we come, all merry (only my eye troubled me, as I said), we found no ferryboat was there, nor no oares to carry us to Deptford. However, afterwards oares was called from the other side at Greenwich; but, when it come, a frolique, being mighty merry, took us, and there we would sleep all night in the coach in the Isle of Doggs. So we did, there being now with us my Lady Scott, and with great pleasure drew up the glasses, and slept till daylight, and then some victuals and wine being brought us, we ate a bit, and so up and took boat, merry as might be; and when come to Sir G. Carteret's, there all to bed.

25th. Our good humour in every body continuing, and there I slept till seven o'clock. Then up and to the office, well refreshed, my eye only troubling me, which by keeping a little covered with my handkercher and washing now and then with cold water grew better by night. At noon to the 'Change, which was very thin, and thence homeward, and was called in by Mr. Rawlinson, with whom I dined and some good company very harmlessly merry. But sad the story of the plague in the City, it growing mightily. This day my Lord Brunker did give me Mr. Grant's' book upon the Bills of Mortality, new printed and enlarged. Thence to my office awhile, full of business, and thence by coach to the Duke of Albemarle's, not meeting one coach going nor coming from my house thither and back again, which is very strange. One of my chief errands was to speak to Sir W. Clerke about my wife's brother, who importunes me, and I doubt he do want mightily, but I can do little for him there as to employment in the army, and out of my purse I dare not for fear of a precedent, and letting him come often to me is troublesome and dangerous too, he living in the dangerous part of the town, but I will do what I can possibly for him and as soon as I can. Mightily troubled all this afternoon with masters coming to me about Bills of Exchange and my signing them upon my Goldsmiths, but I did send for them all and hope to ease myself this weeke of all the clamour. These two or three days Mr. Shaw at Alderman Backewell's hath lain sick, like to die, and is feared will not live a day to an end. At night home and to bed, my head full of business, and among others, this day come a letter to me from Paris from my Lord Hinchingbroke, about his coming over; and I have sent this night an order from the Duke of Albemarle for a ship of 36 guns to [go] to Calais to fetch him.

26th. Up, and after doing a little business, down to Deptford with Sir W. Batten, and there left him, and I to Greenwich to the Park, where I hear the King and Duke are come by water this morn from Hampton Court. They asked me several questions. The King mightily pleased with his new buildings there. I followed them to Castle's ship in building, and there, met Sir W. Batten, and thence to Sir G. Carteret's, where all the morning with them; they not having any but the Duke of Monmouth, and Sir W. Killigrew, and one gentleman, and a page more. Great variety of talk, and was often led to speak to the King and Duke. By and by they to dinner, and all to dinner and sat down to the King saving myself, which, though I could not in modesty expect, yet, God forgive my pride! I was sorry I was there, that Sir W. Batten should say that he could sit down where I could not, though he had twenty times more reason than I, but this was my pride and folly. I down and walked with Mr. Castle, who told me the design of Ford and Rider to oppose and do all the hurt they can to Captain Taylor in his new ship "The London," and how it comes, and that they are a couple of false persons, which I believe, and withal that he himself is a knave too. He and I by and by to dinner mighty nobly, and the King having dined, he come down, and I went in the barge with him, I sitting at the door. Down to Woolwich (and there I just saw and kissed my wife, and saw some of her painting, which is very curious; and away again to the King) and back again with him in the barge, hearing him and the Duke talk, and seeing and observing their manner of discourse. And God forgive me! though I admire them with all the duty possible, yet the more a man considers and observes them, the less he finds of difference between them and other men, though (blessed be God!) they are both princes of great nobleness and spirits. The barge put me into another boat that come to our side, Mr. Holder with a bag of gold to the Duke, and so they away and I home to the office. The Duke of Monmouth is the most skittish leaping gallant that ever I saw, always in action, vaulting or leaping, or clambering. Thence mighty full of the honour of this day, I took coach and to Kate Joyce's, but she not within, but spoke with Anthony, who tells me he likes well of my proposal for Pall to Harman, but I fear that less than L500 will not be taken, and that I shall not be able to give, though I did not say so to him. After a little other discourse and the sad news of the death of so many in the parish of the plague, forty last night, the bell always going, I back to the Exchange, where I went up and sat talking with my beauty, Mrs. Batelier, a great while, who is indeed one of the finest women I ever saw in my life. After buying some small matter, I home, and there to the office and saw Sir J. Minnes now come from Portsmouth, I home to set my Journall for these four days in order, they being four days of as great content and honour and pleasure to me as ever I hope to live or desire, or think any body else can live. For methinks if a man would but reflect upon this, and think that all these things are ordered by God Almighty to make me contented, and even this very marriage now on foot is one of the things intended to find me content in, in my life and matter of mirth, methinks it should make one mightily more satisfied in the world than he is. This day poor Robin Shaw at Backewell's died, and Backewell himself now in Flanders. The King himself asked about Shaw, and being told he was dead, said he was very sorry for it. The sicknesse is got into our parish this week, and is got, indeed, every where; so that I begin to think of setting things in order, which I pray God enable me to put both as to soul and body.

27th. Called up at 4 o'clock. Up and to my preparing some papers for Hampton Court, and so by water to Fox Hall, and there Mr. Gauden's coach took me up, and by and by I took up him, and so both thither, a brave morning to ride in and good discourse with him. Among others he begun with me to speak of the Tangier Victuallers resigning their employment, and his willingness to come on. Of which I was glad, and took the opportunity to answer him with all kindness and promise of assistance. He told me a while since my Lord Berkeley did speak of it to him, and yesterday a message from Sir Thomas Ingram. When I come to Hampton Court I find Sir T. Ingram and Creed ready with papers signed for the putting of Mr. Gawden in, upon a resignation signed to by Lanyon and sent to Sir Thos. Ingram. At this I was surprized but yet was glad, and so it passed but with respect enough to those that are in, at least without any thing ill taken from it. I got another order signed about the boats, which I think I shall get something by. So dispatched all my business, having assurance of continuance of all hearty love from Sir W. Coventry, and so we staid and saw the King and Queene set out toward Salisbury, and after them the Duke and Duchesse, whose hands I did kiss. And it was the first time I did ever, or did see any body else, kiss her hand, and it was a most fine white and fat hand. But it was pretty to see the young pretty ladies dressed like men, in velvet coats, caps with ribbands, and with laced bands, just like men. Only the Duchesse herself it did not become. They gone, we with great content took coach again, and hungry come to Clapham about one o'clock, and Creed there too before us, where a good dinner, the house having dined, and so to walk up and down in the gardens, mighty pleasant. By and by comes by promise to me Sir G. Carteret, and viewed the house above and below, and sat and drank there, and I had a little opportunity to kiss and spend some time with the ladies above, his daughter, a buxom lass, and his sister Fissant, a serious lady, and a little daughter of hers, that begins to sing prettily. Thence, with mighty pleasure, with Sir G. Carteret by coach, with great discourse of kindnesse with him to my Lord Sandwich, and to me also; and I every day see more good by the alliance. Almost at Deptford I 'light and walked over to Half-way House, and so home, in my way being shown my cozen Patience's house, which seems, at distance, a pretty house. At home met the weekly Bill, where above 1000 encreased in the Bill, and of them, in all about 1,700 of the plague, which hath made the officers this day resolve of sitting at Deptford, which puts me to some consideration what to do. Therefore home to think and consider of every thing about it, and without determining any thing eat a little supper and to bed, full of the pleasure of these 6 or 7 last days.

28th. Up betimes, and down to Deptford, where, after a little discourse with Sir G. Carteret, who is much displeased with the order of our officers yesterday to remove the office to Deptford, pretending other things, but to be sure it is with regard to his own house (which is much because his family is going away). I am glad I was not at the order making, and so I will endeavour to alter it. Set out with my Lady all alone with her with six horses to Dagenhams; going by water to the Ferry. And a pleasant going, and good discourse; and when there, very merry, and the young couple now well acquainted. But, Lord! to see in what fear all the people here do live would make one mad, they are afeard of us that come to them, insomuch that I am troubled at it, and wish myself away. But some cause they have; for the chaplin, with whom but a week or two ago we were here mighty high disputing, is since fallen into a fever and dead, being gone hence to a friend's a good way off. A sober and a healthful man. These considerations make us all hasten the marriage, and resolve it upon Monday next, which is three days before we intended it. Mighty merry all of us, and in the evening with full content took coach again and home by daylight with great pleasure, and thence I down to Woolwich, where find my wife well, and after drinking and talking a little we to bed.

29th. Up betimes, and after viewing some of my wife's pictures, which now she is come to do very finely to my great satisfaction beyond what I could ever look for, I went away and by water to the office, where nobody to meet me, but busy all the morning. At noon to dinner, where I hear that my Will is come in thither and laid down upon my bed, ill of the headake, which put me into extraordinary fear; and I studied all I could to get him out of the house, and set my people to work to do it without discouraging him, and myself went forth to the Old Exchange to pay my fair Batelier for some linnen, and took leave of her, they breaking up shop for a while; and so by coach to Kate Joyce's, and there used all the vehemence and rhetorique I could to get her husband to let her go down to Brampton, but I could not prevail with him; he urging some simple reasons, but most that of profit, minding the house, and the distance, if either of them should be ill. However, I did my best, and more than I had a mind to do, but that I saw him so resolved against it, while she was mightily troubled at it. At last he yielded she should go to Windsor, to some friends there. So I took my leave of them, believing that it is great odds that we ever all see one another again; for I dare not go any more to that end of the towne. So home, and to writing of letters--hard, and then at night home, and fell to my Tangier papers till late, and then to bed, in some ease of mind that Will is gone to his lodging, and that he is likely to do well, it being only the headake.

30th (Lord's day). Up, and in my night gowne, cap and neckcloth, undressed all day long, lost not a minute, but in my chamber, setting my Tangier accounts to rights. Which I did by night to my very heart's content, not only that it is done, but I find every thing right, and even beyond what, after so long neglecting them, I did hope for. The Lord of Heaven be praised for it! Will was with me to-day, and is very well again. It was a sad noise to hear our bell to toll and ring so often to-day, either for deaths or burials; I think five or six times. At night weary with my day's work, but full of joy at my having done it, I to bed, being to rise betimes tomorrow to go to the wedding at Dagenhams. So to bed, fearing I have got some cold sitting in my loose garments all this day.

31st. Up, and very betimes by six o'clock at Deptford, and there find Sir G. Carteret, and my Lady ready to go: I being in my new coloured silk suit, and coat trimmed with gold buttons and gold broad lace round my hands, very rich and fine. By water to the Ferry, where, when we come, no coach there; and tide of ebb so far spent as the horse-boat could not get off on the other side the river to bring away the coach. So we were fain to stay there in the unlucky Isle of Doggs, in a chill place, the morning cool, and wind fresh, above two if not three hours to our great discontent. Yet being upon a pleasant errand, and seeing that it could not be helped, we did bear it very patiently; and it was worth my observing, I thought, as ever any thing, to see how upon these two scores, Sir G. Carteret, the most passionate man in the world, and that was in greatest haste to be gone, did bear with it, and very pleasant all the while, at least not troubled much so as to fret and storm at it. Anon the coach comes: in the mean time there coming a News thither with his horse to go over, that told us he did come from Islington this morning; and that Proctor the vintner of the Miter in Wood-street, and his son, are dead this morning there, of the plague; he having laid out abundance of money there, and was the greatest vintner for some time in London for great entertainments. We, fearing the canonicall hour would be past before we got thither, did with a great deal of unwillingness send away the license and wedding ring. So that when we come, though we drove hard with six horses, yet we found them gone from home; and going towards the church, met them coming from church, which troubled us. But, however, that trouble was soon over; hearing it was well done: they being both in their old cloaths; my Lord Crew giving her, there being three coach fulls of them. The young lady mighty sad, which troubled me; but yet I think it was only her gravity in a little greater degree than usual. All saluted her, but I did not till my Lady Sandwich did ask me whether I had saluted her or no. So to dinner, and very merry we were; but yet in such a sober way as never almost any wedding was in so great families: but it was much better. After dinner company divided, some to cards, others to talk. My Lady Sandwich and I up to settle accounts, and pay her some money. And mighty kind she is to me, and would fain have had me gone down for company with her to Hinchingbroke; but for my life I cannot. At night to supper, and so to talk; and which, methought, was the most extraordinary thing, all of us to prayers as usual, and the young bride and bridegroom too and so after prayers, soberly to bed; only I got into the bridegroom's chamber while he undressed himself, and there was very merry, till he was called to the bride's chamber, and into bed they went. I kissed the bride in bed, and so the curtaines drawne with the greatest gravity that could be, and so good night. But the modesty and gravity of this business was so decent, that it was to me indeed ten times more delightfull than if it had been twenty times more merry and joviall. Whereas I feared I must have sat up all night, we did here all get good beds, and I lay in the same I did before with Mr. Brisband, who is a good scholler and sober man; and we lay in bed, getting him to give me an account of home, which is the most delightfull talke a man can have of any traveller: and so to sleep. My eyes much troubled already with the change of my drink. Thus I ended this month with the greatest joy that ever I did any in my life, because I have spent the greatest part of it with abundance of joy, and honour, and pleasant journeys, and brave entertainments, and without cost of money; and at last live to see the business ended with great content on all sides. This evening with Mr. Brisband, speaking of enchantments and spells; I telling him some of my charms; he told me this of his owne knowledge, at Bourdeaux, in France. The words these:

Voyci un Corps mort,
Royde come un Baston,
Froid comme Marbre,
Leger come un esprit,
Levons to au nom de Jesus Christ.

He saw four little girles, very young ones, all kneeling, each of them, upon one knee; and one begun the first line, whispering in the eare of the next, and the second to the third, and the third to the fourth, and she to the first. Then the first begun the second line, and so round quite through, and, putting each one finger only to a boy that lay flat upon his back on the ground, as if he was dead; at the end of the words, they did with their four fingers raise this boy as high as they could reach, and he [Mr. Brisband] being there, and wondering at it, as also being afeard to see it, for they would have had him to have bore a part in saying the words, in the roome of one of the little girles that was so young that they could hardly make her learn to repeat the words, did, for feare there might be some sleight used in it by the boy, or that the boy might be light, call the cook of the house, a very lusty fellow, as Sir G. Carteret's cook, who is very big, and they did raise him in just the same manner. This is one of the strangest things I ever heard, but he tells it me of his owne knowledge, and I do heartily believe it to be true. I enquired of him whether they were Protestant or Catholique girles; and he told me they were Protestant, which made it the more strange to me. Thus we end this month, as I said, after the greatest glut of content that ever I had; only under some difficulty because of the plague, which grows mightily upon us, the last week being about 1700 or 1800 of the plague. My Lord Sandwich at sea with a fleet of about 100 sail, to the Northward, expecting De Ruyter, or the Dutch East India fleet. My Lord Hinchingbroke coming over from France, and will meet his sister at Scott's-hall. Myself having obliged both these families in this business very much; as both my Lady, and Sir G. Carteret and his Lady do confess exceedingly, and the latter do also now call me cozen, which I am glad of. So God preserve us all friends long, and continue health among us.

THE DIARY OF SAMUEL PEPYS M.A. F.R.S.
CLERK OF THE ACTS AND SECRETARY TO THE ADMIRALTY
TRANSCRIBED FROM THE SHORTHAND MANUSCRIPT IN THE
PEPYSIAN LIBRARY
MAGDALENE COLLEGE CAMBRIDGE BY THE REV. MYNORS
BRIGHT M.A. LATE FELLOW
AND PRESIDENT OF THE COLLEGE
(Unabridged)
WITH LORD BRAYBROOKE'S NOTES
EDITED WITH ADDITIONS BY
HENRY B. WHEATLEY F.S.A.

DIARY OF SAMUEL PEPYS.

AUGUST 1665

August 1st. Slept, and lay long; then up and my Lord [Crew] and Sir G. Carteret being gone abroad, I first to see the bridegroom and bride, and found them both up, and he gone to dress himself. Both red in the face, and well enough pleased this morning with their night's lodging. Thence down and Mr. Brisband and I to billiards: anon come my Lord and Sir G. Carteret in, who have been looking abroad and visiting some farms that Sir G. Carteret hath thereabouts, and, among other things, report the greatest stories of the bigness of the calfes they find there, ready to sell to the butchers, as big, they say, as little Cowes, and that they do give them a piece of chalke to licke, which they hold makes them white in the flesh within. Very merry at dinner, and so to talk and laugh after dinner, and up and down, some to [one] place, some to another, full of content on all sides. Anon about five o'clock, Sir G. Carteret and his lady and I took coach with the greatest joy and kindnesse that could be from the two familys or that ever I saw with so much appearance, and, I believe, reality in all my life. Drove hard home, and it was night ere we got to Deptford, where, with much kindnesse from them to me, I left them, and home to the office, where I find all well, and being weary and sleepy, it being very late, I to bed.

2nd. Up, it being a publique fast, as being the first Wednesday of the month, for the plague; I within doors all day, and upon my monthly accounts late, and there to my great joy settled almost all my private matters of money in my books clearly, and allowing myself several sums which I had hitherto not reckoned myself sure of, because I would not be over sure of any thing, though with reason I might do it, I did find myself really worth L1900, for which the great God of Heaven and Earth be praised! At night to the office to write a few letters, and so home to bed, after fitting myself for tomorrow's journey.

3rd. Up, and betimes to Deptford to Sir G. Carteret's, where, not liking the horse that had been hired by Mr. Uthwayt for me, I did desire Sir G. Carteret to let me ride his new L40 horse, which he did, and so I left my 'hacquenee'-- [Haquenee = an ambling nag fitted for ladies' riding.]--behind, and so after staying a good while in their bedchamber while they were dressing themselves, discoursing merrily, I parted and to the ferry, where I was forced to stay a great while before I could get my horse brought over, and then mounted and rode very finely to Dagenhams; all the way people, citizens, walking to and again to enquire how the plague is in the City this week by the Bill; which by chance, at Greenwich, I had heard was 2,020 of the plague, and 3,000 and odd of all diseases; but methought it was a sad question to be so often asked me. Coming to Dagenhams, I there met our company coming out of the house, having staid as long as they could for me; so I let them go a little before, and went and took leave of my Lady Sandwich, good woman, who seems very sensible of my service in this late business, and having her directions in some things, among others, to get Sir G. Carteret and my Lord to settle the portion, and what Sir G. Carteret is to settle, into land, soon as may be, she not liking that it should lie long undone, for fear of death on either side. So took leave of her, and then down to the buttery, and eat a piece of cold venison pie, and drank and took some bread and cheese in my hand; and so mounted after them, Mr. Marr very kindly staying to lead me the way. By and by met my Lord Crew returning, after having accompanied them a little way, and so after them, Mr. Marr telling me by the way how a mayde servant of Mr. John Wright's (who lives thereabouts) falling sick of the plague, she was removed to an out-house, and a nurse appointed to look to her; who, being once absent, the mayde got out of the house at the window, and run away. The nurse coming and knocking, and having no answer, believed she was dead, and went and told Mr. Wright so; who and his lady were in great strait what to do to get her buried. At last resolved to go to Burntwood hard by, being in the parish, and there get people to do it. But they would not; so he went home full of trouble, and in the way met the wench walking over the common, which frighted him worse than before; and was forced to send people to take her, which he did; and they got one of the pest coaches and put her into it to carry her to a pest house. And passing in a narrow lane, Sir Anthony Browne, with his brother and some friends in the coach, met this coach with the curtains drawn close. The brother being a young man, and believing there might be some lady in it that would not be seen, and the way being narrow, he thrust his head out of his own into her coach, and to look, and there saw somebody look very ill, and in a sick dress, and stunk mightily; which the coachman also cried out upon. And presently they come up to some people that stood looking after it, and told our gallants that it was a mayde of Mr. Wright's carried away sick of the plague; which put the young gentleman into a fright had almost cost him his life, but is now well again. I, overtaking our young people, 'light, and into the coach to them, where mighty merry all the way; and anon come to the Blockehouse, over against Gravesend, where we staid a great while, in a little drinking-house. Sent back our coaches to Dagenhams. I, by and by, by boat to Gravesend, where no newes of Sir G. Carteret come yet; so back again, and fetched them all over, but the two saddle-horses that were to go with us, which could not be brought over in the horseboat, the wind and tide being against us, without towing; so we had some difference with some watermen, who would not tow them over under 20s., whereupon I swore to send one of them to sea and will do it. Anon some others come to me and did it for 10s. By and by comes Sir G. Carteret, and so we set out for Chatham: in my way overtaking some company, wherein was a lady, very pretty, riding singly, her husband in company with her. We fell into talke, and I read a copy of verses which her husband showed me, and he discommended, but the lady commended: and I read them, so as to make the husband turn to commend them. By and by he and I fell into acquaintance, having known me formerly at the Exchequer. His name is Nokes, over against Bow Church. He was servant to Alderman Dashwood. We promised to meet, if ever we come both to London again; and, at parting, I had a fair salute on horseback, in Rochester streets, of the lady, and so parted. Come to Chatham mighty merry, and anon to supper, it being near 9 o'clock ere we come thither. My Lady Carteret come thither in a coach, by herself, before us. Great mind they have to buy a little 'hacquenee' that I rode on from Greenwich, for a woman's horse. Mighty merry, and after supper, all being withdrawn, Sir G. Carteret did take an opportunity to speak with much value and kindness to me, which is of great joy to me. So anon to bed. Mr. Brisband and I together to my content.

4th. Up at five o'clock, and by six walked out alone, with my Lady Slanning, to the Docke Yard, where walked up and down, and so to Mr. Pett's, who led us into his garden, and there the lady, the best humoured woman in the world, and a devout woman (I having spied her on her knees half an houre this morning in her chamber), clambered up to the top of the banquetting-house to gather nuts, and mighty merry, and so walked back again through the new rope house, which is very usefull; and so to the Hill-house to breakfast and mighty merry. Then they took coach, and Sir G. Carteret kissed me himself heartily, and my Lady several times, with great kindnesse, and then the young ladies, and so with much joy, bade "God be with you!" and an end I think it will be to my mirthe for a great while, it having been the passage of my whole life the most pleasing for the time, considering the quality and nature of the business, and my noble usage in the doing of it, and very many fine journys, entertainments and great company. I returned into the house for a while to do business there with Commissioner Pett, and there with the officers of the Chest, where I saw more of Sir W. Batten's business than ever I did before, for whereas he did own once under his hand to them that he was accountable for L2200, of which he had yet paid but L1600, he writes them a letter lately that he hath but about L50 left that is due to the Chest, but I will do something in it and that speedily. That being done I took horse, and Mr. Barrow with me bore me company to Gravesend, discoursing of his business, wherein I vexed him, and he me, I seeing his frowardness, but yet that he is in my conscience a very honest man, and some good things he told me, which I shall remember to the King's advantage. There I took boat alone, and, the tide being against me, landed at Blackwall and walked to Wapping, Captain Bowd whom I met with talking with me all the way, who is a sober man. So home, and found all things well, and letters from Dover that my Lord Hinchingbroke is arrived at Dover, and would be at Scott's hall this night, where the whole company will meet. I wish myself with them. After writing a few letters I took boat and down to Woolwich very late, and there found my wife and her woman upon the key hearing a fellow in a barge, that lay by, fiddle. So I to them and in, very merry, and to bed, I sleepy and weary.

5th. In the morning up, and my wife showed me several things of her doing, especially one fine woman's Persian head mighty finely done, beyond what I could expect of her; and so away by water, having ordered in the yarde six or eight bargemen to be whipped, who had last night stolen some of the King's cordage from out of the yarde. I to Deptford, and there by agreement met with my Lord Bruncker, and there we kept our office, he and I, and did what there was to do, and at noon parted to meet at the office next week. Sir W. Warren and I thence did walk through the rain to Half-Way House, and there I eat a piece of boiled beef and he and I talked over several businesses, among others our design upon the mast docke, which I hope to compass and get 2 or L300 by. Thence to Redriffe, where we parted, and I home, where busy all the afternoon. Stepped to Colvill's to set right a business of money, where he told me that for certain De Ruyter is come home, with all his fleete, which is very ill newes, considering the charge we have been at in keeping a fleete to the northward so long, besides the great expectation of snapping him, wherein my Lord Sandwich will I doubt suffer some dishonour. I am told also of a great ryott upon Thursday last in Cheapside; Colonell Danvers, a delinquent, having been taken, and in his way to the Tower was rescued from the captain of the guard, and carried away; only one of the rescuers being taken. I am told also that the Duke of Buckingham is dead, but I know not of a certainty. So home and very late at letters, and then home to supper and to bed.

6th (Lord's day). Dressed and had my head combed by my little girle, to whom I confess 'que je sum demasiado kind, nuper ponendo mes mains in su des choses de son breast, mais il faut que je' leave it lest it bring me to 'alcun major inconvenience'. So to my business in my chamber, look over and settling more of my papers than I could the two last days I have spent about them. In the evening, it raining hard, down to Woolwich, where after some little talk to bed.

7th. Up, and with great pleasure looking over my wife's pictures, and then to see my Lady Pen, whom I have not seen since her coming hither, and after being a little merry with her, she went forth and I staid there talking with Mrs. Pegg and looking over her pictures, and commended them; but, Lord! so far short of my wife's, as no comparison. Thence to my wife, and there spent, talking, till noon, when by appointment Mr. Andrews come out of the country to speake with me about their Tangier business, and so having done with him and dined, I home by water, where by appointment I met Dr. Twisden, Mr. Povy, Mr. Lawson, and Stockdale about settling their business of money; but such confusion I never met with, nor could anything be agreed on, but parted like a company of fools, I vexed to lose so much time and pains to no purpose. They gone, comes Rayner, the boatmaker, about some business, and brings a piece of plate with him, which I refused to take of him, thinking indeed that the poor man hath no reason nor encouragement from our dealings with him to give any of us any presents. He gone, there comes Luellin, about Mr. Deering's business of planke, to have the contract perfected, and offers me twenty pieces in gold, as Deering had done some time since himself, but I both then and now refused it, resolving not to be bribed to dispatch business, but will have it done however out of hand forthwith. So he gone, I to supper and to bed.

8th. Up and to the office, where all the morning we sat. At noon I home to dinner alone, and after dinner Bagwell's wife waited at the door, and went with me to my office . . . . So parted, and I to Sir W. Batten's, and there sat the most of the afternoon talking and drinking too much with my Lord Bruncker, Sir G. Smith, G. Cocke and others very merry. I drunk a little mixed, but yet more than I should do. So to my office a little, and then to the Duke of Albemarle's about some business. The streets mighty empty all the way, now even in London, which is a sad sight. And to Westminster Hall, where talking, hearing very sad stories from Mrs. Mumford; among others, of Mrs. Michell's son's family. And poor Will, that used to sell us ale at the Hall-door, his wife and three children died, all, I think, in a day. So home through the City again, wishing I may have taken no ill in going; but I will go, I think, no more thither. Late at the office, and then home to supper, having taken a pullet home with me, and then to bed. The news of De Kuyter's coming home is certain; and told to the great disadvantage of our fleete, and the praise of De Kuyter; but it cannot be helped, nor do I know what to say to it.

9th. Up betimes to my office, where Tom Hater to the writing of letters with me, which have for a good while been in arreare, and we close at it all day till night, only made a little step out for half an houre in the morning to the Exchequer about striking of tallys, but no good done therein, people being most out of towne. At noon T. Hater dined with me, and so at it all the afternoon. At night home and supped, and after reading a little in Cowley's poems, my head being disturbed with overmuch business to-day, I to bed.

10th. Up betimes, and called upon early by my she-cozen Porter, the turner's wife, to tell me that her husband was carried to the Tower, for buying of some of the King's powder, and would have my helpe, but I could give her none, not daring any more to appear in the business, having too much trouble lately therein. By and by to the office, where we sat all the morning; in great trouble to see the Bill this week rise so high, to above 4,000 in all, and of them above 3,000 of the plague. And an odd story of Alderman Bence's stumbling at night over a dead corps in the streete, and going home and telling his wife, she at the fright, being with child, fell sicke and died of the plague. We sat late, and then by invitation my Lord Brunker, Sir J. Minnes, Sir W. Batten and I to Sir G. Smith's to dinner, where very good company and good cheer. Captain Cocke was there and Jacke Fenn, but to our great wonder Alderman Bence, and tells us that not a word of all this is true, and others said so too, but by his owne story his wife hath been ill, and he fain to leave his house and comes not to her, which continuing a trouble to me all the time I was there. Thence to the office and, after writing letters, home, to draw-over anew my will, which I had bound myself by oath to dispatch by to-morrow night; the town growing so unhealthy, that a man cannot depend upon living two days to an end. So having done something of it, I to bed.

11th. Up, and all day long finishing and writing over my will twice, for my father and my wife, only in the morning a pleasant rencontre happened in having a young married woman brought me by her father, old Delkes, that carries pins always in his mouth, to get her husband off that he should not go to sea, 'une contre pouvait avoir done any cose cum else, but I did nothing, si ni baisser her'. After they were gone my mind run upon having them called back again, and I sent a messenger to Blackwall, but he failed. So I lost my expectation. I to the Exchequer, about striking new tallys, and I find the Exchequer, by proclamation, removing to Nonesuch.--[Nonsuch Palace, near Epsom, where the Exchequer money was kept during the time of the plague.]-- Back again and at my papers, and putting up my books into chests, and settling my house and all things in the best and speediest order I can, lest it should please God to take me away, or force me to leave my house. Late up at it, and weary and full of wind, finding perfectly that so long as I keepe myself in company at meals and do there eat lustily (which I cannot do alone, having no love to eating, but my mind runs upon my business), I am as well as can be, but when I come to be alone, I do not eat in time, nor enough, nor with any good heart, and I immediately begin to be full of wind, which brings my pain, till I come to fill my belly a-days again, then am presently well.

12th. The office now not sitting, but only hereafter on Thursdays at the office, I within all the morning about my papers and setting things still in order, and also much time in settling matters with Dr. Twisden. At noon am sent for by Sir G. Carteret, to meet him and my Lord Hinchingbroke at Deptford, but my Lord did not come thither, he having crossed the river at Gravesend to Dagenhams, whither I dare not follow him, they being afeard of me; but Sir G. Carteret says, he is a most sweet youth in every circumstance. Sir G. Carteret being in haste of going to the Duke of Albemarle and the Archbishop, he was pettish, and so I could not fasten any discourse, but take another time. So he gone, I down to Greenwich and sent away the Bezan, thinking to go with my wife to-night to come back again to-morrow night to the Soveraigne at the buoy off the Nore. Coming back to Deptford, old Bagwell walked a little way with me, and would have me in to his daughter's, and there he being gone 'dehors, ego had my volunte de su hiza'. Eat and drank and away home, and after a little at the office to my chamber to put more things still in order, and late to bed. The people die so, that now it seems they are fain to carry the dead to be buried by day-light, the nights not sufficing to do it in. And my Lord Mayor commands people to be within at nine at night all, as they say, that the sick may have liberty to go abroad for ayre. There is one also dead out of one of our ships at Deptford, which troubles us mightily; the Providence fire-ship, which was just fitted to go to sea. But they tell me to-day no more sick on board. And this day W. Bodham tells me that one is dead at Woolwich, not far from the Rope-yard. I am told, too, that a wife of one of the groomes at Court is dead at Salsbury; so that the King and Queene are speedily to be all gone to Milton. God preserve us!

13th (Lord's day). Up betimes and to my chamber, it being a very wet day all day, and glad am I that we did not go by water to see "The Soveraigne"

["The Sovereign of the Seas" was built at Woolwich in 1637 of timber which had been stripped of its bark while growing in the spring, and not felled till the second autumn afterwards; and it is observed by Dr. Plot ("Phil. Trans." for 1691), in his discourse on the most seasonable time for felling timber, written by the advice of Pepys, that after forty-seven years, "all the ancient timber then remaining in her, it was no easy matter to drive a nail into it" ("Quarterly Review," vol. viii., p. 35).--B.]

to-day, as I intended, clearing all matters in packing up my papers and books, and giving instructions in writing to my executors, thereby perfecting the whole business of my will, to my very great joy; so that I shall be in much better state of soul, I hope, if it should please the Lord to call me away this sickly time. At night to read, being weary with this day's great work, and then after supper to bed, to rise betimes to-morrow, and to bed with a mind as free as to the business of the world as if I were not worth L100 in the whole world, every thing being evened under my hand in my books and papers, and upon the whole I find myself worth, besides Brampton estate, the sum of L2164, for which the Lord be praised!

14th. Up, and my mind being at mighty ease from the dispatch of my business so much yesterday, I down to Deptford to Sir G. Carteret, where with him a great while, and a great deale of private talke concerning my Lord Sandwich's and his matters, and chiefly of the latter, I giving him great deale of advice about the necessity of his having caution concerning Fenn, and the many ways there are of his being abused by any man in his place, and why he should not bring his son in to look after his business, and more, to be a Commissioner of the Navy, which he listened to and liked, and told me how much the King was his good Master, and was sure not to deny him that or any thing else greater than that, and I find him a very cunning man, whatever at other times he seems to be, and among other things he told me he was not for the fanfaroone

[Fanfaron, French, from fanfare, a sounding of trumpets; hence, a swaggerer, or empty boaster.]

to make a show with a great title, as he might have had long since, but the main thing to get an estate; and another thing, speaking of minding of business, "By God," says he, "I will and have already almost brought it to that pass, that the King shall not be able to whip a cat, but I must be at the tayle of it." Meaning so necessary he is, and the King and my Lord Treasurer and all do confess it; which, while I mind my business, is my own case in this office of the

Navy, and I hope shall be more, if God give me life and health. Thence by agreement to Sir J. Minnes's lodgings, where I found my Lord Bruncker, and so by water to the ferry, and there took Sir W. Batten's coach that was sent for us, and to Sir W. Batten's, where very merry, good cheer, and up and down the garden with great content to me, and, after dinner, beat Captain Cocke at billiards, won about 8s. of him and my Lord Bruncker. So in the evening after, much pleasure back again and I by water to Woolwich, where supped with my wife, and then to bed betimes, because of rising to-morrow at four of the clock in order to the going out with Sir G. Carteret toward Cranborne to my Lord Hinchingbrooke in his way to Court. This night I did present my wife with the dyamond ring, awhile since given me by Mr. Dicke Vines's brother, for helping him to be a purser, valued at about L10, the first thing of that nature I did ever give her. Great fears we have that the plague will be a great Bill this weeke.

15th. Up by 4 o'clock and walked to Greenwich, where called at Captain Cocke's and to his chamber, he being in bed, where something put my last night's dream into my head, which I think is the best that ever was dreamt, which was that I had my Lady Castlemayne in my armes and was admitted to use all the dalliance I desired with her, and then dreamt that this could not be awake, but that it was only a dream; but that since it was a dream, and that I took so much real pleasure in it, what a happy thing it would be if when we are in our graves (as Shakespeere resembles it) we could dream, and dream but such dreams as this, that then we should not need to be so fearful of death, as we are this plague time. Here I hear that news is brought Sir G. Carteret that my Lord Hinchingbrooke is not well, and so cannot meet us at Cranborne to-night. So I to Sir G. Carteret's; and there was sorry with him for our disappointment. So we have put off our meeting there till Saturday next. Here I staid talking with Sir G. Carteret, he being mighty free with me in his business, and among other things hath ordered Rider and Cutler to put into my hands copper to the value of L5,000 (which Sir G. Carteret's share it seems come to in it), which is to raise part of the money he is to layout for a purchase for my Lady Jemimah. Thence he and I to Sir J. Minnes's by invitation, where Sir W. Batten and my Lady, and my Lord Bruncker, and all of us dined upon a venison pasty and other good meat, but nothing well dressed. But my pleasure lay in getting some bills signed by Sir G. Carteret, and promise of present payment from Mr. Fenn, which do rejoice my heart, it being one of the heaviest things I had upon me, that so much of the little I have should lie (viz. near L1000) in the King's hands. Here very merry and (Sir G. Carteret being gone presently after dinner) to Captain Cocke's, and there merry, and so broke up and I by water to the Duke of Albemarle, with whom I spoke a great deale in private, they being designed to send a fleete of ships privately to the Streights. No news yet from our fleete, which is much wondered at, but the Duke says for certain guns have been heard to the northward very much. It was dark before I could get home, and so land at Church-yard stairs, where, to my great trouble, I met a dead corps of the plague, in the narrow ally just bringing down a little pair of stairs. But I thank God I was not much disturbed at it. However, I shall beware of being late abroad again.

16th. Up, and after doing some necessary business about my accounts at home, to the office, and there with Mr. Hater wrote letters, and I did deliver to him my last will, one part of it to deliver to my wife when I am dead. Thence to the Exchange, where I have not been a great while. But, Lord! how sad a sight it is to see the streets empty of people, and very few upon the 'Change. Jealous of every door that one sees shut up, lest it should be the plague; and about us two shops in three, if not more, generally shut up. From the 'Change to Sir G. Smith's' with Mr. Fenn, to whom I am nowadays very complaisant, he being under payment of my bills to me, and some other sums at my desire, which he readily do. Mighty merry with Captain Cocke and Fenn at Sir G. Smith's, and a brave dinner, but I think Cocke is the greatest epicure that is, eats and drinks with the greatest pleasure and liberty that ever man did. Very contrary newes to-day upon the 'Change, some that our fleete hath taken some of the Dutch East India ships, others that we did attaque it at Bergen and were repulsed, others that our fleete is in great danger after this attaque by meeting with the great body now gone out of Holland, almost 100 sayle of men of warr. Every body is at a great losse and nobody can tell. Thence among the goldsmiths to get some money, and so home, settling some new money matters, and to my great joy have got home L500 more of the money due to me, and got some more money to help Andrews first advanced. This day I had the ill news from Dagenhams, that my poor lord of Hinchingbroke his indisposition is turned to the small-pox. Poor gentleman! that he should be come from France so soon to fall sick, and of that disease too, when he should be gone to see a fine lady, his mistresse. I am most heartily sorry for it. So late setting papers to rights, and so home to bed.

17th. Up and to the office, where we sat all the morning, and at noon dined together upon some victuals I had prepared at Sir W. Batten's upon the King's charge, and after dinner, I having dispatched some business and set things in order at home, we down to the water and by boat to Greenwich to the Bezan yacht, where Sir W. Batten, Sir J. Minnes, my Lord Bruncker and myself, with some servants (among others Mr. Carcasse, my Lord's clerk, a very civil gentleman), embarked in the yacht and down we went most pleasantly, and noble discourse I had with my Lord Bruneker, who is a most excellent person. Short of Gravesend it grew calme, and so we come to an anchor, and to supper mighty merry, and after it, being moonshine, we out of the cabbin to laugh and talk, and then, as we grew sleepy, went in and upon velvet cushions of the King's that belong to the yacht fell to sleep, which we all did pretty well till 3 or 4 of the clock, having risen in the night to look for a new comet which is said to have lately shone, but we could see no such thing.

18th. Up about 5 o'clock and dressed ourselves, and to sayle again down to the Soveraigne at the buoy of the Nore, a noble ship, now rigged and fitted and manned; we did not stay long, but to enquire after her readinesse and thence to Sheernesse, where we walked up and down, laying out the ground to be taken in for a yard to lay provisions for cleaning and repairing of ships, and a most proper place it is for the purpose. Thence with great pleasure up the Meadeway, our yacht contending with Commissioner Pett's, wherein he met us from

Chatham, and he had the best of it. Here I come by, but had not tide enough to stop at Quinbrough, a with mighty pleasure spent the day in doing all and seeing these places, which I had never done before. So to the Hill house at Chatham and there dined, and after dinner spent some time discoursing of business. Among others arguing with the Commissioner about his proposing the laying out so much money upon Sheerenesse, unless it be to the slighting of Chatham yarde, for it is much a better place than Chatham, which however the King is not at present in purse to do, though it were to be wished he were. Thence in Commissioner Pett's coach (leaving them there). I late in the darke to Gravesend, where great is the plague, and I troubled to stay there so long for the tide. At 10 at night, having supped, I took boat alone, and slept well all the way to the Tower docke about three o'clock in the morning. So knocked up my people, and to bed.

19th. Slept till 8 o'clock, and then up and met with letters from the King and Lord Arlington, for the removal of our office to Greenwich. I also wrote letters, and made myself ready to go to Sir G. Carteret, at Windsor; and having borrowed a horse of Mr. Blackbrough, sent him to wait for me at the Duke of Albemarle's door: when, on a sudden, a letter comes to us from the Duke of Albemarle, to tell us that the fleete is all come back to Solebay, and are presently to be dispatched back again. Whereupon I presently by water to the Duke of Albemarle to know what news; and there I saw a letter from my Lord Sandwich to the Duke of Albemarle, and also from Sir W. Coventry and Captain Teddiman; how my Lord having commanded Teddiman with twenty-two ships

[A news letter of August 19th (Salisbury), gives the following account of this affair:--"The Earl of Sandwich being on the Norway coast, ordered Sir Thomas Teddeman with 20 ships to attack 50 Dutch merchant ships in Bergen harbour; six convoyers had so placed themselves that only four or five of the ships could be reached at once. The Governor of Bergen fired on our ships, and placed 100 pieces of ordnance and two regiments of foot on the rocks to attack them, but they got clear without the loss of a ship, only 500 men killed or wounded, five or six captains among them. The fleet has gone to Sole Bay to repair losses and be ready to encounter the Dutch fleet, which is gone northward" ("Calendar of State Papers," 1664-65, pp. 526, 527). Medals were struck in Holland, the inscription in Dutch on one of these is thus translated: "Thus we arrest the pride of the English, who extend their piracy even against their friends, and who insulting the forts of Norway, violate the rights of the harbours of King Frederick; but, for the reward of their audacity, see their vessels destroyed by the balls of the Dutch" (Hawkins's "Medallic Illustrations of the History of Great Britain and Ireland," ed. Franks and Grueber, 1885, vol. i., p. 508). Sir Gilbert Talbot's "True Narrative of the Earl of Sandwich's Attempt upon Bergen with the English Fleet on the 3rd of August, 1665, and the Cause of his Miscarriage thereupon," is in the British Museum (Harl.

MS., No. 6859). It is printed in "Archaeologia," vol. xxii., p. 33. The Earl of Rochester also gave an account of the action in a letter to his mother (Wordsworth's "Ecclesiastical Biography," fourth edition, vol. iv., p. 611). Sir John Denham, in his "Advice to a Painter," gives a long satirical account of the affair. A coloured drawing of the attack upon Bergen, on vellum, showing the range of the ships engaged, is in the British Museum. Shortly after the Bergen affair forty of the Dutch merchant vessels, on their way to Holland, fell into the hands of the English, and in Penn's "Memorials of Sir William Penn," vol. ii., p. 364, is a list of the prizes taken on the 3rd and 4th September. The troubles connected with these prizes and the disgrace into which Lord Sandwich fell are fully set forth in subsequent pages of the Diary. Evelyn writes in his Diary (November 27th, 1665): "There was no small suspicion of my Lord Sandwich having permitted divers commanders who were at ye taking of ye East India prizes to break bulk and take to themselves jewels, silkes, &c., tho' I believe some whom I could name fill'd their pockets, my Lo. Sandwich himself had the least share. However, he underwent the blame, and it created him enemies, and prepossess'd ye Lo. Generall [Duke of Albemarle], for he spake to me of it with much zeale and concerne, and I believe laid load enough on Lo. Sandwich at Oxford."]

(of which but fifteen could get thither, and of those fifteen but eight or nine could come up to play) to go to Bergen; where, after several messages to and fro from the Governor of the Castle, urging that Teddiman ought not to come thither with more than five ships, and desiring time to think of it, all the while he suffering the Dutch ships to land their guns to their best advantage; Teddiman on the second pretence, began to play at the Dutch ships, (wherof ten East India-men,) and in three hours' time (the town and castle, without any provocation, playing on our ships,) they did cut all our cables, so as the wind being off the land, did force us to go out, and rendered our fire-ships useless; without doing any thing, but what hurt of course our guns must have done them: we having lost five commanders, besides Mr. Edward Montagu, and Mr. Windham.

[This Mr. Windham had entered into a formal engagement with the Earl of Rochester, "not without ceremonies of religion, that if either of them died, he should appear, and give the other notice of the future state, if there was any." He was probably one of the brothers of Sir William Wyndham, Bart. See Wordsworth's "Ecclesiastical Biography," fourth. edition, vol. iv., p. 615.--B.]

Our fleete is come home to our great grief with not above five weeks' dry, and six days' wet provisions: however, must out again; and the Duke hath ordered the Soveraigne, and all other ships ready, to go out to the fleete to strengthen them. This news troubles us all, but cannot be helped. Having read all this news, and received commands of the Duke with great content, he giving me the words which to my great joy he hath several times said to me, that his greatest reliance is upon me. And my Lord Craven also did come out to talk with me, and told me that I am in mighty esteem with the Duke, for which I bless God. Home, and having given my fellow-officers an account hereof, to Chatham, and wrote other letters, I by water to Charing-Cross, to the post-house, and there the people tell me they are shut up; and so I went to the new post-house, and there got a guide and horses to Hounslow, where I was mightily taken with a little girle, the daughter of the master of the house (Betty Gysby), which, if she lives, will make a great beauty. Here I met with a fine fellow who, while I staid for my horses, did enquire newes, but I could not make him remember Bergen in Norway, in 6 or 7 times telling, so ignorant he was. So to Stanes, and there by this time it was dark night, and got a guide who lost his way in the forest, till by help of the moone (which recompenses me for all the pains I ever took about studying of her motions,) I led my guide into the way back again; and so we made a man rise that kept a gate, and so he carried us to Cranborne. Where in the dark I perceive an old house new building with a great deal of rubbish, and was fain to go up a ladder to Sir G. Carteret's chamber. And there in his bed I sat down, and told him all my bad newes, which troubled him mightily; but yet we were very merry, and made the best of it; and being myself weary did take leave, and after having spoken with Mr. Fenn in bed, I to bed in my Lady's chamber that she uses to lie in, and where the Duchesse of York, that now is, was born. So to sleep; being very well, but weary, and the better by having carried with me a bottle of strong water; whereof now and then a sip did me good.

20th (Lord's day). Sir G. Carteret come and walked by my bedside half an houre, talking and telling me how my Lord is in this unblameable in all this ill-successe, he having followed orders; and that all ought to be imputed to the falsenesse of the King of Denmarke, who, he told me as a secret, had promised to deliver up the Dutch ships to us, and we expected no less; and swears it will, and will easily, be the ruine of him and his kingdom, if we fall out with him, as we must in honour do; but that all that can be, must be to get the fleete out again to intercept De Witt, who certainly will be coming home with the East India ships, he being gone thither. He being gone, I up and with Fenn, being ready to walk forth to see the place; and I find it to be a very noble seat in a noble forest, with the noblest prospect towards Windsor, and round about over many countys, that can be desired; but otherwise a very melancholy place, and little variety save only trees. I had thoughts of going home by water, and of seeing Windsor Chappell and Castle, but finding at my coming in that Sir G. Carteret did prevent me in speaking for my sudden return to look after business, I did presently eat a bit off the spit about 10 o'clock, and so took horse for Stanes, and thence to Brainford to Mr. Povy's, the weather being very pleasant to ride in. Mr. Povy not being at home I lost my labour, only eat and drank there with his lady, and told my bad newes, and hear the plague is round about them there. So away to Brainford; and there at the inn that goes down to the water-side, I 'light and paid off my post-horses, and so slipped on my shoes, and laid my things by, the tide not serving, and to church, where a dull sermon, and many Londoners. After church to my inn, and eat and drank, and so about seven o'clock by water, and got between nine and ten to Queenhive, very dark. And I could not get my waterman to go elsewhere for fear of the plague. Thence with a lanthorn, in great fear of meeting of dead corpses, carried to be buried; but, blessed be God, met none, but did see now and then a linke (which is the mark of them) at a distance. So got safe home about 10 o'clock, my people not all abed, and after supper I weary to bed.

21st. Called up, by message from Lord Bruncker and the rest of my fellows, that they will meet me at the Duke of Albemarle's this morning; so I up, and weary, however, got thither before them, and spoke with my Lord, and with him and other gentlemen to walk in the Parke, where, I perceive, he spends much of his time, having no whither else to go; and here I hear him speake of some Presbyter people that he caused to be apprehended yesterday, at a private meeting in Covent Garden, which he would have released upon paying L5 per man to the poor, but it was answered, they would not pay anything; so he ordered them to another prison from the guard. By and by comes my fellow-officers, and the Duke walked in, and to counsel with us; and that being done we departed, and Sir W. Batten and I to the office, where, after I had done a little business, I to his house to dinner, whither comes Captain Cocke, for whose epicurisme a dish of partriges was sent for, and still gives me reason to think is the greatest epicure in the world. Thence, after dinner, I by water to Sir W. Warren's and with him two hours, talking of things to his and my profit, and particularly good advice from him what use to make of Sir G. Carteret's kindnesse to me and my interest in him, with exceeding good cautions for me not using it too much nor obliging him to fear by prying into his secrets, which it were easy for me to do. Thence to my Lord Bruncker, at Greenwich, and Sir J. Minnes by appointment, to looke after the lodgings appointed for us there for our office, which do by no means please me, they being in the heart of all the labourers and workmen there, which makes it as unsafe as to be, I think, at London. Mr. Hugh May, who is a most ingenuous man, did show us the lodgings, and his acquaintance I am desirous of. Thence walked, it being now dark, to Sir J. Minnes's, and there staid at the door talking with him an hour while messengers went to get a boat for me, to carry me to Woolwich, but all to no purpose; so I was forced to walk it in the darke, at ten o'clock at night, with Sir J. Minnes's George with me, being mightily troubled for fear of the doggs at Coome farme, and more for fear of rogues by the way, and yet more because of the plague which is there, which is very strange, it being a single house, all alone from the towne, but it seems they use to admit beggars, for their owne safety, to lie in their barns, and they brought it to them; but I bless God I got about eleven of the clock well to my wife, and giving 4s. in recompence to George, I to my wife, and having first viewed her last piece of drawing since I saw her, which is seven or eight days, which pleases me beyond any thing in the world, to bed with great content but weary.

22nd. Up, and after much pleasant talke and being importuned by my wife and her two mayds, which are both good wenches, for me to buy a necklace of pearle for her, and I promising to give her one of L60 in two years at furthest, and in less if she pleases me in her painting, I went away and walked to Greenwich, in my way seeing a coffin with a dead body therein, dead of the plague, lying in an open close belonging to Coome farme, which was carried out last night, and the parish have not appointed any body to bury it; but only set a watch there day and night, that nobody should go thither or come thence, which is a most cruel thing: this disease making us more cruel to one another than if we are doggs. So to the King's House, and there met my Lord Bruncker and Sir J. Minnes, and to our lodgings again that are appointed for us, which do please me better to day than last night, and are set a doing. Thence I to Deptford, where by appointment I find Mr. Andrews come, and to the Globe, where we dined together and did much business as to our Plymouth gentlemen; and after a good dinner and good discourse, he being a very good man, I think verily, we parted and I to the King's yard, walked up and down, and by and by out at the back gate, and there saw the Bagwell's wife's mother and daughter, and went to them, and went in to the daughter's house with the mother, and 'faciebam le cose que ego tenebam a mind to con elle', and drinking and talking, by and by away, and so walked to Redriffe, troubled to go through the little lane, where the plague is, but did and took water and home, where all well; but Mr. Andrews not coming to even accounts, as I expected, with relation to something of my own profit, I was vexed that I could not settle to business, but home to my viall, though in the evening he did come to my satisfaction. So after supper (he being gone first) I to settle my journall and to bed.

23rd. Up, and whereas I had appointed Mr. Hater and Will to come betimes to the office to meet me about business there, I was called upon as soon as ready by Mr. Andrews to my great content, and he and I to our Tangier accounts, where I settled, to my great joy, all my accounts with him, and, which is more, cleared for my service to the contractors since the last sum I received of them, L222 13s. profit to myself, and received the money actually in the afternoon. After he was gone comes by a pretence of mine yesterday old Delks the waterman, with his daughter Robins, and several times to and again, he leaving her with me, about the getting of his son Robins off, who was pressed yesterday again . . . . All the afternoon at my office mighty busy writing letters, and received a very kind and good one from my Lord Sandwich of his arrival with the fleete at Solebay, and the joy he has at my last newes he met with, of the marriage of my Lady Jemimah; and he tells me more, the good newes that all our ships, which were in such danger that nobody would insure upon them, from the Eastland,

[Eastland was a name given to the eastern countries of Europe. The Eastland Company, or Company of Merchants trading to the East

Country, was incorporated in Queen Elizabeth's reign (anno 21), and the charter was confirmed 13 Car. II. They were also called "The Merchants of Elbing."]

were all safe arrived, which I am sure is a great piece of good luck, being in much more danger than those of Hambrough which were lost, and their value much greater at this time to us. At night home, much contented with this day's work, and being at home alone looking over my papers, comes a neighbour of ours hard by to speak with me about business of the office, one Mr. Fuller, a great merchant, but not my acquaintance, but he come drunk, and would have had me gone and drunk with him at home, or have let him send for wine hither, but I would do neither, nor offered him any, but after some sorry discourse parted, and I up to [my] chamber and to bed.

24th. Up betimes to my office, where my clerks with me, and very busy all the morning writing letters. At noon down to Sir J. Minnes and Lord Bruncker to Greenwich to sign some of the Treasurer's books, and there dined very well; and thence to look upon our rooms again at the King's house, which are not yet ready for us. So home and late writing letters, and so, weary with business, home to supper and to bed.

25th. Up betimes to the office, and there, as well as all the afternoon, saving a little dinner time, all alone till late at night writing letters and doing business, that I may get beforehand with my business again, which hath run behind a great while, and then home to supper and to bed. This day I am told that Dr. Burnett, my physician, is this morning dead of the plague; which is strange, his man dying so long ago, and his house this month open again. Now himself dead. Poor unfortunate man!

26th. Up betimes, and prepared to my great satisfaction an account for the board of my office disbursements, which I had suffered to run on to almost L120. That done I down by water to Greenwich, where we met the first day my Lord Bruncker, Sir J. Minnes, and I, and I think we shall do well there, and begin very auspiciously to me by having my account abovesaid passed, and put into a way of having it presently paid. When we rose I find Mr. Andrews and Mr. Yeabsly, who is just come from Plymouth, at the door, and we walked together toward my Lord Brunker's, talking about their business, Yeabsly being come up on purpose to discourse with me about it, and finished all in a quarter of an hour, and is gone again. I perceive they have some inclination to be going on with their victualling-business for a while longer before they resign it to Mr. Gauden, and I am well contented, for it brings me very good profit with certainty, yet with much care and some pains. We parted at my Lord Bruncker's doore, where I went in, having never been there before, and there he made a noble entertainment for Sir J. Minnes, myself, and Captain Cocke, none else saving some painted lady that dined there, I know not who she is. But very merry we were, and after dinner into the garden, and to see his and her chamber, where some good pictures, and a very handsome young woman for my lady's woman. Thence I by water home, in my way seeing a man taken up dead, out of the hold of a small catch that lay at Deptford. I doubt it might be the plague, which, with the thought of Dr. Burnett, did something disturb me, so that I did not what I intended and should have done at the office, as to business, but home sooner than ordinary, and after supper, to read melancholy alone, and then to bed.

27th (Lord's day). Very well in the morning, and up and to my chamber all the morning to put my things and papers yet more in order, and so to dinner. Thence all the afternoon at my office till late making up my papers and letters there into a good condition of order, and so home to supper, and after reading a good while in the King's works,--[Charles I.'s Works, now in the Pepysian Library]--which is a noble book, to bed.

28th. Up, and being ready I out to Mr. Colvill, the goldsmith's, having not for some days been in the streets; but now how few people I see, and those looking like people that had taken leave of the world. I there, and made even all accounts in the world between him and I, in a very good condition, and I would have done the like with Sir Robert Viner, but he is out of towne, the sicknesse being every where thereabouts. I to the Exchange, and I think there was not fifty people upon it, and but few more like to be as they told me, Sir G. Smith and others. Thus I think to take adieu to-day of the London streets, unless it be to go again to Viner's. Home to dinner, and there W. Hewer brings me L119 he hath received for my office disbursements, so that I think I have L1800 and more in the house, and, blessed be God! no money out but what I can very well command and that but very little, which is much the best posture I ever was in in my life, both as to the quantity and the certainty I have of the money I am worth; having most of it in my own hand. But then this is a trouble to me what to do with it, being myself this day going to be wholly at Woolwich; but for the present I am resolved to venture it in an iron chest, at least for a while. In the afternoon I sent down my boy to Woolwich with some things before me, in order to my lying there for good and all, and so I followed him. Just now comes newes that the fleete is gone, or going this day, out again, for which God be praised! and my Lord Sandwich hath done himself great right in it, in getting so soon out again. I pray God, he may meet the enemy. Towards the evening, just as I was fitting myself, comes W. Hewer and shows me a letter which Mercer had wrote to her mother about a great difference between my wife and her yesterday, and that my wife will have her go away presently. This, together with my natural jealousy that some bad thing or other may be in the way, did trouble me exceedingly, so as I was in a doubt whether to go thither or no, but having fitted myself and my things I did go, and by night got thither, where I met my wife walking to the waterside with her paynter, Mr. Browne, and her mayds. There I met Commissioner Pett, and my Lord Brunker, and the lady at his house had been thereto-day, to see her. Commissioner Pett staid a very little while, and so I to supper with my wife and Mr. Shelden, and so to bed with great pleasure.

29th. In the morning waking, among other discourse my wife begun to tell me the difference between her and Mercer, and that it was only from restraining her to gad abroad to some Frenchmen that were in the town, which I do not wholly yet in part believe, and for my quiet would not enquire into it. So rose and dressed myself, and away by land walking a good way, then remembered that I had promised Commissioner Pett to go with him in his coach, and therefore I went back again to him, and so by his coach to Greenwich, and called at Sir Theophilus Biddulph's, a sober, discreet man, to discourse of the preventing of the plague in Greenwich, and Woolwich, and Deptford, where in every place it begins to grow very great. We appointed another meeting, and so walked together to Greenwich and there parted, and Pett and I to the office, where all the morning, and after office done I to Sir J. Minnes and dined with him, and thence to Deptford thinking to have seen Bagwell, but did not, and so straight to Redriffe, and home, and late at my business to dispatch away letters, and then home to bed, which I did not intend, but to have staid for altogether at Woolwich, but I made a shift for a bed for Tom, whose bed is gone to Woolwich, and so to bed.

30th. Up betimes and to my business of settling my house and papers, and then abroad and met with Hadley, our clerke, who, upon my asking how the plague goes, he told me it encreases much, and much in our parish; for, says he, there died nine this week, though I have returned but six: which is a very ill practice, and makes me think it is so in other places; and therefore the plague much greater than people take it to be. Thence, as I intended, to Sir R. Viner's, and there found not Mr. Lewes ready for me, so I went forth and walked towards Moorefields to see (God forbid my presumption!) whether I could see any dead corps going to the grave; but, as God would have it, did not. But, Lord! how every body's looks, and discourse in the street is of death, and nothing else, and few people going up and down, that the towne is like a place distressed and forsaken. After one turne there back to Viner's, and there found my business ready for me, and evened all reckonings with them to this day to my great content. So home, and all day till very late at night setting my Tangier and private accounts in order, which I did in both, and in the latter to my great joy do find myself yet in the much best condition that ever I was in, finding myself worth L2180 and odd, besides plate and goods, which I value at L250 more, which is a very great blessing to me. The Lord make me thankfull! and of this at this day above L1800 in cash in my house, which speaks but little out of my hands in desperate condition, but this is very troublesome to have in my house at this time. So late to bed, well pleased with my accounts, but weary of being so long at them.

31st. Up and, after putting several things in order to my removal, to Woolwich; the plague having a great encrease this week, beyond all expectation of almost 2,000, making the general Bill 7,000, odd 100; and the plague above 6,000. I down by appointment to Greenwich, to our office, where I did some business, and there dined with our company and Sir W. Boreman, and Sir The. Biddulph, at Mr. Boreman's, where a good venison pasty, and after a good merry dinner I to my office, and there late writing letters, and then to Woolwich by water, where pleasant with my wife and people, and after supper to bed. Thus this month ends with great sadness upon the publick, through the greatness of the plague every where through the kingdom almost. Every day sadder and sadder news of its encrease. In the City died this week 7,496 and of them 6,102 of the plague. But it is feared that the true number of the dead, this week is near 10,000; partly from the poor that cannot be taken notice of, through the greatness of the number, and partly from the Quakers and others that will not have any bell ring for them. Our fleete gone out to find the Dutch, we having about 100 sail in our fleete, and in them the Soveraigne one; so that it is a better fleete than the former with the Duke was. All our fear is that the Dutch should be got in before them; which would be a very great sorrow to the publick, and to me particularly, for my Lord Sandwich's sake. A great deal of money being spent, and the kingdom not in a condition to spare, nor a parliament without much difficulty to meet to give more. And to that; to have it said, what hath been done by our late fleetes? As to myself I am very well, only in fear of the plague, and as much of an ague by being forced to go early and late to Woolwich, and my family to lie there continually. My late gettings have been very great to my great content, and am likely to have yet a few more profitable jobbs in a little while; for which Tangier, and Sir W. Warren I am wholly obliged to.

THE DIARY OF SAMUEL PEPYS M.A. F.R.S.
CLERK OF THE ACTS AND SECRETARY TO THE ADMIRALTY
TRANSCRIBED FROM THE SHORTHAND MANUSCRIPT IN THE
PEPYSIAN LIBRARY
MAGDALENE COLLEGE CAMBRIDGE BY THE REV. MYNORS
BRIGHT M.A. LATE FELLOW
AND PRESIDENT OF THE COLLEGE
(Unabridged)
WITH LORD BRAYBROOKE'S NOTES
EDITED WITH ADDITIONS BY
HENRY B. WHEATLEY F.S.A.

DIARY OF SAMUEL PEPYS.

SEPTEMBER 1665

September 1st. Up, and to visit my Lady Pen and her daughter at the Ropeyarde where I did breakfast with them and sat chatting a good while. Then to my lodging at Mr. Shelden's, where I met Captain Cocke and eat a little bit of dinner, and with him to Greenwich by water, having good discourse with him by the way. After being at Greenwich a little while, I to London, to my house, there put many more things in order for my totall remove, sending away my girle Susan and other goods down to Woolwich, and I by water to the Duke of Albemarle, and thence home late by water. At the Duke of Albemarle's I overheard some examinations of the late plot that is discoursed of and a great deale of do there is about it. Among other discourses, I heard read, in the presence of the Duke, an examination and discourse of Sir Philip Howard's, with one of the plotting party. In many places these words being, "Then," said Sir P. Howard, "if you so come over to the King, and be faithfull to him, you shall be maintained, and be set up with a horse and armes," and I know not what. And then said such a one, "Yes, I will be true to the King." "But, damn me," said Sir Philip, "will you so and so?" And thus I believe twelve times Sir P. Howard answered him a "damn me," which was a fine way of rhetorique to persuade a Quaker or Anabaptist from his persuasion. And this was read in the hearing of Sir P. Howard, before the Duke and twenty more officers, and they make sport of it, only without any reproach, or he being anything ashamed of it!

[This republican plot was described by the Lord Chancellor in a speech delivered on October 9th, when parliament met at Oxford.]

But it ended, I remember, at last, "But such a one (the plotter) did at last bid them remember that he had not told them what King he would be faithfull to."

2nd. This morning I wrote letters to Mr. Hill and Andrews to come to dine with me to-morrow, and then I to the office, where busy, and thence to dine with Sir J. Minnes, where merry, but only that Sir J. Minnes who hath lately lost two coach horses, dead in the stable, has a third now a dying. After dinner I to

Deptford, and there took occasion to 'entrar a la casa de la gunaica de ma Minusier', and did what I had a mind . . . To Greenwich, where wrote some letters, and home in pretty good time.

3rd (Lord's day). Up; and put on my coloured silk suit very fine, and my new periwigg, bought a good while since, but durst not wear, because the plague was in Westminster when I bought it; and it is a wonder what will be the fashion after the plague is done, as to periwiggs, for nobody will dare to buy any haire, for fear of the infection, that it had been cut off of the heads of people dead of the plague. Before church time comes Mr. Hill (Mr. Andrews failing because he was to receive the Sacrament), and to church, where a sorry dull parson, and so home and most excellent company with Mr. Hill and discourse of musique. I took my Lady Pen home, and her daughter Pegg, and merry we were; and after dinner I made my wife show them her pictures, which did mad Pegg Pen, who learns of the same man and cannot do so well. After dinner left them and I by water to Greenwich, where much ado to be suffered to come into the towne because of the sicknesse, for fear I should come from London, till I told them who I was. So up to the church, where at the door I find Captain Cocke in my Lord Brunker's coach, and he come out and walked with me in the church-yarde till the church was done, talking of the ill government of our Kingdom, nobody setting to heart the business of the Kingdom, but every body minding their particular profit or pleasures, the King himself minding nothing but his ease, and so we let things go to wracke. This arose upon considering what we shall do for money when the fleete comes in, and more if the fleete should not meet with the Dutch, which will put a disgrace upon the King's actions, so as the Parliament and Kingdom will have the less mind to give more money, besides so bad an account of the last money, we fear, will be given, not half of it being spent, as it ought to be, upon the Navy. Besides, it is said that at this day our Lord Treasurer cannot tell what the profit of Chimney money is, what it comes to per annum, nor looks whether that or any other part of the revenue be duly gathered as it ought; the very money that should pay the City the L200,000 they lent the King, being all gathered and in the hands of the Receiver and hath been long and yet not brought up to pay the City, whereas we are coming to borrow 4 or L500,000 more of the City, which will never be lent as is to be feared. Church being done, my Lord Bruncker, Sir J. Minnes, and I up to the Vestry at the desire of the justices of the Peace, Sir Theo. Biddulph and Sir W. Boreman and Alderman Hooker, in order to the doing something for the keeping of the plague from growing; but Lord! to consider the madness of the people of the town, who will (because they are forbid) come in crowds along with the dead corps to see them buried; but we agreed on some orders for the prevention thereof. Among other stories, one was very passionate, methought, of a complaint brought against a man in the towne for taking a child from London from an infected house. Alderman Hooker told us it was the child of a very able citizen in Gracious Street, a saddler, who had buried all the rest of his children of the plague, and himself and wife now being shut up and in despair of escaping, did desire only to save the life of this little child; and so prevailed to have it received stark-naked into the arms of a friend, who brought it (having put it into new fresh clothes) to Greenwich; where upon hearing the story, we did agree it should be permitted to be received and kept in the towne. Thence with my Lord Bruncker to Captain Cocke's, where we mighty merry and supped, and very late I by water to Woolwich, in great apprehensions of an ague. Here was my Lord Bruncker's lady of pleasure, who, I perceive, goes every where with him; and he, I find, is obliged to carry her, and make all the courtship to her that can be.

4th. Writing letters all the morning, among others to my Lady Carteret, the first I have wrote to her, telling her the state of the city as to health and other sorrowfull stories, and thence after dinner to Greenwich, to Sir J. Minnes, where I found my Lord Bruncker, and having staid our hour for the justices by agreement, the time being past we to walk in the Park with Mr. Hammond and Turner, and there eat some fruit out of the King's garden and walked in the Parke, and so back to Sir J. Minnes, and thence walked home, my Lord Bruncker giving me a very neat cane to walk with; but it troubled me to pass by Coome farme where about twenty-one people have died of the plague, and three or four days since I saw a dead corps in a coffin lie in the Close unburied, and a watch is constantly kept there night and day to keep the people in, the plague making us cruel, as doggs, one to another.

5th. Up, and walked with some Captains and others talking to me to Greenwich, they crying out upon Captain Teddiman's management of the business of Bergen, that he staid treating too long while he saw the Dutch fitting themselves, and that at first he might have taken every ship, and done what he would with them. How true I cannot tell. Here we sat very late and for want of money, which lies heavy upon us, did nothing of business almost. Thence home with my Lord Bruncker to dinner where very merry with him and his doxy. After dinner comes Colonell Blunt in his new chariot made with springs; as that was of wicker, wherein a while since we rode at his house. And he hath rode, he says, now this journey, many miles in it with one horse, and out-drives any coach, and out-goes any horse, and so easy, he says. So for curiosity I went into it to try it, and up the hill to the heath, and over the cart-rutts and found it pretty well, but not so easy as he pretends, and so back again, and took leave of my Lord and drove myself in the chariot to the office, and there ended my letters and home pretty betimes and there found W. Pen, and he staid supper with us and mighty merry talking of his travells and the French humours, etc., and so parted and to bed.

6th. Busy all the morning writing letters to several, so to dinner, to London, to pack up more things thence; and there I looked into the street and saw fires burning in the street, as it is through the whole City, by the Lord Mayor's order. Thence by water to the Duke of Albemarle's: all the way fires on each side of the Thames, and strange to see in broad daylight two or three burials upon the Bankeside, one at the very heels of another: doubtless all of the plague; and yet at least forty or fifty people going along with every one of them. The Duke mighty pleasant with me; telling me that he is certainly informed that the Dutch were not come home upon the 1st instant, and so he hopes our fleete may meet with them, and here to my great joy I got him to sign bills for the several sums I have paid on Tangier business by his single letter, and so now I can get more hands to them. This was a great joy to me: Home to Woolwich late by water, found wife in bed, and yet late as [it] was to write letters in order to my rising betimes to go to Povy to-morrow. So to bed, my wife asking me to-night about a letter of hers I should find, which indeed Mary did the other day give me as if she had found it in my bed, thinking it had been mine, brought to her from a man without name owning great kindness to her and I know not what. But looking it over seriously, and seeing it bad sense and ill writ, I did believe it to be her brother's and so had flung it away, but finding her now concerned at it and vexed with Mary about it, it did trouble me, but I would take no notice of it to-night, but fell to sleep as if angry.

7th. Up by 5 of the clock, mighty full of fear of an ague, but was obliged to go, and so by water, wrapping myself up warm, to the Tower, and there sent for the Weekely Bill, and find 8,252 dead in all, and of them 6,878 of the plague; which is a most dreadfull number, and shows reason to fear that the plague hath got that hold that it will yet continue among us. Thence to Brainford, reading "The Villaine," a pretty good play, all the way. There a coach of Mr. Povy's stood ready for me, and he at his house ready to come in, and so we together merrily to Swakely, Sir R. Viner's. A very pleasant place, bought by him of Sir James Harrington's lady. He took us up and down with great respect, and showed us all his house and grounds; and it is a place not very moderne in the garden nor house, but the most uniforme in all that ever I saw; and some things to excess. Pretty to see over the screene of the hall (put up by Sir J. Harrington, a Long Parliamentman) the King's head, and my Lord of Essex on one side, and Fairfax on the other; and upon the other side of the screene, the parson of the parish, and the lord of the manor and his sisters. The window-cases, door-cases, and chimnys of all the house are marble. He showed me a black boy that he had, that died of a consumption, and being dead, he caused him to be dried in an oven, and lies there entire in a box. By and by to dinner, where his lady I find yet handsome, but hath been a very handsome woman; now is old. Hath brought him near L100,000 and now he lives, no man in England in greater plenty, and commands both King and Council with his credit he gives them. Here was a fine lady a merchant's wife at dinner with us, and who should be here in the quality of a woman but Mrs. Worship's daughter, Dr. Clerke's niece, and after dinner Sir Robert led us up to his long gallery, very fine, above stairs (and better, or such, furniture I never did see), and there Mrs. Worship did give us three or four very good songs, and sings very neatly, to my great delight. After all this, and ending the chief business to my content about getting a promise of some money of him, we took leave, being exceedingly well treated here, and a most pleasant journey we had back, Povy and I, and his company most excellent in anything but business, he here giving me an account of as many persons at Court as I had a mind or thought of enquiring after. He tells me by a letter he showed me, that the King is not, nor hath been of late, very well, but quite out of humour; and, as some think, in a consumption, and weary of every thing. He showed me my Lord Arlington's house that he was born in, in a towne called Harlington: and so carried me through a most pleasant country to Brainford, and there put me into my boat, and good night. So I wrapt myself warm, and by water got to Woolwich about one in the morning, my wife and all in bed.

8th. Waked, and fell in talk with my wife about the letter, and she satisfied me that she did not know from whence it come, but believed it might be from her cozen Franke Moore lately come out of France. The truth is the thing I think cannot have much in it, and being unwilling (being in other things so much at ease) to vex myself in a strange place at a melancholy time, passed all by and were presently friends. Up, and several with me about business. Anon comes my Lord Bruncker, as I expected, and we to the enquiring into the business of the late desertion of the Shipwrights from worke, who had left us for three days together for want of money, and upon this all the morning, and brought it to a pretty good issue, that they, we believe, will come to-morrow to work. To dinner, having but a mean one, yet sufficient for him, and he well enough pleased, besides that I do not desire to vye entertainments with him or any else. Here was Captain Cocke also, and Mr. Wayth. We staid together talking upon one business or other all the afternoon. In the evening my Lord Bruncker hearing that Mr. Ackeworth's clerke, the Dutchman who writes and draws so well, was transcribing a book of Rates and our ships for Captain Millet a gallant of his mistress's, we sent for him for it. He would not deliver it, but said it was his mistress's and had delivered it to her. At last we were forced to send to her for it; she would come herself, and indeed the book was a very neat one and worth keeping as a rarity, but we did think fit, and though much against my will, to cancell all that he had finished of it, and did give her the rest, which vexed her, and she bore it discreetly enough, but with a cruel deal of malicious rancour in her looks. I must confess I would have persuaded her to have let us have it to the office, and it may be the board would not have censured too hardly of it, but my intent was to have had it as a Record for the office, but she foresaw what would be the end of it and so desired it might rather be cancelled, which was a plaguy deal of spite. My Lord Bruncker being gone and company, and she also, afterwards I took my wife and people and walked into the fields about a while till night, and then home, and so to sing a little and then to bed. I was in great trouble all this day for my boy Tom who went to Greenwich yesterday by my order and come not home till to-night for fear of the plague, but he did come home to-night, saying he staid last night by Mr. Hater's advice hoping to have me called as I come home with my boat to come along with me.

9th. Up and walked to Greenwich, and there we sat and dispatched a good deal of business I had a mind to. At noon, by invitation, to my Lord Bruncker's, all of us, to dinner, where a good venison pasty, and mighty merry. Here was Sir W. Doyly, lately come from Ipswich about the sicke and wounded, and Mr. Evelyn and Captain Cocke. My wife also was sent for by my Lord Bruncker, by Cocke, and was here. After dinner, my Lord and his mistress would see her home again, it being a most cursed rainy afternoon, having had none a great while before, and I, forced to go to the office on foot through all the rain, was almost wet to my skin, and spoiled my silke breeches almost. Rained all the afternoon and evening, so as my letters being done, I was forced to get a bed at Captain Cocke's, where I find Sir W. Doyly, and he, and Evelyn at supper; and I with them full of discourse of the neglect of our masters, the great officers of State, about all business, and especially that of money: having now some thousands prisoners, kept to no purpose at a great charge, and no money provided almost for the doing of it. We fell to talk largely of the want of some persons understanding to look after businesses, but all goes to rack. "For," says Captain Cocke, "my Lord Treasurer, he minds his ease, and lets things go how they will: if he can have his L8000 per annum, and a game at l'ombre,--[Spanish card game]--he is well. My Lord Chancellor he minds getting of money and nothing else; and my Lord Ashly will rob the Devil and the Alter, but he will get money if it be to be got." But that that put us into this great melancholy, was newes brought to-day, which Captain Cocke reports as a certain truth, that all the Dutch fleete, men-of-war and merchant East India ships, are got every one in from Bergen the 3d of this month, Sunday last; which will make us all ridiculous. The fleete come home with shame to require a great deale of money, which is not to be had, to discharge many men that must get the plague then or continue at greater charge on shipboard, nothing done by them to encourage the Parliament to give money, nor the Kingdom able to spare any money, if they would, at this time of the plague, so that, as things look at present, the whole state must come to ruine. Full of these melancholy thoughts, to bed; where, though I lay the softest I ever did in my life, with a downe bed, after the Danish manner, upon me, yet I slept very ill, chiefly through the thoughts of my Lord Sandwich's concernment in all this ill successe at sea.

10th (Lord's day). Walked home; being forced thereto by one of my watermen falling sick yesterday, and it was God's great mercy I did not go by water with them yesterday, for he fell sick on Saturday night, and it is to be feared of the plague. So I sent him away to London with his fellow; but another boat come to me this morning, whom I sent to Blackewall for Mr. Andrews. I walked to Woolwich, and there find Mr. Hill, and he and I all the morning at musique and a song he hath set of three parts, methinks, very good. Anon comes Mr. Andrews, though it be a very ill day, and so after dinner we to musique and sang till about 4 or 5 o'clock, it blowing very hard, and now and then raining, and wind and tide being against us, Andrews and I took leave and walked to Greenwich. My wife before I come out telling me the ill news that she hears that her father is very ill, and then I told her I feared of the plague, for that the house is shut up. And so she much troubled she did desire me to send them something; and I said I would, and will do so. But before I come out there happened newes to come to the by an expresse from Mr. Coventry, telling me the most happy news of my Lord Sandwich's meeting with part of the Dutch; his taking two of their East India ships, and six or seven others, and very good prizes and that he is in search of the rest of the fleet, which he hopes to find upon the Wellbancke, with the loss only of the Hector, poor Captain Cuttle.

This newes do so overjoy me that I know not what to say enough to express it, but the better to do it I did walk to Greenwich, and there sending away Mr. Andrews, I to Captain Cocke's, where I find my Lord Bruncker and his mistress, and Sir J. Minnes. Where we supped (there was also Sir W. Doyly and Mr. Evelyn); but the receipt of this newes did put us all into such an extacy of joy, that it inspired into Sir J. Minnes and Mr. Evelyn such a spirit of mirth, that in all my life I never met with so merry a two hours as our company this night was. Among other humours, Mr. Evelyn's repeating of some verses made up of nothing but the various acceptations of may and can, and doing it so aptly upon occasion of something of that nature, and so fast, did make us all die almost with laughing, and did so stop the mouth of Sir J. Minnes in the middle of all his mirth (and in a thing agreeing with his own manner of genius), that I never saw any man so out-done in all my life; and Sir J. Minnes's mirth too to see himself out-done, was the crown of all our mirth. In this humour we sat till about ten at night, and so my Lord and his mistress home, and we to bed, it being one of the times of my life wherein I was the fullest of true sense of joy.

11th. Up and walked to the office, there to do some business till ten of the clock, and then by agreement my Lord, Sir J. Minnes, Sir W. Doyly, and I took boat and over to the ferry, where Sir W. Batten's coach was ready for us, and to Walthamstow drove merrily, excellent merry discourse in the way, and most upon our last night's revells; there come we were very merry, and a good plain venison dinner. After dinner to billiards, where I won an angel,

[A gold coin, so called because it bore the image of an angel, varying in value from six shillings and eightpence to ten shillings.]

and among other sports we were merry with my pretending to have a warrant to Sir W. Hickes (who was there, and was out of humour with Sir W. Doyly's having lately got a warrant for a leash of buckes, of which we were now eating one) which vexed him, and at last would compound with me to give my Lord Bruncker half a buck now, and me a Doe for it a while hence when the season comes in, which we agreed to and had held, but that we fear Sir W. Doyly did betray our design, which spoiled all; however, my Lady Batten invited herself to dine with him this week, and she invited us all to dine with her there, which we agreed to, only to vex him, he being the most niggardly fellow, it seems, in the world. Full of good victuals and mirth we set homeward in the evening, and very merry all the way. So to Greenwich, where when come I find my Lord Rutherford and Creed come from Court, and among other things have brought me several orders for money to pay for Tangier; and, among the rest L7000 and more, to this Lord, which is an excellent thing to consider, that, though they can do nothing else, they can give away the King's money upon their progresse. I did give him the best answer I could to pay him with tallys, and that is all they could get from me. I was not in humour to spend much time with them, but walked a little before Sir J. Minnes's door and then took leave, and I by water to Woolwich, where with my wife to a game at tables,

[The old name for backgammon, used by Shakespeare and others. The following lines are from an epitaph entirely made up of puns on backgammon

"Man's life's a game at tables, and he may
Mend his bad fortune by his wiser play."

Wit's Recre., i. 250, reprint, 1817.]

and to bed.

12th. Up, and walked to the office, where we sat late, and thence to dinner home with Sir J. Minnes, and so to the office, where writing letters, and home in the evening, where my wife shews me a letter from her brother speaking of their father's being ill, like to die, which, God forgive me! did not trouble me so much as it should, though I was indeed sorry for it. I did presently resolve to send him something in a letter from my wife, viz. 20s. So to bed.

13th. Up, and walked to Greenwich, taking pleasure to walk with my minute watch in my hand, by which I am come now to see the distances of my way from Woolwich to Greenwich, and do find myself to come within two minutes constantly to the same place at the end of each quarter of an houre. Here we rendezvoused at Captain Cocke's, and there eat oysters, and so my Lord Bruncker, Sir J. Minnes, and I took boat, and in my Lord's coach to Sir W. Hickes's, whither by and by my Lady Batten and Sir William comes. It is a good seat, with a fair grove of trees by it, and the remains of a good garden; but so let to run to ruine, both house and every thing in and about it, so ill furnished and miserably looked after, I never did see in all my life. Not so much as a latch to his dining-room door; which saved him nothing, for the wind blowing into the room for want thereof, flung down a great bow pott that stood upon the side-table, and that fell upon some Venice glasses, and did him a crown's worth of hurt. He did give us the meanest dinner (of beef, shoulder and umbles of venison

[Dr. Johnson was puzzled by the following passage in "The Merry Wives of Windsor," act v., sc. 3: "Divide me like a bribe-buck, each a haunch. I will keep the sides to myself; my shoulders for the fellow of this walk." If he could have read the account of Sir William Hickes's dinner, he would at once have understood the allusion to the keeper's perquisites of the shoulders of all deer killed in his walk.--B.]

which he takes away from the keeper of the Forest, and a few pigeons, and all in the meanest manner) that ever I did see, to the basest degree. After dinner we officers of the Navy stepped aside to read some letters and consider some business, and so in again. I was only pleased at a very fine picture of the Queene-Mother, when she was young, by Van-Dike; a very good picture, and a lovely sweet face. Thence in the afternoon home, and landing at Greenwich I saw Mr. Pen walking my way, so we walked together, and for discourse I put him into talk of France, when he took delight to tell me of his observations, some good, some impertinent, and all ill told, but it served for want of better, and so to my house, where I find my wife abroad, and hath been all this day, nobody knows where, which troubled me, it being late and a cold evening. So being invited to his mother's to supper, we took Mrs. Barbara, who was mighty finely dressed, and in my Lady's coach, which we met going for my wife, we thither, and there after some discourse went to supper. By and by comes my wife and Mercer, and had been with Captain Cocke all day, he coming and taking her out to go see his boy at school at Brumly [Bromley], and brought her home again with great respect. Here pretty merry, only I had no stomach, having dined late, to eat. After supper Mr. Pen and I fell to discourse about some words in a French song my wife was saying, "D'un air tout interdict," wherein I laid twenty to one against him which he would not agree with me, though I know myself in the right as to the sense of the word, and almost angry we were, and were an houre and more upon the dispute, till at last broke up not satisfied, and so home in their coach and so to bed. H. Russell did this day deliver my 20s. to my wife's father or mother, but has not yet told us how they do.

14th. Up, and walked to Greenwich, and there fitted myself in several businesses to go to London, where I have not been now a pretty while. But before I went from the office newes is brought by word of mouth that letters are now just now brought from the fleete of our taking a great many more of the Dutch fleete, in which I did never more plainly see my command of my temper in my not admitting myself to receive any kind of joy from it till I had heard the certainty of it, and therefore went by water directly to the Duke of Albemarle, where I find a letter of the Lath from Solebay, from my Lord Sandwich, of the fleete's meeting with about eighteen more of the Dutch fleete, and his taking of most of them; and the messenger says, they had taken three after the letter was wrote and sealed; which being twenty-one, and the fourteen took the other day, is forty-five sail; some of which are good, and others rich ships, which is so great a cause of joy in us all that my Lord and everybody is highly joyed thereat. And having taken a copy of my Lord's letter, I away back again to the Beare at the Bridge foot, being full of wind and out of order, and there called for a biscuit and a piece of cheese and gill of sacke, being forced to walk over the Bridge, toward the 'Change, and the plague being all thereabouts. Here my news was highly welcome, and I did wonder to see the 'Change so full, I believe 200 people; but not a man or merchant of any fashion, but plain men all. And Lord! to see how I did endeavour all I could to talk with as few as I could, there being now no observation of shutting up of houses infected, that to be sure we do converse and meet with people that have the plague upon them. I to Sir Robert Viner's, where my main business was about settling the business of Debusty's L5000 tallys, which I did for the present to enable me to have some money, and so home, buying some things for my wife in the way. So home, and put up several things to carry to Woolwich, and upon serious thoughts I am advised by

W. Griffin to let my money and plate rest there, as being as safe as any place, nobody imagining that people would leave money in their houses now, when all their families are gone. So for the present that being my opinion, I did leave them there still. But, Lord! to see the trouble that it puts a man to, to keep safe what with pain a man hath been getting together, and there is good reason for it. Down to the office, and there wrote letters to and again about this good newes of our victory, and so by water home late. Where, when I come home I spent some thoughts upon the occurrences of this day, giving matter for as much content on one hand and melancholy on another, as any day in all my life. For the first; the finding of my money and plate, and all safe at London, and speeding in my business of money this day. The hearing of this good news to such excess, after so great a despair of my Lord's doing anything this year; adding to that, the decrease of 500 and more, which is the first decrease we have yet had in the sickness since it begun: and great hopes that the next week it will be greater. Then, on the other side, my finding that though the Bill in general is abated, yet the City within the walls is encreased, and likely to continue so, and is close to our house there. My meeting dead corpses of the plague, carried to be buried close to me at noon-day through the City in Fanchurch-street. To see a person sick of the sores, carried close by me by Gracechurch in a hackney-coach. My finding the Angell tavern, at the lower end of Tower-hill, shut up, and more than that, the alehouse at the Tower-stairs, and more than that, the person was then dying of the plague when I was last there, a little while ago, at night, to write a short letter there, and I overheard the mistresse of the house sadly saying to her husband somebody was very ill, but did not think it was of the plague. To hear that poor Payne, my waiter, hath buried a child, and is dying himself. To hear that a labourer I sent but the other day to Dagenhams, to know how they did there, is dead of the plague; and that one of my own watermen, that carried me daily, fell sick as soon as he had landed me on Friday morning last, when I had been all night upon the water (and I believe he did get his infection that day at Brainford), and is now dead of the plague. To hear that Captain Lambert and Cuttle are killed in the taking these ships; and that Mr. Sidney Montague is sick of a desperate fever at my Lady Carteret's, at Scott's-hall. To hear that Mr. Lewes hath another daughter sick. And, lastly, that both my servants, W. Hewer and Tom Edwards, have lost their fathers, both in St. Sepulchre's parish, of the plague this week, do put me into great apprehensions of melancholy, and with good reason. But I put off the thoughts of sadness as much as I can, and the rather to keep my wife in good heart and family also. After supper (having eat nothing all this day) upon a fine tench of Mr. Shelden's taking, we to bed.

15th. Up, it being a cold misting morning, and so by water to the office, where very busy upon several businesses. At noon got the messenger, Marlow, to get me a piece of bread and butter and cheese and a bottle of beer and ale, and so I went not out of the office but dined off that, and my boy Tom, but the rest of my clerks went home to dinner. Then to my business again, and by and by sent my waterman to see how Sir W. Warren do, who is sicke, and for which I have reason to be very sorry, he being the friend I have got most by of most friends in England but the King: who returns me that he is pretty well again, his disease being an ague. I by water to Deptford, thinking to have seen my valentine, but I could not, and so come back again, and to the office, where a little business, and thence with Captain Cocke, and there drank a cup of good drink, which I am fain to allow myself during this plague time, by advice of all, and not contrary to my oathe, my physician being dead, and chyrurgeon out of the way, whose advice I am obliged to take, and so by water home and eat my supper, and to bed, being in much pain to think what I shall do this winter time; for go every day to Woolwich I cannot, without endangering my life; and staying from my wife at Greenwich is not handsome.

16th. Up, and walked to Greenwich reading a play, and to the office, where I find Sir J. Minnes gone to the fleete, like a doating foole, to do no good, but proclaim himself an asse; for no service he can do there, nor inform my Lord, who is come in thither to the buoy of the Nore, in anything worth his knowledge. At noon to dinner to my Lord Bruncker, where Sir W. Batten and his Lady come, by invitation, and very merry we were, only that the discourse of the likelihood of the increase of the plague this weeke makes us a little sad, but then again the thoughts of the late prizes make us glad. After dinner, by appointment, comes Mr. Andrews, and he and I walking alone in the garden talking of our Tangier business, and I endeavoured by the by to offer some encouragements for their continuing in the business, which he seemed to take hold of, and the truth is my profit is so much concerned that I could wish they would, and would take pains to ease them in the business of money as much as was possible. He being gone (after I had ordered him L2000, and he paid me my quantum out of it) I also walked to the office, and there to my business; but find myself, through the unfitness of my place to write in, and my coming from great dinners, and drinking wine, that I am not in the good temper of doing business now a days that I used to be and ought still to be. At night to Captain Cocke's, meaning to lie there, it being late, and he not being at home, I walked to him to my Lord Bruncker's, and there staid a while, they being at tables; and so by and by parted, and walked to his house; and, after a mess of good broth, to bed, in great pleasure, his company being most excellent.

17th (Lord's day). Up, and before I went out of my chamber did draw a musique scale, in order to my having it at any time ready in my hand to turn to for exercise, for I have a great mind in this Vacation to perfect myself in my scale, in order to my practising of composition, and so that being done I down stairs, and there find Captain Cocke under the barber's hands, the barber that did heretofore trim Commissioner Pett, and with whom I have been. He offered to come this day after dinner with his violin to play me a set of Lyra-ayres upon it, which I was glad of, hoping to be merry thereby. Being ready we to church, where a company of fine people to church, and a fine Church, and very good sermon, Mr. Plume' being a very excellent scholler and preacher. Coming out of the church I met Mrs. Pierce, whom I was ashamed to see, having not been with her since my coming to town, but promised to visit her. Thence with Captain Cocke, in his coach, home to dinner, whither comes by invitation my Lord

Bruncker and his mistresse and very good company we were, but in dinner time comes Sir J. Minnes from the fleete, like a simple weak man, having nothing to say of what he hath done there, but tells of what value he imagines the prizes to be, and that my Lord Sandwich is well, and mightily concerned to hear that I was well. But this did put me upon a desire of going thither; and, moving of it to my Lord, we presently agreed upon it to go this very tide, we two and Captain Cocke. So every body prepared to fit himself for his journey, and I walked to Woolwich to trim and shift myself, and by the time I was ready they come down in the Bezan yacht, and so I aboard and my boy Tom, and there very merrily we sailed to below Gravesend, and there come to anchor for all night, and supped and talked, and with much pleasure at last settled ourselves to sleep having very good lodging upon cushions in the cabbin.

18th. By break of day we come to within sight of the fleete, which was a very fine thing to behold, being above 100 ships, great and small; with the flag-ships of each squadron, distinguished by their several flags on their main, fore, or mizen masts. Among others, the Soveraigne, Charles, and Prince; in the last of which my Lord Sandwich was. When we called by her side his Lordshipp was not stirring, so we come to anchor a little below his ship, thinking to have rowed on board him, but the wind and tide was so strong against us that we could not get up to him, no, though rowed by a boat of the Prince's that come to us to tow us up; at last however he brought us within a little way, and then they flung out a rope to us from the Prince and so come on board, but with great trouble and tune and patience, it being very cold; we find my Lord newly up in his night-gown very well. He received us kindly; telling us the state of the fleet, lacking provisions, having no beer at all, nor have had most of them these three weeks or month, and but few days' dry provisions. And indeed he tells us that he believes no fleete was ever set to sea in so ill condition of provision, as this was when it went out last. He did inform us in the business of Bergen,

[Lord Sandwich was not so successful in convincing other people as to the propriety of his conduct at Bergen as he was with Pepys.]

so as to let us see how the judgment of the world is not to be depended on in things they know not; it being a place just wide enough, and not so much hardly, for ships to go through to it, the yardarmes sticking in the very rocks. He do not, upon his best enquiry, find reason to except against any part of the management of the business by Teddiman; he having staid treating no longer than during the night, whiles he was fitting himself to fight, bringing his ship a-breast, and not a quarter of an hour longer (as is said); nor could more ships have been brought to play, as is thought. Nor could men be landed, there being 10,000 men effectively always in armes of the Danes; nor, says he, could we expect more from the Dane than he did, it being impossible to set fire on the ships but it must burn the towne. But that wherein the Dane did amisse is, that he did assist them, the Dutch, all the while, while he was treating with us, while he should have been neutrall to us both. But, however, he did demand but the treaty of us; which is, that we should not come with more than five ships. A flag of truce is said, and confessed by my Lord, that he believes it was hung out; but while they did hang it out, they did shoot at us; so that it was not either seen perhaps, or fit to cease upon sight of it, while they continued actually in action against us. But the main thing my Lord wonders at, and condemns the Dane for, is, that the blockhead, who is so much in debt to the Hollander, having now a treasure more by much than all his Crowne was worth, and that which would for ever have beggared the Hollanders, should not take this time to break with the Hollander, and, thereby paid his debt which must have been forgiven him, and got the greatest treasure into his hands that ever was together in the world. By and by my Lord took me aside to discourse of his private matters, who was very free with me touching the ill condition of the fleete that it hath been in, and the good fortune that he hath had, and nothing else that these prizes are to be imputed to. He also talked with me about Mr. Coventry's dealing with him in sending Sir W. Pen away before him, which was not fair nor kind; but that he hath mastered and cajoled Sir W. Pen, that he hath been able to do, nothing in the fleete, but been obedient to him; but withal tells me he is a man that is but of very mean parts, and a fellow not to be lived with, so false and base he is; which I know well enough to be very true, and did, as I had formerly done, give my Lord my knowledge of him. By and by was called a Council of Warr on board, when come Sir W. Pen there, and Sir Christopher Mings, Sir Edward Spragg, Sir Jos. Jordan, Sir Thomas Teddiman, and Sir Roger Cuttance, and so the necessity of the fleete for victuals, clothes, and money was discoursed, but by the discourse there of all but my Lord, that is to say, the counterfeit grave nonsense of Sir W. Pen and the poor mean discourse of the rest, methinks I saw how the government and management of the greatest business of the three nations is committed to very ordinary heads, saving my Lord, and in effect is only upon him, who is able to do what he pleases with them, they not having the meanest degree of reason to be able to oppose anything that he says, and so I fear it is ordered but like all the rest of the King's publique affayres. The council being up they most of them went away, only Sir W. Pen who staid to dine there and did so, but the wind being high the ship (though the motion of it was hardly discernible to the eye) did make me sick, so as I could not eat any thing almost. After dinner Cocke did pray me to helpe him to L500 of W. How, who is deputy Treasurer, wherein my Lord Bruncker and I am to be concerned and I did aske it my Lord, and he did consent to have us furnished with L500, and I did get it paid to Sir Roger Cuttance and Mr. Pierce in part for above L1000 worth of goods, Mace, Nutmegs, Cynamon, and Cloves, and he tells us we may hope to get L1500 by it, which God send! Great spoil, I hear, there hath been of the two East India ships, and that yet they will come in to the King very rich: so that I hope this journey will be worth L100 to me.

[There is a shorthand journal of proceedings relating to Pepys's purchase of some East India prize goods among the Rawlinson MSS. in the Bodleian Library.]

After having paid this money, we took leave of my Lord and so to our Yacht again, having seen many of my friends there. Among others I hear that W. Howe will grow very rich by this last business and grows very proud and insolent by it; but it is what I ever expected. I hear by every body how much my poor Lord of Sandwich was concerned for me during my silence a while, lest I had been dead of the plague in this sickly time. No sooner come into the yacht, though overjoyed with the good work we have done to-day, but I was overcome with sea sickness so that I begun to spue soundly, and so continued a good while, till at last I went into the cabbin and shutting my eyes my trouble did cease that I fell asleep, which continued till we come into Chatham river where the water was smooth, and then I rose and was very well, and the tide coming to be against us we did land before we come to Chatham and walked a mile, having very good discourse by the way, it being dark and it beginning to rain just as we got thither. At Commissioner Pett's we did eat and drink very well and very merry we were, and about 10 at night, it being moonshine and very cold, we set out, his coach carrying us, and so all night travelled to Greenwich, we sometimes sleeping a little and then talking and laughing by the way, and with much pleasure, but that it was very horrible cold, that I was afeard of an ague. A pretty passage was that the coach stood of a sudden and the coachman come down and the horses stirring, he cried, Hold! which waked me, and the coach[man] standing at the boote to [do] something or other and crying, Hold! I did wake of a sudden and not knowing who he was, nor thinking of the coachman between sleeping and waking I did take up the heart to take him by the shoulder, thinking verily he had been a thief. But when I waked I found my cowardly heart to discover a fear within me and that I should never have done it if I had been awake.

19th. About 4 or 5 of the clock we come to Greenwich, and, having first set down my Lord Bruncker, Cocke and I went to his house, it being light, and there to our great trouble, we being sleepy and cold, we met with the ill newes that his boy Jacke was gone to bed sicke, which put Captain Cocke and me also into much trouble, the boy, as they told us, complaining of his head most, which is a bad sign it seems. So they presently betook themselves to consult whither and how to remove him. However I thought it not fit for me to discover too much fear to go away, nor had I any place to go to. So to bed I went and slept till 10 of the clock and then comes Captain Cocke to wake me and tell me that his boy was well again. With great joy I heard the newes and he told it, so I up and to the office where we did a little, and but a little business. At noon by invitation to my Lord Bruncker's where we staid till four of the clock for my Lady Batten and she not then coming we to dinner and pretty merry but disordered by her making us stay so long. After dinner I to the office, and there wrote letters and did business till night and then to Sir J. Minnes's, where I find my Lady Batten come, and she and my Lord Bruncker and his mistresse, and the whole house-full there at cards. But by and by my Lord Bruncker goes away and others of the company, and when I expected Sir J. Minnes and his sister should have staid to have made Sir W. Batten and Lady sup, I find they go up in snuffe to bed without taking any manner of leave of them, but left them with Mr. Boreman. The reason of this I could not presently learn, but anon I hear it is that Sir J. Minnes did expect and intend them a supper, but they without respect to him did first apply themselves to Boreman, which makes all this great feude. However I staid and there supped, all of us being in great disorder from this, and more from Cocke's boy's being ill, where my Lady Batten and Sir W. Batten did come to town with an intent to lodge, and I was forced to go seek a lodging which my W. Hewer did get me, viz., his own chamber in the towne, whither I went and found it a very fine room, and there lay most excellently.

20th. Called up by Captain Cocke (who was last night put into great trouble upon his boy's being rather worse than better, upon which he removed him out of his house to his stable), who told me that to my comfort his boy was now as well as ever he was in his life. So I up, and after being trimmed, the first time I have been touched by a barber these twelvemonths, I think, and more, went to Sir J. Minnes's, where I find all out of order still, they having not seen one another till by and by Sir J. Minnes and Sir W. Batten met, to go into my Lord Bruncker's coach, and so we four to Lambeth, and thence to the Duke of Albemarle, to inform him what we have done as to the fleete, which is very little, and to receive his direction. But, Lord! what a sad time it is to see no boats upon the River; and grass grows all up and down White Hall court, and nobody but poor wretches in the streets! And, which is worst of all, the Duke showed us the number of the plague this week, brought in the last night from the Lord Mayor; that it is encreased about 600 more than the last, which is quite contrary to all our hopes and expectations, from the coldness of the late season. For the whole general number is 8,297, and of them the plague 7,165; which is more in the whole by above 50, than the biggest Bill yet; which is very grievous to us all. I find here a design in my Lord Bruncker and Captain Cocke to have had my Lord Bruncker chosen as one of us to have been sent aboard one of the East Indiamen, and Captain Cocke as a merchant to be joined with him, and Sir J. Minnes for the other, and Sir G. Smith to be joined with him. But I did order it so that my Lord Bruncker and Sir J. Minnes were ordered, but I did stop the merchants to be added, which would have been a most pernicious thing to the King I am sure. In this I did, I think, a very good office, though I cannot acquit myself from some envy of mine in the business to have the profitable business done by another hand while I lay wholly imployed in the trouble of the office. Thence back again by my Lord's coach to my Lord Bruncker's house, where I find my Lady Batten, who is become very great with Mrs. Williams (my Lord Bruncker's whore), and there we dined and were mighty merry. After dinner I to the office there to write letters, to fit myself for a journey to-morrow to Nonsuch to the Exchequer by appointment. That being done I to Sir J. Minnes where I find Sir W. Batten and his Lady gone home to Walthamstow in great snuffe as to Sir J. Minnes, but yet with some necessity, hearing that a mayde-servant of theirs is taken ill. Here I staid and resolved of my going in my Lord

Bruncker's coach which he would have me to take, though himself cannot go with me as he intended, and so to my last night's lodging to bed very weary.

21st. Up between five and six o'clock; and by the time I was ready, my Lord's coach comes for me; and taking Will Hewer with me, who is all in mourning for his father, who is lately dead of the plague, as my boy Tom's is also, I set out, and took about L100 with me to pay the fees there, and so rode in some fear of robbing. When I come thither, I find only Mr. Ward, who led me to Burgess's bedside, and Spicer's, who, watching of the house, as it is their turns every night, did lie long in bed to-day, and I find nothing at all done in my business, which vexed me. But not seeing how to helpe it I did walk up and down with Mr. Ward to see the house; and by and by Spicer and Mr. Falconbrige come to me and he and I to a towne near by, Yowell, there drink and set up my horses and also bespoke a dinner, and while that is dressing went with Spicer and walked up and down the house and park; and a fine place it hath heretofore been, and a fine prospect about the house. A great walk of an elme and a walnutt set one after another in order. And all the house on the outside filled with figures of stories, and good painting of Rubens' or Holben's doing. And one great thing is, that most of the house is covered, I mean the posts, and quarters in the walls; covered with lead, and gilded. I walked into the ruined garden, and there found a plain little girle, kinswoman of Mr. Falconbridge, to sing very finely by the eare only, but a fine way of singing, and if I come ever to lacke a girle again I shall think of getting her. Thence to the towne, and there Spicer, Woodruffe, and W. Bowyer and I dined together and a friend of Spicer's; and a good dinner I had for them. Falconbrige dined somewhere else, by appointment. Strange to see how young W. Bowyer looks at 41 years; one would not take him for 24 or more, and is one of the greatest wonders I ever did see. After dinner, about 4 of the clock we broke up, and I took coach and home (in fear for the money I had with me, but that this friend of Spicer's, one of the Duke's guard did ride along the best part of the way with us). I got to my Lord Bruncker's before night, and there I sat and supped with him and his mistresse, and Cocke whose boy is yet ill. Thence, after losing a crowne betting at Tables-- [Cribbage]--, we walked home, Cocke seeing me at my new lodging, where I went to bed. All my worke this day in the coach going and coming was to refresh myself in my musique scale, which I would fain have perfecter than ever I had yet.

22nd. Up betimes and to the office, meaning to have entered my last 5 or 6 days' Journall, but was called away by my Lord Bruncker and Sir J. Minnes, and to Blackwall, there to look after the storehouses in order to the laying of goods out of the East India ships when they shall be unloaden. That being done, we into Johnson's house, and were much made of, eating and drinking. But here it is observable what he tells us, that in digging his late Docke, he did 12 foot under ground find perfect trees over-covered with earth. Nut trees, with the branches and the very nuts upon them; some of whose nuts he showed us. Their shells black with age, and their kernell, upon opening, decayed, but their shell perfectly hard as ever. And a yew tree he showed us (upon which, he says, the very ivy was taken up whole about it), which upon cutting with an addes [adze], we found to be rather harder than the living tree usually is. They say, very much, but I do not know how hard a yew tree naturally is.

[The same discovery was made in 1789, in digging the Brunswick Dock, also at Blackwall, and elsewhere in the neighbourhood.]

The armes, they say, were taken up at first whole, about the body, which is very strange. Thence away by water, and I walked with my Lord Bruncker home, and there at dinner comes a letter from my Lord Sandwich to tell me that he would this day be at Woolwich, and desired me to meet him. Which fearing might have lain in Sir J. Minnes' pocket a while, he sending it me, did give my Lord Bruncker, his mistress, and I occasion to talk of him as the most unfit man for business in the world. Though at last afterwards I found that he was not in this faulty, but hereby I have got a clear evidence of my Lord Bruncker's opinion of him. My Lord Bruncker presently ordered his coach to be ready and we to Woolwich, and my Lord Sandwich not being come, we took a boat and about a mile off met him in his Catch, and boarded him, and come up with him; and, after making a little halt at my house, which I ordered, to have my wife see him, we all together by coach to Mr. Boreman's, where Sir J. Minnes did receive him very handsomely, and there he is to lie; and Sir J. Minnes did give him on the sudden, a very handsome supper and brave discourse, my Lord Bruncker, and Captain Cocke, and Captain Herbert being there, with myself. Here my Lord did witness great respect to me, and very kind expressions, and by other occasions, from one thing to another did take notice how I was overjoyed at first to see the King's letter to his Lordship, and told them how I did kiss it, and that, whatever he was, I did always love the King. This my Lord Bruncker did take such notice [of] as that he could not forbear kissing me before my Lord, professing his finding occasion every day more and more to love me, and Captain Cocke has since of himself taken notice of that speech of my Lord then concerning me, and may be of good use to me. Among other discourse concerning long life, Sir J. Minnes saying that his great-grandfather was alive in Edward the Vth's time; my Lord Sandwich did tell us how few there have been of his family since King Harry the VIIIth; that is to say, the then Chiefe Justice, and his son the Lord Montagu, who was father to Sir Sidney,

[These are the words in the MS., and not "his son and the Lord Montagu," as in some former editions. Pepys seems to have written Lord Montagu by mistake for Sir Edward Montagu.]

who was his father. And yet, what is more wonderfull, he did assure us from the mouth of my Lord Montagu himself, that in King James's time ([when he] had a mind to get the King to cut off the entayle of some land which was given in Harry the VIIIth's time to the family, with the remainder in the Crowne); he did answer the King in showing how unlikely it was that ever it could revert to the Crown, but that it would be a present convenience to him; and did show that at that time there were 4,000 persons derived from the very body of the Chiefe Justice. It seems the number of daughters in the family having been very great, and they too had most of them many children, and grandchildren, and great-grandchildren. This he tells as a most known and certain truth. After supper, my Lord Bruncker took his leave, and I also did mine, taking Captain Herbert home to my lodging to lie with me, who did mighty seriously inquire after who was that in the black dress with my wife yesterday, and would not believe that it was my wife's mayde, Mercer, but it was she.

23rd. Up, and to my Lord Sandwich, who did advise alone with me how far he might trust Captain Cocke in the business of the prize-goods, my Lord telling me that he hath taken into his hands 2 or L3000 value of them: it being a good way, he says, to get money, and afterwards to get the King's allowance thereof, it being easier, he observes, to keepe money when got of the King than to get it when it is too late. I advised him not to trust Cocke too far, and did therefore offer him ready money for a L1000 or two, which he listens to and do agree to, which is great joy to me, hoping thereby to get something! Thence by coach to Lambeth, his Lordship, and all our office, and Mr. Evelyn, to the Duke of Albemarle, where, after the compliment with my Lord very kind, we sat down to consult of the disposing and supporting of the fleete with victuals and money, and for the sicke men and prisoners; and I did propose the taking out some goods out of the prizes, to the value of L10,000, which was accorded to, and an order, drawn up and signed by the Duke and my Lord, done in the best manner I can, and referred to my Lord Bruncker and Sir J. Minnes, but what inconveniences may arise from it I do not yet see, but fear there may be many. Here we dined, and I did hear my Lord Craven whisper, as he is mightily possessed with a good opinion of me, much to my advantage, which my good Lord did second, and anon my Lord Craven did speak publiquely of me to the Duke, in the hearing of all the rest; and the Duke did say something of the like advantage to me; I believe, not much to the satisfaction of my brethren; but I was mightily joyed at it. Thence took leave, leaving my Lord Sandwich to go visit the Bishop of Canterbury, and I and Sir W. Batten down to the Tower, where he went further by water, and I home, and among other things took out all my gold to carry along with me to-night with Captain Cocke downe to the fleete, being L180 and more, hoping to lay out that and a great deal more to good advantage. Thence down to Greenwich to the office, and there wrote several letters, and so to my Lord Sandwich, and mighty merry and he mighty kind to me in the face of all, saying much in my favour, and after supper I took leave and with Captain Cocke set out in the yacht about ten o'clock at night, and after some discourse, and drinking a little, my mind full of what we are going about and jealous of Cocke's outdoing me. So to sleep upon beds brought by Cocke on board mighty handsome, and never slept better than upon this bed upon the floor in the Cabbin.

24th (Lord's day). Waked, and up and drank, and then to discourse; and then being about Grayes, and a very calme, curious morning, we took our wherry, and to the fishermen, and bought a great deal of fine fish, and to Gravesend to White's, and had part of it dressed; and, in the meantime, we to walk about a mile from the towne, and so back again; and there, after breakfast, one of our watermen told us he had heard of a bargain of cloves for us, and we went to a blind alehouse at the further end wretched dirty seamen, who, of the towne to a couple of poor wretches, had got together about 37 lb. of cloves and to 10 of nutmeggs, and we bought them of them, the first at 5s. 6d. per lb. and the latter at 4s.; and paid them in gold; but, Lord! to see how silly these men are in the selling of it, and easily to be persuaded almost to anything, offering a bag to us to pass as 20 lbs. of cloves, which upon weighing proved 25 lbs. But it would never have been allowed by my conscience to have wronged the poor wretches, who told us how dangerously they had got some, and dearly paid for the rest of these goods. This being done we with great content herein on board again and there Captain Cocke and I to discourse of our business, but he will not yet be open to me, nor am I to him till I hear what he will say and do with Sir Roger Cuttance. However, this discourse did do me good, and got me a copy of the agreement made the other day on board for the parcel of Mr. Pierce and Sir Roger Cuttance, but this great parcel is of my Lord Sandwich's. By and by to dinner about 3 o'clock and then I in the cabbin to writing down my journall for these last seven days to my, great content, it having pleased God that in this sad time of the plague every thing else has conspired to my happiness and pleasure more for these last three months than in all my, life before in so little time. God long preserve it and make me thankful) for it! After finishing my Journal), then to discourse and to read, and then to supper and to bed, my mind not being at full ease, having not fully satisfied myself how Captain Cocke will deal with me as to the share of the profits.

25th. Found ourselves come to the fleete, and so aboard the Prince; and there, after a good while in discourse, we did agree a bargain of L5,000 with Sir Roger Cuttance for my Lord Sandwich for silk, cinnamon, nutmeggs, and indigo. And I was near signing to an undertaking for the payment of the whole sum; but I did by chance escape it; having since, upon second thoughts, great cause to be glad of it, reflecting upon the craft and not good condition, it may be, of Captain Cocke. I could get no trifles for my wife. Anon to dinner and thence in great haste to make a short visit to Sir W. Pen, where I found them and his lady and daughter and many commanders at dinner. Among others Sir G. Askue, of whom whatever the matter is, the world is silent altogether. But a very pretty dinner there was, and after dinner Sir W. Pen made a bargain with Cocke for ten bales of silke, at 16s. per lb., which, as Cocke says, will be a good pennyworth, and so away to the Prince and presently comes my Lord on board from Greenwich, with whom, after a little discourse about his trusting of Cocke, we parted and to our yacht; but it being calme, we to make haste, took our wherry toward Chatham; but, it growing darke, we were put to great difficultys, our simple, yet confident waterman, not knowing a step of the way; and we found ourselves to go backward and forward, which, in the darke night and a wild place, did vex us mightily. At last we got a fisher boy by chance, and took him into the boat, and being an odde kind of boy, did vex us too; for he would not answer us aloud when we spoke to him, but did carry us safe thither, though with a mistake or two; but I wonder they were not more. In our way I was [surprised] and so were we all, at the strange nature of the sea-water in a darke night, that it seemed like fire upon every stroke of the oare, and, they say, is a sign of winde. We went to the Crowne Inne, at Rochester, and there to supper, and made ourselves merry with our poor fisher-boy, who told us he had not been in a bed in the whole seven years since he came to 'prentice, and hath two or three more years to serve. After eating something, we in our clothes to bed.

26th. Up by five o'clock and got post horses and so set out for Greenwich, calling and drinking at Dartford. Being come to Greenwich and shifting myself I to the office, from whence by and by my Lord Bruncker and Sir J. Minnes set out toward Erith to take charge of the two East India shipps, which I had a hand in contriving for the King's service and may do myself a good office too thereby. I to dinner with Mr. Wright to his father-in-law in Greenwich, one of the most silly, harmless, prating old men that ever I heard in my life. Creed dined with me, and among other discourses got of me a promise of half that he could get my Lord Rutherford to give me upon clearing his business, which should not be less, he says, than L50 for my half, which is a good thing, though cunningly got of him. By and by Luellin comes, and I hope to get something of Deering shortly. They being gone, Mr. Wright and I went into the garden to discourse with much trouble for fear of losing all the profit and principal of what we have laid out in buying of prize goods, and therefore puts me upon thoughts of flinging up my interest, but yet I shall take good advice first. Thence to the office, and after some letters down to Woolwich, where I have not lain with my wife these eight days I think, or more. After supper, and telling her my mind in my trouble in what I have done as to buying' of these goods, we to bed.

27th. Up, and saw and admired my wife's picture of our Saviour,

[This picture by Mrs. Pepys may have given trouble when Pepys was unjustifiably attacked for having Popish pictures in his house.]

now finished, which is very pretty. So by water to Greenwich, where with Creed and Lord Rutherford, and there my Lord told me that he would give me L100 for my pains, which pleased me well, though Creed, like a cunning rogue, hath got a promise of half of it from me. We to the King's Head, the great musique house, the first time I was ever there, and had a good breakfast, and thence parted, I being much troubled to hear from Creed, that he was told at Salsbury that I am come to be a great swearer and drinker, though I know the contrary; but, Lord! to see how my late little drinking of wine is taken notice of by envious men to my disadvantage. I thence to Captain Cocke's, [and] (he not yet come from town) to Mr. Evelyn's, where much company; and thence in his coach with him to the Duke of Albemarle by Lambeth, who was in a mighty pleasant humour; there the Duke tells us that the Dutch do stay abroad, and our fleet must go out again, or to be ready to do so. Here we got several things ordered as we desired for the relief of the prisoners, and sick and wounded men. Here I saw this week's Bill of Mortality, wherein, blessed be God! there is above 1800 decrease, being the first considerable decrease we have had. Back again the same way and had most excellent discourse of Mr. Evelyn touching all manner of learning; wherein I find him a very fine gentleman, and particularly of paynting, in which he tells me the beautifull Mrs. Middleton is rare, and his own wife do brave things. He brought me to the office, whither comes unexpectedly Captain Cocke, who hath brought one parcel of our goods by waggons, and at first resolved to have lodged them at our office; but then the thoughts of its being the King's house altered our resolution, and so put them at his friend's, Mr. Glanvill's, and there they are safe. Would the rest of them were so too! In discourse, we come to mention my profit, and he offers me L500 clear, and I demand L600 for my certain profit. We part to-night, and I lie there at Mr. Glanvill's house, there being none there but a maydeservant and a young man; being in some pain, partly from not knowing what to do in this business, having a mind to be at a certainty in my profit, and partly through his having Jacke sicke still, and his blackemore now also fallen sicke. So he being gone, I to bed.

28th. Up, and being mightily pleased with my night's lodging, drank a cup of beer, and went out to my office, and there did some business, and so took boat and down to Woolwich (having first made a visit to Madam Williams, who is going down to my Lord Bruncker) and there dined, and then fitted my papers and money and every thing else for a journey to Nonsuch to-morrow. That being done I walked to Greenwich, and there to the office pretty late expecting Captain Cocke's coming, which he did, and so with me to my new lodging (and there I chose rather to lie because of my interest in the goods that we have brought there to lie), but the people were abed, so we knocked them up, and so I to bed, and in the night was mightily troubled with a looseness (I suppose from some fresh damp linen that I put on this night), and feeling for a chamber-pott, there was none, I having called the mayde up out of her bed, she had forgot I suppose to put one there; so I was forced in this strange house to rise and shit in the chimney twice; and so to bed and was very well again, and

29th. To sleep till 5 o'clock, when it is now very dark, and then rose, being called up by order by Mr. Marlow, and so up and dressed myself, and by and by comes Mr. Lashmore on horseback, and I had my horse I borrowed of Mr. Gillthropp, Sir W. Batten's clerke, brought to me, and so we set out and rode hard and was at Nonsuch by about eight o'clock, a very fine journey and a fine day. There I come just about chappell time and so I went to chappell with them and thence to the several offices about my tallys, which I find done, but strung for sums not to my purpose, and so was forced to get them to promise me to have them cut into other sums. But, Lord! what ado I had to persuade the dull fellows to it, especially Mr. Warder, Master of the Pells, and yet without any manner of reason for their scruple. But at last I did, and so left my tallies there against another day, and so walked to Yowell, and there did spend a peece upon them, having a whole house full, and much mirth by a sister of the mistresse of the house, an old mayde lately married to a lieutenant of a company that quarters there, and much pleasant discourse we had and, dinner being done, we to horse again and come to Greenwich before night, and so to my lodging, and there being a little weary sat down and fell to order some of my pocket papers, and then comes Captain Cocke, and after a great deal of discourse with him seriously upon the disorders of our state through lack of men to mind the public business and to understand it, we broke up, sitting up talking very late. We spoke a little of my late business propounded of taking profit for my money laid out for these goods, but he finds I rise in my demand, he offering me still L500 certain. So we did give it over, and I to bed. I hear for certain this night upon the road that Sir Martin Noell is this day dead of the plague in London, where he hath lain sick of it these eight days.

30th. Up and to the office, where busy all the morning, and at noon with Sir W. Batten to Coll. Cleggat to dinner, being invited, where a very pretty dinner to my full content and very merry. The great burden we have upon us at this time at the office, is the providing for prisoners and sicke men that are recovered, they lying before our office doors all night and all day, poor wretches. Having been on shore, the captains won't receive them on board, and other ships we have not to put them on, nor money to pay them off, or provide for them. God remove this difficulty! This made us followed all the way to this gentleman's house and there are waited for our coming out after dinner. Hither come Luellin to me and would force me to take Mr. Deering's 20 pieces in gold he did offer me a good while since, which I did, yet really and sincerely against my will and content, I seeing him a man not likely to do well in his business, nor I to reap any comfort in having to do with, and be beholden to, a man that minds more his pleasure and company than his business. Thence mighty merry and much pleased with the dinner and company and they with me I parted and there was set upon by the poor wretches, whom I did give good words and some little money to, and the poor people went away like lambs, and in good earnest are not to be censured if their necessities drive them to bad courses of stealing or the like, while they lacke wherewith to live. Thence to the office, and there wrote a letter or two and dispatched a little business, and then to Captain Cocke's, where I find Mr. Temple, the fat blade, Sir Robert. Viner's chief man. And we three and two companions of his in the evening by agreement took ship in the Bezan and the tide carried us no further than Woolwich about 8 at night, and so I on shore to my wife, and there to my great trouble find my wife out of order, and she took me downstairs and there alone did tell me her falling out with both her mayds and particularly Mary, and how Mary had to her teeth told her she would tell me of something that should stop her mouth and words of that sense. Which I suspect may be about Brown, but my wife prays me to call it to examination, and this, I being of myself jealous, do make me mightily out of temper, and seeing it not fit to enter into the dispute did passionately go away, thinking to go on board again. But when I come to the stairs I considered the Bezan would not go till the next ebb, and it was best to lie in a good bed and, it may be, get myself into a better humour by being with my wife. So I back again and to bed and having otherwise so many reasons to rejoice and hopes of good profit, besides considering the ill that trouble of mind and melancholly may in this sickly time bring a family into, and that if the difference were never so great, it is not a time to put away servants, I was resolved to salve up the business rather than stir in it, and so become pleasant with my wife and to bed, minding nothing of this difference. So to sleep with a good deal of content, and saving only this night and a day or two about the same business a month or six weeks ago, I do end this month with the greatest content, and may say that these last three months, for joy, health, and profit, have been much the greatest that ever I received in all my life in any twelve months almost in my life, having nothing upon me but the consideration of the sicklinesse of the season during this great plague to mortify mee. For all which the Lord God be praised!

THE DIARY OF SAMUEL PEPYS M.A. F.R.S.
CLERK OF THE ACTS AND SECRETARY TO THE ADMIRALTY
TRANSCRIBED FROM THE SHORTHAND MANUSCRIPT IN THE
PEPYSIAN LIBRARY
MAGDALENE COLLEGE CAMBRIDGE BY THE REV. MYNORS
BRIGHT M.A. LATE FELLOW
AND PRESIDENT OF THE COLLEGE
(Unabridged)
WITH LORD BRAYBROOKE'S NOTES
EDITED WITH ADDITIONS BY
HENRY B. WHEATLEY F.S.A.

DIARY OF SAMUEL PEPYS.

OCTOBER 1665

October 1st (Lord's day). Called up about 4 of the clock and so dressed myself and so on board the Bezan, and there finding all my company asleep I would not wake them, but it beginning to be break of day I did stay upon the decke walking, and then into the Maister's cabbin and there laid and slept a little, and so at last was waked by Captain Cocke's calling of me, and so I turned out, and then to chat and talk and laugh, and mighty merry. We spent most of the morning talking and reading of "The Siege of Rhodes," which is certainly (the more I read it the more I think so) the best poem that ever was wrote. We breakfasted betimes and come to the fleete about two of the clock in the afternoon, having a fine day and a fine winde. My Lord received us mighty kindly, and after discourse with us in general left us to our business, and he to his officers, having called a council of wary, we in the meantime settling of papers with Mr. Pierce and everybody else, and by and by with Captain Cuttance. Anon called down to my Lord, and there with him till supper talking and discourse; among other things, to my great joy, he did assure me that he had wrote to the King and Duke about these prize-goods, and told me that they did approve of what he had done, and that he would owne what he had done, and would have me to tell all the world so, and did, under his hand, give Cocke and me his certificate of our bargains, and giving us full power of disposal of what we have so bought. This do ease my mind of all my fear, and makes my heart lighter by L100 than it was before. He did discourse to us of the Dutch fleete being abroad, eighty-five of them still, and are now at the Texell, he believes, in expectation of our Eastland ships coming home with masts and hempe, and our loaden Hambrough ships going to Hambrough. He discoursed against them that would have us yield to no conditions but conquest over the Dutch, and seems to believe that the Dutch will call for the protection of the King of France and come under his power, which were to be wished they might be brought to do under ours by fair means, and to that end would have all Dutch men and familys, that would come hither and settled, to be declared denizens; and my Lord did whisper to me alone that things here must break in pieces, nobody minding any thing, but every man his owne business of profit or pleasure, and the King some little designs of his owne, and that certainly the kingdom could not stand in this condition long, which I fear and believe is very true. So to supper and there my Lord the kindest man to me, before all the table talking of me to my advantage and with tenderness too that it overjoyed me. So after supper Captain Cocke and I and Temple on board the Bezan, and there to cards for a while and then to read again in "Rhodes" and so to sleep. But, Lord! the mirth which it caused me to be waked in the night by their snoaring round about me; I did laugh till I was ready to burst, and waked one of the two companions of Temple, who could not a good while tell where he was that he heard one laugh so, till he recollected himself, and I told him what it was at, and so to sleep again, they still snoaring.

2nd. We having sailed all night (and I do wonder how they in the dark could find the way) we got by morning to Gillingham, and thence all walked to Chatham; and there with Commissioner Pett viewed the Yard; and among other things, a teame of four horses come close by us, he being with me, drawing a piece of timber that I am confident one man could easily have carried upon his back. I made the horses be taken away, and a man or two to take the timber away with their hands. This the Commissioner did see, but said nothing, but I think had cause to be ashamed of. We walked, he and I and Cocke, to the Hill-house, where we find Sir W. Pen in bed and there much talke and much dissembling of kindnesse from him, but he is a false rogue, and I shall not trust him, but my being there did procure his consent to have his silk carried away before the money received, which he would not have done for Cocke I am sure. Thence to Rochester, walked to the Crowne, and while dinner was getting ready, I did there walk to visit the old Castle ruines, which hath been a noble place, and there going up I did upon the stairs overtake three pretty mayds or women and took them up with me, and I did 'baiser sur mouches et toucher leur mains' and necks to my great pleasure: but, Lord! to see what a dreadfull thing it is to look down the precipices, for it did fright me mightily, and hinder me of much pleasure which I would have made to myself in the company of these three, if it had not been for that. The place hath been very noble and great and strong in former ages. So to walk up and down the Cathedral, and thence to the Crowne, whither Mr. Fowler, the Mayor of the towne, was come in his gowne, and is a very reverend magistrate. After I had eat a bit, not staying to eat with them, I went away, and so took horses and to Gravesend, and there staid not, but got a boat, the sicknesse being very much in the towne still, and so called on board my Lord Bruncker and Sir John Minnes, on board one of the East Indiamen at Erith, and there do find them full of envious complaints for the pillageing of the ships, but I did pacify them, and discoursed about making money of some of the goods, and do hope to be the better by it honestly. So took leave (Madam Williams being here also with my Lord), and about 8 o'clock got to Woolwich and there supped and mighty pleasant with my wife, who is, for ought I see, all friends with her mayds, and so in great joy and content to bed.

3rd. Up, and to my great content visited betimes by Mr. Woolly, my uncle Wight's cozen, who comes to see what work I have for him about these East India goods, and I do find that this fellow might have been of great use, and hereafter may be of very great use to me, in this trade of prize goods, and glad I am fully of his coming hither. While I dressed myself, and afterwards in walking to Greenwich we did discourse over all the business of the prize goods, and he puts me in hopes I may get some money in what I have done, but not so much as I expected, but that I may hereafter do more. We have laid a design of getting more, and are to talk again of it a few days hence. To the office, where nobody to meet me, Sir W. Batten being the only man and he gone this day to meet to adjourne the Parliament to Oxford. Anon by appointment comes one to tell me my Lord Rutherford is come; so I to the King's Head to him, where I find his lady, a fine young Scotch lady, pretty handsome and plain. My wife also, and Mercer, by and by comes, Creed bringing them; and so presently to dinner and very merry; and after to even our accounts, and I to give him tallys, where he do allow me L100, of which to my grief the rogue Creed has trepanned me out of L50. But I do foresee a way how it may be I may get a greater sum of my Lord to his content by getting him allowance of interest upon his tallys. That being done, and some musique and other diversions, at last away goes my Lord and Lady, and I sent my wife to visit Mrs. Pierce, and so I to my office, where wrote important letters to the Court, and at night (Creed having clownishly left my wife), I to Mrs. Pierces and brought her and Mrs. Pierce to the King's Head and there spent a piece upon a supper for her and mighty merry and pretty discourse, she being as pretty as ever, most of our mirth being upon "my Cozen" (meaning my Lord Bruncker's ugly mistress, whom he calls cozen), and to my trouble she tells me that the fine Mrs. Middleton is noted for carrying about her body a continued sour base smell, that is very offensive, especially if she be a little hot. Here some bad musique to close the night and so away and all of us saw Mrs. Belle Pierce (as pretty as ever she was almost) home, and so walked to Will's lodging where I used to lie, and there made shift for a bed for Mercer, and mighty pleasantly to bed. This night I hear that of our two watermen that use to carry our letters, and were well on Saturday last, one is dead, and the other dying sick of the plague. The plague, though decreasing elsewhere, yet being greater about the Tower and thereabouts.

4th. Up and to my office, where Mr. Andrews comes, and reckoning with him I get L64 of him. By and by comes Mr. Gawden, and reckoning with him he gives me L60 in his account, which is a great mercy to me. Then both of them met and discoursed the business of the first man's resigning and the other's taking up the business of the victualling of Tangier, and I do not think that I shall be able to do as well under Mr. Gawden as under these men, or within a little as to profit and less care upon me. Thence to the King's Head to dinner, where we three and Creed and my wife and her woman dined mighty merry and sat long talking, and so in the afternoon broke up, and I led my wife to our lodging again, and I to the office where did much business, and so to my wife. This night comes Sir George Smith to see me at the office, and tells me how the plague is decreased this week 740, for which God be praised! but that it encreases at our end of the town still, and says how all the towne is full of Captain Cocke's being in some ill condition about prize-goods, his goods being taken from him, and I know not what. But though this troubles me to have it said, and that it is likely to be a business in Parliament, yet I am not much concerned at it, because yet I believe this newes is all false, for he would have wrote to me sure about it. Being come to my wife, at our lodging, I did go to bed, and left my wife with her people to laugh and dance and I to sleep.

5th. Lay long in bed talking among other things of my sister Pall, and my wife of herself is very willing that I should give her L400 to her portion, and would have her married soon as we could; but this great sicknesse time do make it unfit to send for her up. I abroad to the office and thence to the Duke of Albemarle, all my way reading a book of Mr. Evelyn's translating and sending me as a present, about directions for gathering a Library;

> [Instructions concerning erecting of a Library, presented to my Lord the President De Mesme by Gilbert Naudeus, and now interpreted by Jo. Evelyn, Esquire. London, 1661: This little book was dedicated to Lord Clarendon by the translator. It was printed while Evelyn was abroad, and is full of typographical errors; these are corrected in a copy mentioned in Evelyn's "Miscellaneous Writings," 1825, p. xii, where a letter to Dr. Godolphin on the subject is printed.]

but the book is above my reach, but his epistle to my Lord Chancellor is a very fine piece. When I come to the Duke it was about the victuallers' business, to put it into other hands, or more hands, which I do advise in, but I hope to do myself a jobb of work in it. So I walked through Westminster to my old house the Swan, and there did pass some time with Sarah, and so down by water to Deptford and there to my Valentine.

> [A Mrs. Bagwell. See ante, February 14th, 1664-65]

Round about and next door on every side is the plague, but I did not value it, but there did what I would 'con elle', and so away to Mr. Evelyn's to discourse of our confounded business of prisoners, and sick and wounded seamen, wherein he and we are so much put out of order.

> [Each of the Commissioners for the Sick and Wounded was appointed to a particular district, and Evelyn's district was Kent and Sussex. On September 25th, 1665, Evelyn wrote in his Diary: "My Lord Admiral being come from ye fleete to Greenewich, I went thence with him to ye Cockpit to consult with the Duke of Albemarle. I was peremptory that unless we had L10,000 immediately, the prisoners would starve, and 'twas proposed it should be rais'd out of the E. India prizes now taken by Lord Sandwich. They being but two of ye

Commission, and so not impower'd to determine, sent an expresse to his Majesty and Council to know what they should do."]

And here he showed me his gardens, which are for variety of evergreens, and hedge of holly, the finest things I ever saw in my life.

[Evelyn purchased Sayes Court, Deptford, in 1653, and laid out his gardens, walks, groves, enclosures, and plantations, which afterwards became famous for their beauty. When he took the place in hand it was nothing but an open field of one hundred acres, with scarcely a hedge in it.]

Thence in his coach to Greenwich, and there to my office, all the way having fine discourse of trees and the nature of vegetables. And so to write letters, I very late to Sir W. Coventry of great concernment, and so to my last night's lodging, but my wife is gone home to Woolwich. The Bill, blessed be God! is less this week by 740 of what it was the last week. Being come to my lodging I got something to eat, having eat little all the day, and so to bed, having this night renewed my promises of observing my vowes as I used to do; for I find that, since I left them off, my mind is run a'wool-gathering and my business neglected.

6th. Up, and having sent for Mr. Gawden he come to me, and he and I largely discoursed the business of his Victualling, in order to the adding of partners to him or other ways of altering it, wherein I find him ready to do anything the King would have him do. So he and I took his coach and to Lambeth and to the Duke of Albemarle about it, and so back again, where he left me. In our way discoursing of the business and contracting a great friendship with him, and I find he is a man most worthy to be made a friend, being very honest and gratefull, and in the freedom of our discourse he did tell me his opinion and knowledge of Sir W. Pen to be, what I know him to be, as false a man as ever was born, for so, it seems, he hath been to him. He did also tell me, discoursing how things are governed as to the King's treasure, that, having occasion for money in the country, he did offer Alderman Maynell to pay him down money here, to be paid by the Receiver in some county in the country, upon whom Maynell had assignments, in whose hands the money also lay ready. But Maynell refused it, saying that he could have his money when he would, and had rather it should lie where it do than receive it here in towne this sickly time, where he hath no occasion for it. But now the evil is that he hath lent this money upon tallys which are become payable, but he finds that nobody looks after it, how long the money is unpaid, and whether it lies dead in the Receiver's hands or no, so the King he pays Maynell 10 per cent. while the money lies in his Receiver's hands to no purpose but the benefit of the Receiver. I to dinner to the King's Head with Mr. Woolly, who is come to instruct me in the business of my goods, but gives me not so good comfort as I thought I should have had. But, however, it will be well worth my time though not above

2 or L300. He gone I to my office, where very busy drawing up a letter by way of discourse to the Duke of Albemarle about my conception how the business of the Victualling should be ordered, wherein I have taken great pains, and I think have hitt the right if they will but follow it. At this very late and so home to our lodgings to bed.

7th. Up and to the office along with Mr. Childe, whom I sent for to discourse about the victualling business, who will not come into partnership (no more will Captain Beckford), but I do find him a mighty understanding man, and one I will keep a knowledge of. Did business, though not much, at the office; because of the horrible crowd and lamentable moan of the poor seamen that lie starving in the streets for lack of money. Which do trouble and perplex me to the heart; and more at noon when we were to go through them, for then a whole hundred of them followed us; some cursing, some swearing, and some praying to us. And that that made me more troubled was a letter come this afternoon from the Duke of Albemarle, signifying the Dutch to be in sight, with 80 sayle, yesterday morning, off of Solebay, coming right into the bay. God knows what they will and may do to us, we having no force abroad able to oppose them, but to be sacrificed to them. Here come Sir W. Rider to me, whom I sent for about the victualling business also, but he neither will not come into partnership, but desires to be of the Commission if there be one. Thence back the back way to my office, where very late, very busy. But most of all when at night come two waggons from Rochester with more goods from Captain Cocke; and in houseing them at Mr. Tooker's lodgings come two of the Custome-house to seize them, and did seize them but I showed them my 'Transire'. However, after some hot and angry words, we locked them up, and sealed up the key, and did give it to the constable to keep till Monday, and so parted. But, Lord! to think how the poor constable come to me in the dark going home; "Sir," says he, "I have the key, and if you would have me do any service for you, send for me betimes to-morrow morning, and I will do what you would have me." Whether the fellow do this out of kindness or knavery, I cannot tell; but it is pretty to observe. Talking with him in the high way, come close by the bearers with a dead corpse of the plague; but, Lord! to see what custom is, that I am come almost to think nothing of it. So to my lodging, and there, with Mr. Hater and Will, ending a business of the state of the last six months' charge of the Navy, which we bring to L1,000,000 and above, and I think we do not enlarge much in it if anything. So to bed.

8th (Lord's day). Up and, after being trimmed, to the office, whither I upon a letter from the Duke of Albemarle to me, to order as many ships forth out of the river as I can presently, to joyne to meet the Dutch; having ordered all the Captains of the ships in the river to come to me, I did some business with them, and so to Captain Cocke's to dinner, he being in the country. But here his brother Solomon was, and, for guests, myself, Sir G. Smith, and a very fine lady, one Mrs. Penington, and two more gentlemen. But, both [before] and after dinner, most witty discourse with this lady, who is a very fine witty lady, one of the best I ever heard speake, and indifferent handsome. There after dinner an houre or two, and so to the office, where ended my business with the Captains; and I think of twenty-two ships we shall make shift to get out seven. (God helpe us! men being sick, or provisions lacking.) And so to write letters to Sir Ph. Warwicke, Sir W. Coventry, and Sir G. Carteret to Court about the last six months' accounts, and sent away by an express to-night. This day I hear the Pope is dead;--[a false report]--and one said, that the newes is, that the King of France is stabbed, but that the former is very true, which will do great things sure, as to the troubling of that part of the world, the King of Spayne

[Philip IV., King of Spain, who succeeded to the throne in 1621, died in 1665. He was succeeded by his son Charles II.]

being so lately dead. And one thing more, Sir Martin Noell's lady is dead with griefe for the death of her husband and nothing else, as they say, in the world; but it seems nobody can make anything of his estate, whether he be dead worth anything or no, he having dealt in so many things, publique and private, as nobody can understand whereabouts his estate is, which is the fate of these great dealers at everything. So after my business being done I home to my lodging and to bed,

9th. Up, my head full of business, and called upon also by Sir John Shaw, to whom I did give a civil answer about our prize goods, that all his dues as one of the Farmers of the Customes are paid, and showed him our Transire; with which he was satisfied, and parted, ordering his servants to see the weight of them. I to the office, and there found an order for my coming presently to the Duke of Albemarle, and what should it be, but to tell me, that, if my Lord Sandwich do not come to towne, he do resolve to go with the fleete to sea himself, the Dutch, as he thinks, being in the Downes, and so desired me to get a pleasure boat for to take him in to-morrow morning, and do many other things, and with a great liking of me, and my management especially, as that coxcombe my Lord Craven do tell me, and I perceive it, and I am sure take pains enough to deserve it. Thence away and to the office at London, where I did some business about my money and private accounts, and there eat a bit of goose of Mr. Griffin's, and so by water, it raining most miserably, to Greenwich, calling on several vessels in my passage. Being come there I hear another seizure hath been made of our goods by one Captain Fisher that hath been at Chatham by warrant of the Duke of Albemarle, and is come in my absence to Tooker's and viewed them, demanding the key of the constable, and so sealed up the door. I to the house, but there being no officers nor constable could do nothing, but back to my office full of trouble about this, and there late about business, vexed to see myself fall into this trouble and concernment in a thing that I want instruction from my Lord Sandwich whether I should appear in it or no, and so home to bed, having spent two hours, I and my boy, at Mr. Glanvill's removing of faggots to make room to remove our goods to, but when done I thought it not fit to use it. The newes of the killing of the [King of] France is wholly untrue, and they say that of the Pope too.

10th. Up, and receive a stop from the Duke of Albemarle of setting out any more ships, or providing a pleasure boat for himself, which I am glad of, and do see, what I thought yesterday, that this resolution of his was a sudden one and silly. By and by comes Captain Cocke's Jacob to tell me that he is come from Chatham this morning, and that there are four waggons of goods at hand coming to towne, which troubles me. I directed him to bring them to his master's house. But before I could send him away to bring them thither, newes is brought me that they are seized on in the towne by this Captain Fisher and they will carry them to another place. So I to them and found our four waggons in the streete stopped by the church by this Fisher and company and 100 or 200 people in the streetes gazing. I did give them good words, and made modest desires of carrying the goods to Captain Cocke's, but they would have them to a house of their hiring, where in a barne the goods were laid. I had transires to show for all, and the tale was right, and there I spent all the morning seeing this done. At which Fisher was vexed that I would not let it be done by any body else for the merchant, and that I must needs be concerned therein, which I did not think fit to owne. So that being done, I left the goods to be watched by men on their part and ours, and so to the office by noon, whither by and by comes Captain Cocke, whom I had with great care sent for by expresse the last night, and so I with him to his house and there eat a bit, and so by coach to Lambeth, and I took occasion first to go to the Duke of Albemarle to acquaint him with some thing of what had been done this morning in behalf of a friend absent, which did give a good entrance and prevented their possessing the Duke with anything of evil of me by their report, and by and by in comes Captain Cocke and tells his whole story. So an order was made for the putting him in possession upon giving security to, be accountable for the goods, which for the present did satisfy us, and so away, giving Locke that drew the order a piece. (Lord! to see how unhappily a man may fall into a necessity of bribing people to do him right in a thing, wherein he hath done nothing but fair, and bought dear.) So to the office, there to write my letters, and Cocke comes to tell me that Fisher is come to him, and that he doubts not to cajole Fisher and his companion and make them friends with drink and a bribe. This night comes Sir Christopher Mings to towne, and I went to see him, and by and by he being then out of the town comes to see me. He is newly come from Court, and carries direction for the making a show of getting out the fleete again to go fight the Dutch, but that it will end in a fleete of 20 good sayling frigates to go to the Northward or Southward, and that will be all. I enquired, but he would not be to know that he had heard any thing at Oxford about the business of the prize goods, which I did suspect, but he being gone, anon comes Cocke and tells me that he hath been with him a great while, and that he finds him sullen and speaking very high what disrespect he had received of my Lord, saying that he hath walked 3 or 4 hours together at that Earle's cabbin door for audience and could not be received, which, if true, I am sorry for. He tells me that Sir G. Ascue says, that he did from the beginning declare against these [prize] goods, and would not receive his dividend; and that he and Sir W. Pen are at odds about it, and that he fears Mings hath been doing ill offices to my Lord. I did tonight give my Lord an account of all this, and so home and to bed.

11th. Up, and so in my chamber staid all the morning doing something toward my Tangier accounts, for the stating of them, and also comes up my landlady, Mrs. Clerke, to make an agreement for the time to come; and I, for the having room enough, and to keepe out strangers, and to have a place to retreat to for my wife, if the sicknesse should come to Woolwich, am contented to pay dear; so for three rooms and a dining-room, and for linen and bread and beer and butter, at nights and mornings, I am to give her L5 10s. per month, and I wrote and we signed to an agreement. By and by comes Cocke to tell me that Fisher and his fellow were last night mightily satisfied and promised all friendship, but this morning he finds them to have new tricks and shall be troubled with them. So he being to go down to Erith with them this afternoon about giving security, I advised him to let them go by land, and so he and I (having eat something at his house) by water to Erith, but they got thither before us, and there we met Mr. Seymour, one of the Commissioners for Prizes, and a Parliament-man, and he was mighty high, and had now seized our goods on their behalf; and he mighty imperiously would have all forfeited, and I know not what. I thought I was in the right in a thing I said and spoke somewhat earnestly, so we took up one another very smartly, for which I was sorry afterwards, shewing thereby myself too much concerned, but nothing passed that I valued at all. But I could not but think [it odd] that a Parliament-man, in a serious discourse before such persons as we and my Lord Bruncker, and Sir John Minnes, should quote Hudibras, as being the book I doubt he hath read most. They I doubt will stand hard for high security, and Cocke would have had me bound with him for his appearing, but I did stagger at it, besides Seymour do stop the doing it at all till he has been with the Duke of Albemarle. So there will be another demurre. It growing late, and I having something to do at home, took my leave alone, leaving Cocke there for all night, and so against tide and in the darke and very cold weather to Woolwich, where we had appointed to keepe the night merrily; and so, by Captain Cocke's coach, had brought a very pretty child, a daughter of one Mrs. Tooker's, next door to my lodging, and so she, and a daughter and kinsman of Mrs. Pett's made up a fine company at my lodgings at Woolwich, where my wife and Mercer, and Mrs. Barbara danced, and mighty merry we were, but especially at Mercer's dancing a jigg, which she does the best I ever did see, having the most natural way of it, and keeps time the most perfectly I ever did see. This night is kept in lieu of yesterday, for my wedding day of ten years; for which God be praised! being now in an extreme good condition of health and estate and honour, and a way of getting more money, though at this houre under some discomposure, rather than damage, about some prize goods that I have bought off the fleete, in partnership with Captain Cocke; and for the discourse about the world concerning my Lord Sandwich, that he hath done a thing so bad; and indeed it must needs have been a very rash act; and the rather because of a Parliament now newly met to give money, and will have some account of what hath already been spent, besides the precedent for a

General to take what prizes he pleases, and the giving a pretence to take away much more than he intended, and all will lie upon him; and not giving to all the Commanders, as well as the Flaggs, he displeases all them, and offends even some of them, thinking others to be better served than themselves; and lastly, puts himself out of a power of begging anything again a great while of the King. Having danced with my people as long as I saw fit to sit up, I to bed and left them to do what they would. I forgot that we had W. Hewer there, and Tom, and Golding, my barber at Greenwich, for our fiddler, to whom I did give 10s.

12th. Called up before day, and so I dressed myself and down, it being horrid cold, by water to my Lord Bruncker's ship, who advised me to do so, and it was civilly to show me what the King had commanded about the prize-goods, to examine most severely all that had been done in the taking out any with or without order, without respect to my Lord Sandwich at all, and that he had been doing of it, and find him examining one man, and I do find that extreme ill use was made of my Lord's order. For they did toss and tumble and spoil, and breake things in hold to a great losse and shame to come at the fine goods, and did take a man that knows where the fine goods were, and did this over and over again for many days, Sir W. Berkeley being the chief hand that did it, but others did the like at other times, and they did say in doing it that my Lord Sandwich's back was broad enough to bear it. Having learned as much as I could, which was, that the King and Duke were very severe in this point, whatever order they before had given my Lord in approbation of what he had done, and that all will come out and the King see, by the entries at the Custome House, what all do amount to that had been taken, and so I took leave, and by water, very cold, and to Woolwich where it was now noon, and so I staid dinner and talking part of the afternoon, and then by coach, Captain Cocke's, to Greenwich, taking the young lady home, and so to Cocke, and he tells me that he hath cajolled with Seymour, who will be our friend; but that, above all, Seymour tells him, that my Lord Duke did shew him to-day an order from Court, for having all respect paid to the Earle of Sandwich, and what goods had been delivered by his order, which do overjoy us, and that to-morrow our goods shall be weighed, and he doubts not possession to-morrow or next day. Being overjoyed at this I to write my letters, and at it very late. Good newes this week that there are about 600 less dead of the plague than the last. So home to bed.

13th. Lay long, and this morning comes Sir Jer. Smith

[Captain Jeremiah Smith (or Smyth), knighted June, 1665; Admiral of the Blue in 1666. He succeeded Sir William Penn as Comptroller of the Victualling Accounts in 1669, and held the office until 1675.]

to see me in his way to Court, and a good man he is, and one that I must keep fair with, and will, it being I perceive my interest to have kindnesse with the Commanders. So to the office, and there very busy till about noon comes Sir W. Warren, and he goes and gets a bit of meat ready at the King's Head for us, and I by and by thither, and we dined together, and I am not pleased with him about a little business of Tangier that I put to him to do for me, but however, the hurt is not much, and his other matters of profit to me continue very likely to be good. Here we spent till 2 o'clock, and so I set him on shore, and I by water to the Duke of Albemarle, where I find him with Lord Craven and Lieutenant of the Tower about him; among other things, talking of ships to get of the King to fetch coles for the poore of the city, which is a good worke. But, Lord! to hear the silly talke between these three great people! Yet I have no reason to find fault, the Duke and Lord Craven being my very great friends. Here did the business I come about, and so back home by water, and there Cocke comes to me and tells me that he is come to an understanding with Fisher, and that he must give him L100, and that he shall have his goods in possession to-morrow, they being all weighed to-day, which pleases me very well. This day the Duke tells me that there is no news heard of the Dutch, what they do or where they are, but believes that they are all gone home, for none of our spyes can give us any tideings of them. Cocke is fain to keep these people, Fisher and his fellow, company night and day to keep them friends almost and great troubles withal. My head is full of settling the victualling business also, that I may make some profit out of it, which I hope justly to do to the King's advantage. To-night come Sir J. Bankes to me upon my letter to discourse it with him, and he did give me the advice I have taken almost as fully as if I had been directed by him what to write. The business also of my Tangier accounts to be sent to Court is upon my hands in great haste; besides, all my owne proper accounts are in great disorder, having been neglected now above a month, which grieves me, but it could not be settled sooner. These together and the feare of the sicknesse and providing for my family do fill my head very full, besides the infinite business of the office, and nobody here to look after it but myself. So late from my office to my lodgings, and to bed.

14th. Up, and to the office, where mighty busy, especially with Mr. Gawden, with whom I shall, I think, have much to do, and by and by comes the Lieutenant of the Tower by my invitation yesterday, but I had got nothing for him, it is to discourse about the Cole shipps. So he went away to Sheriffe Hooker's, and I staid at the office till he sent for me at noon to dinner, I very hungry. When I come to the Sheriffe's he was not there, nor in many other places, nor could find him at all, so was forced to come to the office and get a bit of meat from the taverne, and so to my business. By and by comes the Lieutenant and reproaches me with my not treating him as I ought, but all in jest, he it seemed dined with Mr. Adrian May. Very late writing letters at the office, and much satisfied to hear from Captain Cocke that he had got possession of some of his goods to his own house, and expected to have all to-night. The towne, I hear, is full of talke that there are great differences in the fleete among the great Commanders, and that Mings at Oxford did impeach my Lord of something, I think about these goods, but this is but talke. But my heart and head to-night is full of the Victualling business, being overjoyed and proud at my success in my proposal about it, it being read before the King, Duke, and the Caball with complete applause and satisfaction. This Sir G. Carteret and Sir

W. Coventry both writ me, besides Sir W. Coventry's letter to the Duke of Albemarle, which I read yesterday, and I hope to find my profit in it also. So late home to bed.

15th (Lord's day). Up, and while I staid for the barber, tried to compose a duo of counterpoint, and I think it will do very well, it being by Mr. Berckenshaw's rule. By and by by appointment comes Mr. Povy's coach, and, more than I expected, him himself, to fetch me to Brainford: so he and I immediately set out, having drunk a draft of mulled sacke; and so rode most nobly, in his most pretty and best contrived charriott in the world, with many new conveniences, his never having till now, within a day or two, been yet finished; our discourse upon Tangier business, want of money, and then of publique miscarriages, nobody minding the publique, but every body himself and his lusts. Anon we come to his house, and there I eat a bit, and so with fresh horses, his noble fine horses, the best confessedly in England, the King having none such, he sent me to Sir Robert Viner's, whom I met coming just from church, and so after having spent half-an-hour almost looking upon the horses with some gentlemen that were in company, he and I into his garden to discourse of money, but none is to be had, he confessing himself in great straits, and I believe it. Having this answer, and that I could not get better, we fell to publique talke, and to think how the fleete and seamen will be paid, which he protests he do not think it possible to compass, as the world is now: no money got by trade, nor the persons that have it by them in the City to be come at. The Parliament, it seems, have voted the King L1,250,000 at L50,000 per month, tax for the war; and voted to assist the King against the Dutch, and all that shall adhere to them; and thanks to be given him for his care of the Duke of Yorke, which last is a very popular vote on the Duke's behalf. He tells me how the taxes of the last assessment, which should have been in good part gathered, are not yet laid, and that even in part of the City of London; and the Chimny-money comes almost to nothing, nor any thing else looked after. Having done this I parted, my mind not eased by any money, but only that I had done my part to the King's service. And so in a very pleasant evening back to Mr. Povy's, and there supped, and after supper to talke and to sing, his man Dutton's wife singing very pleasantly (a mighty fat woman), and I wrote out one song from her and pricked the tune, both very pretty. But I did never heare one sing with so much pleasure to herself as this lady do, relishing it to her very heart, which was mighty pleasant.

16th. Up about seven o'clock; and, after drinking, and I observing Mr. Povy's being mightily mortifyed in his eating and drinking, and coaches and horses, he desiring to sell his best, and every thing else, his furniture of his house, he walked with me to Syon,

[Sion House, granted by Edward VI. to his uncle, the Duke of Somerset. After his execution, 1552, it was forfeited, and given to John Dudley, Duke of Northumberland. The duke being beheaded in 1553, it reverted to the Crown, and was granted in 1604 to Henry Percy, Earl of Northumberland. It still belongs to the Duke of Northumberland.]

and there I took water, in our way he discoursing of the wantonnesse of the Court, and how it minds nothing else, and I saying that that would leave the King shortly if he did not leave it, he told me "No," for the King do spend most of his time in feeling and kissing them naked . . . But this lechery will never leave him. Here I took boat (leaving him there) and down to the Tower, where I hear the Duke of Albemarle is, and I to Lumbard Streete, but can get no money. So upon the Exchange, which is very empty, God knows! and but mean people there. The newes for certain that the Dutch are come with their fleete before Margett, and some men were endeavouring to come on shore when the post come away, perhaps to steal some sheep. But, Lord! how Colvill talks of the businesse of publique revenue like a madman, and yet I doubt all true; that nobody minds it, but that the King and Kingdom must speedily be undone, and rails at my Lord about the prizes, but I think knows not my relation to him. Here I endeavoured to satisfy all I could, people about Bills of Exchange from Tangier, but it is only with good words, for money I have not, nor can get. God knows what will become of all the King's matters in a little time, for he runs in debt every day, and nothing to pay them looked after. Thence I walked to the Tower; but, Lord! how empty the streets are and melancholy, so many poor sick people in the streets full of sores; and so many sad stories overheard as I walk, every body talking of this dead, and that man sick, and so many in this place, and so many in that. And they tell me that, in Westminster, there is never a physician and but one apothecary left, all being dead; but that there are great hopes of a great decrease this week: God send it! At the Tower found my Lord Duke and Duchesse at dinner; so I sat down. And much good cheer, the Lieutenant and his lady, and several officers with the Duke. But, Lord! to hear the silly talk that was there, would make one mad; the Duke having none almost but fools about him. Much of their talke about the Dutch coming on shore, which they believe they may some of them have been and steal sheep, and speak all in reproach of them in whose hands the fleete is; but, Lord helpe him, there is something will hinder him and all the world in going to sea, which is want of victuals; for we have not wherewith to answer our service; and how much better it would have been if the Duke's advice had been taken for the fleete to have gone presently out; but, God helpe the King! while no better counsels are given, and what is given no better taken. Thence after dinner receiving many commands from the Duke, I to our office on the Hill, and there did a little business and to Colvill's again, and so took water at the Tower, and there met with Captain Cocke, and he down with me to Greenwich, I having received letters from my Lord Sandwich to-day, speaking very high about the prize goods, that he would have us to fear nobody, but be very confident in what we have done, and not to confess any fault or doubt of what he hath done; for the King hath allowed it, and do now confirm it, and sent orders, as he says, for nothing to be disturbed that his Lordshipp hath ordered therein as to the division of the goods to the fleete; which do comfort us, but my Lord writes to me that both he and I may hence learn by what we see in this business. But that which pleases me best is that Cocke tells me that he now understands that Fisher was set on in this business by the design of some of the Duke of Albemarle's people, Warcupp and others, who lent him money to set him out in it, and he has spent high. Who now curse him for a rogue to take L100 when he might have had as well L1,500, and they are mightily fallen out about it. Which in due time shall be discovered, but that now that troubles me afresh is, after I am got to the office at Greenwich that some new troubles are come, and Captain Cocke's house is beset before and behind with guards, and more, I do fear they may come to my office here to search for Cocke's goods and find some small things of my clerk's. So I assisted them in helping to remove their small trade, but by and by I am told that it is only the Custome House men who came to seize the things that did lie at Mr. Glanville's, for which they did never yet see our Transire, nor did know of them till to-day. So that my fear is now over, for a transire is ready for them. Cocke did get a great many of his goods to London to-day. To the Still Yarde, which place, however, is now shut up of the plague; but I was there, and we now make no bones of it. Much talke there is of the Chancellor's speech and the King's at the Parliament's meeting, which are very well liked; and that we shall certainly, by their speeches, fall out with France at this time, together with the Dutch, which will find us work. Late at the office entering my Journall for 8 days past, the greatness of my business hindering me of late to put it down daily, but I have done it now very true and particularly, and hereafter will, I hope, be able to fall into my old way of doing it daily. So to my lodging, and there had a good pullet to my supper, and so to bed, it being very cold again, God be thanked for it!

17th. Up, and all day long busy at the office, mighty busy, only stepped to my lodging and had a fowl for my dinner, and at night my wife and Mercer comes to me, which troubled me a little because I am to be mighty busy to-morrow all day seriously about my accounts. So late from my office to her, and supped, and so to bed.

18th. Up, and after some pleasant discourse with my wife (though my head full of business) I out and left her to go home, and myself to the office, and thence by water to the Duke of Albemarle's, and so back again and find my wife gone. So to my chamber at my lodgings, and to the making of my accounts up of Tangier, which I did with great difficulty, finding the difference between short and long reckonings where I have had occasion to mix my moneys, as I have of late done my Tangier treasure upon other occasions, and other moneys upon that. However, I was at it late and did it pretty perfectly, and so, after eating something, to bed, my mind eased of a great deal of figures and castings.

19th. Up, and to my accounts again, and stated them very clear and fair, and at noon dined at my lodgings with Mr. Hater and W. Hewer at table with me, I being come to an agreement yesterday with my landlady for L6 per month, for so many rooms for myself, them, and my wife and mayde, when she shall come, and to pay besides for my dyett. After dinner I did give them my accounts and letters to write against I went to the Duke of Albemarle's this evening, which I did; and among other things, spoke to him for my wife's brother, Balty, to be of his guard, which he kindly answered that he should. My business of the Victualling goes on as I would have it; and now my head is full how to make some profit of it to myself or people. To that end, when I came home, I wrote a letter to Mr. Coventry, offering myself to be the Surveyor Generall, and am apt to think he will assist me in it, but I do not set my heart much on it, though it would be a good helpe. So back to my office, and there till past one before I could get all these letters and papers copied out, which vexed me, but so sent them away without hopes of saving the post, and so to my lodging to bed.

20th. Up, and had my last night's letters brought back to me, which troubles me, because of my accounts, lest they should be asked for before they come, which I abhorr, being more ready to give than they can be to demand them: so I sent away an expresse to Oxford with them, and another to Portsmouth, with a copy of my letter to Mr. Coventry about my victualling business, for fear he should be gone from Oxford, as he intended, thither. So busy all the morning and at noon to Cocke, and dined there. He and I alone, vexed that we are not rid of all our trouble about our goods, but it is almost over, and in the afternoon to my lodging, and there spent the whole afternoon and evening with Mr. Hater, discoursing of the business of the office, where he tells me that among others Thomas Willson do now and then seem to hint that I do take too much business upon me, more than I can do, and that therefore some do lie undone. This I confess to my trouble is true, but it arises from my being forced to take so much on me, more than is my proper task to undertake. But for this at last I did advise to him to take another clerk if he thinks fit, I will take care to have him paid. I discoursed also much with him about persons fit to be put into the victualling business, and such as I could spare something out of their salaries for them, but without trouble I cannot, I see, well do it, because Thomas Willson must have the refusal of the best place which is London of L200 per annum, which I did intend for Tooker, and to get L50 out of it as a help to Mr. Hater. How[ever], I will try to do something of this kind for them. Having done discourse with him late, I to enter my Tangier accounts fair, and so to supper and to bed.

21 st. Up, and to my office, where busy all the morning, and then with my two clerks home to dinner, and so back again to the office, and there very late very busy, and so home to supper and to bed.

22nd (Lord's day). Up, and after ready and going to Captain Cocke's, where I find we are a little further safe in some part of our goods, I to Church, in my way was meeting with some letters, which made me resolve to go after church to my Lord Duke of Albemarle's, so, after sermon, I took Cocke's chariott, and to Lambeth; but, in going and getting over the water, and through White Hall, I spent so much time, the Duke had almost dined. However, fresh meat was brought for me to his table, and there I dined, and full of discourse and very kind. Here they are again talking of the prizes, and my Lord Duke did speake very broad that my Lord Sandwich and Pen should do what they would, and answer for themselves. For his part, he would lay all before the King. Here he tells me the Dutch Embassador at Oxford is clapped up, but since I hear it is not true. Thence back again, it being evening before I could get home, and there Cocke not being within, I and Mr. Salomon to Mr. Glanville's, and there we found Cocke and sat and supped, and was mighty merry with only Madam Penington, who is a fine, witty lady. Here we spent the evening late with great mirth, and so home and to bed.

23rd. Up, and after doing some business I down by water, calling to see my wife, with whom very merry for ten minutes, and so to Erith, where my Lord Bruncker and I kept the office, and dispatched some business by appointment on the Bezan. Among other things about the slopsellers, who have trusted us so long, they are not able, nor can be expected to trust us further, and I fear this winter the fleete will be undone by that particular. Thence on board the East India ship, where my Lord Bruncker had provided a great dinner, and thither comes by and by Sir John Minnes and before him Sir W. Warren and anon a Perspective glasse maker, of whom we, every one, bought a pocket glasse. But I am troubled with the much talke and conceitedness of Mrs. Williams and her impudence, in case she be not married to my Lord. They are getting themselves ready to deliver the goods all out to the East India Company, who are to have the goods in their possession and to advance two thirds of the moderate value thereof and sell them as well as they can and the King to give them 6 per cent. for the use of the money they shall so advance. By this means the company will not suffer by the King's goods bringing down the price of their own. Thence in the evening back again with Sir W. Warren and Captain Taylor in my boat, and the latter went with me to the office, and there he and I reckoned; and I perceive I shall get L100 profit by my services of late to him, which is a very good thing. Thence to my lodging, where I find my Lord Rutherford, of which I was glad. We supped together and sat up late, he being a mighty wanton man with a daughter in law of my landlady's, a pretty conceited woman big with child, and he would be handling her breasts, which she coyly refused. But they gone, my Lord and I to business, and he would have me forbear paying Alderman Backewell the money ordered him, which I, in hopes to advantage myself, shall forbear, but do not think that my Lord will do any thing gratefully more to me than he hath done, not that I shall get any thing as I pretended by helping him to interest for his last L7700, which I could do, and do him a courtesy too. Discourse being done, he to bed in my chamber and I to another in the house.

24th. Lay long, having a cold. Then to my Lord and sent him going to Oxford, and I to my office, whither comes Sir William Batten now newly from Oxford. I can gather nothing from him about my Lord Sandwich about the business of the prizes, he being close, but he shewed me a bill which hath been read in the House making all breaking of bulke for the time to come felony, but it is a foolish Act, and will do no great matter, only is calculated to my Lord Sandwich's case. He shewed me also a good letter printed from the Bishopp of Munster to the States of Holland shewing the state of their case. Here we did some business and so broke up and I to Cocke, where Mr. Evelyn was, to dinner, and there merry, yet vexed again at publique matters, and to see how little heed is had to the prisoners and sicke and wounded. Thence to my office, and no sooner there but to my great surprise am told that my Lord Sandwich is come to towne; so I presently to Boreman's, where he is and there found him: he mighty kind to me, but no opportunity of discourse private yet, which he tells me he must have with me; only his business is sudden to go to the fleece, to get out a few ships to drive away the Dutch. I left him in discourse with Sir W. Batten and others, and myself to the office till about 10 at night and so, letters being done, I to him again to Captain Cocke's, where he supped, and lies, and never saw him more merry, and here is Charles Herbert, who the King hath lately knighted.

> [This person, erroneously called by Pepys Sir C. Herbert, will be best defined by subjoining the inscription on his monument in Westminster Abbey: "Sir Charles Harbord, Knight, third son of Sir Charles Harbord, Knight, Surveyor-General, and First Lieutenant of the Royall James, under the most noble and illustrious Captaine, Edward, Earle of Sandwich, Vice-Admirall of England, which, after a terrible fight, maintained to admiration against a squadron of the Holland fleet, above six hours, neere the Suffolk coast, having put off two fireships; at last, being utterly disabled, and few of her men remaining unhurt, was, by a third, unfortunately set on fire. But he (though he swome well) neglected to save himselfe, as some did, and out of perfect love to that worthy Lord, whom, for many yeares, he had constantly accompanyed, in all his honourable employments, and in all the engagements of the former warre, dyed with him, at the age of xxxii., much bewailed by his father, whom he never offended; and much beloved by all for his knowne piety, vertue, loyalty, fortitude, and fidelity."--B.]

My Lord, to my great content, did tell me before them, that never anything was read to the King and Council, all the chief Ministers of State being there, as my letter about the Victualling was, and no more said upon it than a most thorough consent to every word was said, and directed, that it be pursued and practised. After much mirth, and my Lord having travelled all night last night, he to bed, and we all parted, I home.

25th. Up and to my Lord Sandwich's, where several Commanders, of whom I took the state of all their ships, and of all could find not above four capable of going out. The truth is, the want of victuals being the whole overthrow of this yeare both at sea, and now at the Nore here and Portsmouth, where all the fleete lies. By and by comes down my Lord, and then he and I an houre together alone upon private discourse. He tells me that Mr. Coventry and he are not reconciled, but declared enemies: the only occasion of it being, he tells me, his ill usage from him about the first fight, wherein he had no right done him, which, methinks, is a poor occasion, for, in my conscience, that was no design of Coventry's. But, however, when I asked my Lord whether it were not best, though with some condescension, to be friends with him, he told me it was not possible, and so I stopped. He tells me, as very private, that there are great factions at the Court between the King's party and the Duke of Yorke's, and that the King, which is a strange difficulty, do favour my Lord in opposition to the Duke's party; that my Lord Chancellor, being, to be sure, the patron of the Duke's, it is a mystery whence it should be that Mr. Coventry is looked upon by him [Clarendon] as an enemy to him; that if he had a mind himself to be out of this employment, as Mr. Coventry, he believes, wishes, and himself and I do incline to wish it also, in many respects, yet he believes he shall not be able, because of the King, who will keepe him in on purpose, in opposition to the other party; that Prince Rupert and he are all possible friends in the world; that Coventry hath aggravated this business of the prizes, though never so great plundering in the world as while the Duke and he were at sea; and in Sir John Lawson's time he could take and pillage, and then sink a whole ship in the Streights, and Coventry say nothing to it; that my Lord Arlington is his fast friend; that the Chancellor is cold to him, and though I told him that I and the world do take my Lord Chancellor, in his speech the other day, to have said as much as could be wished, yet he thinks he did not. That my Lord Chancellor do from hence begin to be cold to him, because of his seeing him and Arlington so great: that nothing at Court is minded but faction and pleasure, and nothing intended of general good to the kingdom by anybody heartily; so that he believes with me, in a little time confusion will certainly come over all the nation. He told me how a design was carried on a while ago, for the Duke of Yorke to raise an army in the North, and to be the Generall of it, and all this without the knowledge or advice of the Duke of Albemarle, which when he come to know, he was so vexed, they were fain to let it fall to content him: that his matching with the family of Sir G. Carteret do make the difference greater between Coventry and him, they being enemies; that the Chancellor did, as every body else, speak well of me the other day, but yet was, at the Committee for Tangier, angry that I should offer to suffer a bill of exchange to be protested. So my Lord did bid me take heed, for that I might easily suppose I could not want enemies, no more than others. In all he speaks with the greatest trust and love and confidence in what I say or do, that a man can do. After this discourse ended we sat down to dinner and mighty merry, among other things, at the Bill brought into the House to make it felony to break bulke, which, as my Lord says well, will make that no prizes shall be taken, or, if taken, shall be sunke after plundering; and the Act for the method of gathering this last L1,250,000 now voted, and how paid wherein are several strange imperfections. After dinner my Lord by a ketch down to Erith, where the Bezan was, it blowing these last two days and now both night and day very hard southwardly, so that it has certainly drove the Dutch off the coast. My Lord being gone I to the office, and there find Captain Ferrers, who tells me his wife is come to town to see him, having not seen him since 15 weeks ago at his first going to sea last. She is now at a Taverne and stays all night, so I was obliged to give him my house and chamber to lie in, which he with great modesty and after much force took, and so I got Mr. Evelyn's coach to carry her thither, and the coach coming back, I with Mr. Evelyn to Deptford, where a little while with him doing a little business, and so in his coach back again to my lodgings, and there sat with Mrs. Ferrers two hours, and with my little girle, Mistress Frances Tooker, and very pleasant. Anon the Captain comes, and then to supper very merry, and so I led them to bed. And so to bed myself, having seen my pretty little girle home first at the next door.

26th. Up, and, leaving my guests to make themselves ready, I to the office, and thither comes Sir Jer. Smith and Sir Christopher Mings to see me, being just come from Portsmouth and going down to the Fleete. Here I sat and talked with them a good while and then parted, only Sir Christopher Mings and I together by water to the Tower; and I find him a very witty well-spoken fellow, and mighty free to tell his parentage, being a shoemaker's son, to whom he is now going, and I to the 'Change, where I hear how the French have taken two and sunk one of our merchant-men in the Streights, and carried the ships to Toulon; so that there is no expectation but we must fall out with them. The 'Change pretty full, and the town begins to be lively again, though the streets very empty, and most shops shut. So back again I and took boat and called for Sir Christopher Mings at St. Katharine's, who was followed with some ordinary friends, of which, he says, he is proud, and so down to Greenwich, the wind furious high, and we with our sail up till I made it be taken down. I took him, it being 3 o'clock, to my lodgings and did give him a good dinner and so parted, he being pretty close to me as to any business of the fleete, knowing me to be a servant of my Lord Sandwich's. He gone I to the office till night, and then they come and tell me my wife is come to towne, so I to her vexed at her coming, but it was upon innocent business, so I was pleased and made her stay, Captain Ferrers and his lady being yet there, and so I left them to dance, and I to the office till past nine at night, and so to them and there saw them dance very prettily, the Captain and his wife, my wife and Mrs. Barbary, and Mercer and my landlady's daughter, and then little Mistress Frances Tooker and her mother, a pretty woman come to see my wife. Anon to supper, and then to dance again (Golding being our fiddler, who plays very well and all tunes) till past twelve at night, and then we broke up and every one to bed, we make shift for all our company, Mrs. Tooker being gone.

27th. Up, and after some pleasant discourse with my wife, I out, leaving her and Mrs. Ferrers there, and I to Captain Cocke's, there to do some business, and then away with Cocke in his coach through Kent Streete, a miserable, wretched, poor place, people sitting sicke and muffled up with plasters at every 4 or 5 doors. So to the 'Change, and thence I by water to the Duke of Albemarle's, and there much company, but I staid and dined, and he makes mighty much of me; and here he tells us the Dutch are gone, and have lost above 160 cables and anchors, through the last foule weather. Here he proposed to me from Mr. Coventry, as I had desired of Mr. Coventry, that I should be Surveyor-Generall of the Victualling business, which I accepted. But, indeed, the terms in which Mr. Coventry proposes it for me are the most obliging that ever I could expect from any man, and more; it saying me to be the fittest man in England, and that he is sure, if I will undertake, I will perform it; and that it will be also a very desirable thing that I might have this encouragement, my encouragement in the Navy alone being in no wise proportionable to my pains or deserts. This, added to the letter I had three days since from Mr. Southerne, signifying that the Duke of Yorke had in his master's absence opened my letter, and commanded him to tell me that he did approve of my being the Surveyor-General, do make me joyful beyond myself that I cannot express it, to see that as I do take pains, so God blesses me, and hath sent me masters that do observe that I take pains. After having done here, I back by water and to London, and there met with Captain Cocke's coach again, and I went in it to Greenwich and thence sent my wife in it to Woolwich, and I to the office, and thence home late with Captain Taylor, and he and I settled all accounts between us, and I do find that I do get above L129 of him for my services for him within these six months. At it till almost one in the morning, and after supper he away and I to bed, mightily satisfied in all this, and in a resolution I have taken to-night with Mr. Hater to propose the port of London for the victualling business for Thomas Willson, by which it will be better done and I at more ease, in case he should grumble.

[The Duke of York's letter appointing Thomas Wilson Surveyor of the Victualling of His Majesty's Navy in the Port of London, and referring to Pepys as Surveyor-General of the Victualling Affairs, is printed in "Memoirs of the English Affairs, chiefly Naval, 1660-73," by James, Duke of York, 1729, p. 131.]

So to bed.

28th. Up, and sent for Thomas Willson, and broke the victualling business to him and he is mightily contented, and so am I that I have bestowed it on him, and so I to Mr. Boreman's, where Sir W. Batten is, to tell him what I had proposed to Thomas Willson, and the newes also I have this morning from Sir W. Clerke, which is, that notwithstanding all the care the Duke of Albemarle hath taken about the putting the East India prize goods into the East India Company's hands, and my Lord Bruncker and Sir J. Minnes having laden out a great part of the goods, an order is come from Court to stop all, and to have the goods delivered to the Sub-Commissioners of prizes. At which I am glad, because it do vex this simple weake man, and we shall have a little reparation for the disgrace my Lord Sandwich has had in it. He tells me also that the Parliament hath given the Duke of Yorke L120,000, to be paid him after the L1,250,000 is gathered upon the tax which they have now given the King.

[This sum was granted by the Commons to Charles, with a request that he would bestow it on his brother.--B.]

He tells me that the Dutch have lately launched sixteen new ships; all which is great news. Thence by horsebacke with Mr. Deane to Erith, and so aboard my Lord Bruncker and dined, and very merry with him and good discourse between them about ship building, and, after dinner and a little pleasant discourse, we away and by horse back again to Greenwich, and there I to the office very late, offering my persons for all the victualling posts much to my satisfaction. Also much other business I did to my mind, and so weary home to my lodging, and there after eating and drinking a little I to bed. The King and Court, they say, have now finally resolved to spend nothing upon clothes, but what is of the growth of England; which, if observed, will be very pleasing to the people, and very good for them.

29th (Lord's day). Up, and being ready set out with Captain Cocke in his coach toward Erith, Mr. Deane riding along with us, where we dined and were very merry. After dinner we fell to discourse about the Dutch, Cocke undertaking to prove that they were able to wage warr with us three years together, which, though it may be true, yet, not being satisfied with his arguments, my Lord and I did oppose the strength of his arguments, which brought us to a great heate, he being a conceited man, but of no Logique in his head at all, which made my Lord and I mirth. Anon we parted, and back again, we hardly having a word all the way, he being so vexed at our not yielding to his persuasion. I was set down at Woolwich towne end, and walked through the towne in the darke, it being now night. But in the streete did overtake and almost run upon two women crying and carrying a man's coffin between them. I suppose the husband of one of them, which, methinks, is a sad thing. Being come to Shelden's, I find my people in the darke in the dining room, merry and laughing, and, I thought, sporting one with another, which, God helpe me! raised my jealousy presently. Come in the darke, and one of them touching me (which afterward I found was Susan) made them shreeke, and so went out up stairs, leaving them to light a candle and to run out. I went out and was very vexed till I found my wife was gone with Mr. Hill and Mercer this day to see me at Greenwich, and these people were at supper, and the candle on a sudden falling out of the candlesticke (which I saw as I come through the yarde) and Mrs. Barbary being there I was well at ease again, and so bethought myself what to do, whether to go to Greenwich or stay there; at last go I would, and so with a lanthorne, and 3 or 4 people with me, among others Mr. Browne, who was there, would go, I walked with a lanthorne and discoursed with him about paynting and the several sorts of it. I came in good time to Greenwich, where I found Mr. Hill with my wife, and very glad I was to see him. To supper and discourse of musique and so to bed, I lying with him talking till midnight about Berckenshaw's musique rules, which I did to his great satisfaction inform him in, and so to sleep.

30th. Up, and to my office about business. At noon to dinner, and after some discourse of musique, he and I to the office awhile, and he to get Mr. Coleman, if he can, against night. By and by I back again home, and there find him returned with Mr. Coleman (his wife being ill) and Mr. Laneare, with whom with their Lute we had excellent company and good singing till midnight, and a good supper I did give them, but Coleman's voice is quite spoiled, and when he begins to be drunk he is excellent company, but afterward troublesome and impertinent. Laneare sings in a melancholy method very well, and a sober man he seems to be. They being gone, we to bed. Captain Ferrers coming this day from my Lord is forced to lodge here, and I put him to Mr. Hill.

31st. Up, and to the office, Captain Ferrers going back betimes to my Lord. I to the office, where Sir W. Batten met me, and did tell me that Captain Cocke's black was dead of the plague, which I had heard of before, but took no notice. By and by Captain Cocke come to the office, and Sir W. Batten and I did send to him that he would either forbear the office, or forbear going to his owne office. However, meeting yesterday the Searchers with their rods in their hands coming from Captain Cocke's house, I did overhear them say that the fellow did not die of the plague, but he had I know been ill a good while, and I am told that his boy Jack is also ill. At noon home to dinner, and then to the office again, leaving Mr. Hill if he can to get Mrs. Coleman at night. About nine at night I come home, and there find Mrs. Pierce come and little Fran. Tooker, and Mr. Hill, and other people, a great many dancing, and anon comes Mrs. Coleman with her husband and Laneare. The dancing ended and to sing, which Mrs. Coleman do very finely, though her voice is decayed as to strength but mighty sweet though soft, and a pleasant jolly woman, and in mighty good humour was to-night. Among other things Laneare did, at the request of Mr. Hill, bring two or three the finest prints for my wife to see that ever I did see in all my life. But for singing, among other things, we got Mrs. Coleman to sing part of the Opera, though she won't owne that ever she did get any of it without book in order to the stage; but, above all, her counterfeiting of Captain Cooke's part, in his reproaching his man with cowardice, "Base slave," &c., she do it most excellently. At it till past midnight, and then broke up and to bed. Hill and I together again, and being very sleepy we had little discourse as we had the other night. Thus we end the month merrily; and the more for that, after some fears that the plague would have increased again this week, I hear for certain that there is above 400 [less], the whole number being 1,388, and of them of the plague, 1,031. Want of money in the Navy puts everything out of order. Men grow mutinous; and nobody here to mind the business of the Navy but myself. At least Sir W. Batten for the few days he has been here do nothing. I in great hopes of my place of Surveyor-Generall of the Victualling, which will bring me L300 per annum.

s

THE DIARY OF SAMUEL PEPYS M.A. F.R.S.
CLERK OF THE ACTS AND SECRETARY TO THE ADMIRALTY
TRANSCRIBED FROM THE SHORTHAND MANUSCRIPT IN THE
PEPYSIAN LIBRARY
MAGDALENE COLLEGE CAMBRIDGE BY THE REV. MYNORS
BRIGHT M.A. LATE FELLOW
AND PRESIDENT OF THE COLLEGE
(Unabridged)
WITH LORD BRAYBROOKE'S NOTES
EDITED WITH ADDITIONS BY
HENRY B. WHEATLEY F.S.A.

DIARY OF SAMUEL PEPYS.

NOVEMBER & DECEMBER 1665

November 1st. Lay very long in bed discoursing with Mr. Hill of most things of a man's life, and how little merit do prevail in the world, but only favour; and that, for myself, chance without merit brought me in; and that diligence only keeps me so, and will, living as I do among so many lazy people that the diligent man becomes necessary, that they cannot do anything without him, and so told him of my late business of the victualling, and what cares I am in to keepe myself having to do with people of so different factions at Court, and yet must be fair with them all, which was very pleasant discourse for me to tell, as well as he seemed to take it, for him to hear. At last up, and it being a very foule day for raine and a hideous wind, yet having promised I would go by water to Erith, and bearing sayle was in danger of oversetting, but ordered them take down their sayle, and so cold and wet got thither, as they had ended their dinner. How[ever], I dined well, and after dinner all on shore, my Lord Bruncker with us to Mrs. Williams's lodgings, and Sir W. Batten, Sir Edmund Pooly, and others; and there, it being my Lord's birth-day, had every one a green riband tied in our hats very foolishly; and methinks mighty disgracefully for my Lord to have his folly so open to all the world with this woman. But by and by Sir W. Batten and I took coach, and home to Boreman, and so going home by the backside I saw Captain Cocke 'lighting out of his coach (having been at Erith also with her but not on board) and so he would come along with me to my lodging, and there sat and supped and talked with us, but we were angry a little a while about our message to him the other day about bidding him keepe from the office or his owne office, because of his black dying. I owned it and the reason of it, and would have been glad he had been out of the house, but I could not bid him go, and so supped, and after much other talke of the sad condition and state of the King's matters we broke up, and my friend and I to bed. This night coming with Sir W. Batten into Greenwich we called upon Coll. Cleggatt, who tells us for certaine that the King of Denmark hath declared to stand for the King of England, but since I hear it is wholly false.

2nd. Up, left my wife and to the office, and there to my great content Sir W. Warren come to me to settle the business of the Tangier boates, wherein I shall get above L100, besides L100 which he gives me in the paying for them out of his owne purse. He gone, I home to my lodgings to dinner, and there comes Captain Wagers newly returned from the Streights, who puts me in great fear for our last ships that went to Tangier with provisions, that they will be taken. A brave, stout fellow this Captain is, and I think very honest. To the office again after dinner and there late writing letters, and then about 8 at night set out from my office and fitting myself at my lodgings intended to have gone this night in a Ketch down to the Fleete, but calling in my way at Sir J. Minnes's, who is come up from Erith about something about the prizes, they persuaded me not to go till the morning, it being a horrible darke and a windy night. So I back to my lodging and to bed.

3rd. Was called up about four o'clock and in the darke by lanthorne took boat and to the Ketch and set sayle, sleeping a little in the Cabbin till day and then up and fell to reading of Mr. Evelyn's book about Paynting,

> [This must surely have been Evelyn's "Sculptura, or the History and Art of Chalcography and Engraving in Copper," published in 1662. The translation of Freart's "Idea of the Perfection of Painting demonstrated" was not published until 1668.]

which is a very pretty book. Carrying good victuals and Tom with me I to breakfast about 9 o'clock, and then to read again and come to the Fleete about twelve, where I found my Lord (the Prince being gone in) on board the Royall James, Sir Thomas Allen commander, and with my Lord an houre alone discoursing what was my chief and only errand about what was adviseable for his Lordship to do in this state of things, himself being under the Duke of Yorke's and Mr. Coventry's envy, and a great many more and likely never to do anything honourably but he shall be envied and the honour taken as much as can be from it. His absence lessens his interest at Court, and what is worst we never able to set out a fleete fit for him to command, or, if out, to keepe them out or fit them to do any great thing, or if that were so yet nobody at home minds him or his condition when he is abroad, and lastly the whole affairs of state looking as if they would all on a sudden break in pieces, and then what a sad thing it would be for him to be out of the way. My Lord did concur in every thing and thanked me infinitely for my visit and counsel, telling me that in every thing he concurs, but puts a query, what if the King will not think himself safe, if any man should go but him. How he should go off then? To that I had no answer ready, but the making the King see that he may be of as good use to him here while another goes forth. But for that I am not able to say much. We after this talked of some other little things and so to dinner, where my Lord infinitely kind to me, and after dinner I rose and left him with some Commanders at the table taking tobacco and I took the Bezan back with me, and with a brave gale and tide reached up that night to the Hope, taking great pleasure in learning the seamen's manner of singing when they sound the depths, and then to supper and to sleep, which I did most excellently all night, it being a horrible foule night for wind and raine.

4th. They sayled from midnight, and come to Greenwich about 5 o'clock in the morning. I however lay till about 7 or 8, and so to my office, my head a little akeing, partly for want of natural rest, partly having so much business to do to-day, and partly from the newes I hear that one of the little boys at my lodging is not well; and they suspect, by their sending for plaister and fume, that it may be the plague; so I sent Mr. Hater and W. Hewer to speake with the mother; but they returned to me, satisfied that there is no hurt nor danger, but the boy is well, and offers to be searched, however, I was resolved myself to abstain coming thither for a while. Sir W. Batten and myself at the office all the morning. At noon with him to dinner at Boreman's, where Mr. Seymour with us, who is a most conceited fellow and not over much in him. Here Sir W. Batten told us (which I had not heard before) that the last sitting day his cloake was taken from Mingo he going home to dinner, and that he was beaten by the seamen and swears he will come to Greenwich, but no more to the office till he can sit safe. After dinner I to the office and there late, and much troubled to have 100 seamen all the afternoon there, swearing below and cursing us, and breaking the glasse windows, and swear they will pull the house down on Tuesday next. I sent word of this to Court, but nothing will helpe it but money and a rope. Late at night to Mr. Glanville's there to lie for a night or two, and to bed.

5th (Lord's day). Up, and after being trimmed, by boat to the Cockpitt, where I heard the Duke of Albemarle's chaplin make a simple sermon: among other things, reproaching the imperfection of humane learning, he cried: "All our physicians cannot tell what an ague is, and all our arithmetique is not able to number the days of a man;" which, God knows, is not the fault of arithmetique, but that our understandings reach not the thing. To dinner, where a great deale of silly discourse, but the worst is I hear that the plague increases much at Lambeth, St. Martin's and Westminster, and fear it will all over the city. Thence I to the Swan, thinking to have seen Sarah but she was at church, and so I by water to Deptford, and there made a visit to Mr. Evelyn, who, among other things, showed me most excellent painting in little; in distemper, Indian incke, water colours: graveing; and, above all, the whole secret of mezzo-tinto, and the manner of it, which is very pretty, and good things done with it. He read to me very much also of his discourse, he hath been many years and now is about, about Guardenage; which will be a most noble and pleasant piece. He read me part of a play or two of his making, very good, but not as he conceits them, I think, to be. He showed me his Hortus Hyemalis; leaves laid up in a book of several plants kept dry, which preserve colour, however, and look very finely, better than any Herball. In fine, a most excellent person he is, and must be allowed a little for a little conceitedness; but he may well be so, being a man so much above others. He read me, though with too much gusto, some little poems of his own, that were not transcendant, yet one or two very pretty epigrams;

among others, of a lady looking in at a grate, and being pecked at by an eagle that was there. Here comes in, in the middle of our discourse Captain Cocke, as drunk as a dogg, but could stand, and talk and laugh. He did so joy himself in a brave woman that he had been with all the afternoon, and who should it be but my Lady Robinson, but very troublesome he is with his noise and talke, and laughing, though very pleasant. With him in his coach to Mr. Glanville's, where he sat with Mrs. Penington and myself a good while talking of this fine woman again and then went away. Then the lady and I to very serious discourse and, among other things, of what a bonny lasse my Lady Robinson is, who is reported to be kind to the prisoners, and has said to Sir G. Smith, who is her great crony, "Look! there is a pretty man, I would be content to break a commandment with him," and such loose expressions she will have often. After an houre's talke we to bed, the lady mightily troubled about a pretty little bitch she hath, which is very sicke, and will eat nothing, and the worst was, I could hear her in her chamber bemoaning the bitch, and by and by taking her into bed with her. The bitch pissed and shit a bed, and she was fain to rise and had coals out of my chamber to dry the bed again. This night I had a letter that Sir G. Carteret would be in towne to-morrow, which did much surprize me.

6th. Up, and to my office, where busy all the morning and then to dinner to Captain Cocke's with Mr. Evelyn, where very merry, only vexed after dinner to stay too long for our coach. At last, however, to Lambeth and thence the Cockpitt, where we found Sir G. Carteret come, and in with the Duke and the East India Company about settling the business of the prizes, and they have gone through with it. Then they broke up, and Sir G. Carteret come out, and thence through the garden to the water side and by water I with him in his boat down with Captain Cocke to his house at Greenwich, and while supper was getting ready Sir G. Carteret and I did walk an houre in the garden before the house, talking of my Lord Sandwich's business; what enemies he hath, and how they have endeavoured to bespatter him: and particularly about his leaving of 30 ships of the enemy, when Pen would have gone, and my Lord called him back again: which is most false. However, he says, it was purposed by some hot-heads in the House of Commons, at the same time when they voted a present to the Duke of Yorke, to have voted L10,000 to the Prince, and half-a-crowne to my Lord of Sandwich; but nothing come of it.

[The tide of popular indignation ran high against Lord Sandwich, and he was sent to Spain as ambassador to get him honourably out of the way (see post, December 6th).]

But, for all this, the King is most firme to my Lord, and so is my Lord Chancellor, and my Lord Arlington. The Prince, in appearance, kind; the Duke of Yorke silent, says no hurt; but admits others to say it in his hearing. Sir W. Pen, the falsest rascal that ever was in the world; and that this afternoon the Duke of Albemarle did tell him that Pen was a very cowardly rogue, and one that hath brought all these rogueish fanatick Captains into the fleete, and swears he should never go out with the fleete again. That Sir W. Coventry is most kind to Pen still; and says nothing nor do any thing openly to the prejudice of my Lord. He agrees with me, that it is impossible for the King [to] set out a fleete again the next year; and that he fears all will come to ruine, there being no money in prospect but these prizes, which will bring, it may be, L20,000, but that will signify nothing in the world for it. That this late Act of Parliament for bringing the money into the Exchequer, and making of it payable out there, intended as a prejudice to him and will be his convenience hereafter and ruine the King's business, and so I fear it will and do wonder Sir W. Coventry would be led by Sir G. Downing to persuade the King and Duke to have it so, before they had thoroughly weighed all circumstances; that for my Lord, the King has said to him lately that I was an excellent officer, and that my Lord Chancellor do, he thinks, love and esteem of me as well as he do of any man in England that he hath no more acquaintance with. So having done and received from me the sad newes that we are like to have no money here a great while, not even of the very prizes, I set up my rest

[The phrase "set up my rest" is a metaphor from the once fashionable game of Primero, meaning, to stand upon the cards you have in your hand, in hopes they may prove better than those of your adversary. Hence, to make up your mind, to be determined (see Nares's "Glossary").]

in giving up the King's service to be ruined and so in to supper, where pretty merry, and after supper late to Mr. Glanville's, and Sir G. Carteret to bed. I also to bed, it being very late.

7th. Up, and to Sir G. Carteret, and with him, he being very passionate to be gone, without staying a minute for breakfast, to the Duke of Albemarle's and I with him by water and with Fen: but, among other things, Lord! to see how he wondered to see the river so empty of boats, nobody working at the Custome-house keys; and how fearful he is, and vexed that his man, holding a wine-glasse in his hand for him to drinke out of, did cover his hands, it being a cold, windy, rainy morning, under the waterman's coate, though he brought the waterman from six or seven miles up the river, too. Nay, he carried this glasse with him for his man to let him drink out of at the Duke of Albemarle's, where he intended to dine, though this he did to prevent sluttery, for, for the same reason he carried a napkin with him to Captain Cocke's, making him believe that he should eat with foule linnen. Here he with the Duke walked a good while in the Parke, and I with Fen, but cannot gather that he intends to stay with us, nor thinks any thing at all of ever paying one farthing of money more to us here, let what will come of it. Thence in, and Sir W. Batten comes in by and by, and so staying till noon, and there being a great deal of company there, Sir W. Batten and I took leave of the Duke and Sir G. Carteret, there being no good to be done more for money, and so over the River and by coach to Greenwich, where at Boreman's we dined, it being late. Thence my head being full of business and mind out of order for thinking of the effects which will arise from the want of money, I made an end of my letters by eight o'clock, and so to my lodging and there spent the evening till midnight talking with Mrs. Penington, who is a very discreet, understanding lady and very pretty discourse we had and great variety, and she tells me with great sorrow her bitch is dead this morning, died in her bed. So broke up and to bed.

8th. Up, and to the office, where busy among other things to looke my warrants for the settling of the Victualling business, the warrants being come to me for the Surveyors of the ports and that for me also to be Surveyor-Generall. I did discourse largely with Tom Willson about it and doubt not to make it a good service to the King as well, as the King gives us very good salarys. It being a fast day, all people were at church and the office quiett; so I did much business, and at noon adventured to my old lodging, and there eat, but am not yet well satisfied, not seeing of Christopher, though they say he is abroad. Thence after dinner to the office again, and thence am sent for to the King's Head by my Lord Rutherford, who, since I can hope for no more convenience from him, his business is troublesome to me, and therefore I did leave him as soon as I could and by water to Deptford, and there did order my matters so, walking up and down the fields till it was dark night, that 'je allais a la maison of my valentine,--[Bagwell's wife]--and there 'je faisais whatever je voudrais avec' her, and, about eight at night, did take water, being glad I was out of the towne; for the plague, it seems, rages there more than ever, and so to my lodgings, where my Lord had got a supper and the mistresse of the house, and her daughters, and here staid Mrs. Pierce to speake with me about her husband's business, and I made her sup with us, and then at night my Lord and I walked with her home, and so back again. My Lord and I ended all we had to say as to his business overnight, and so I took leave, and went again to Mr. Glanville's and so to bed, it being very late.

9th. Up, and did give the servants something at Mr. Glanville's and so took leave, meaning to lie to-night at my owne lodging. To my office, where busy with Mr. Gawden running over the Victualling business, and he is mightily pleased that this course is taking and seems sensible of my favour and promises kindnesse to me. At noon by water, to the King's Head at Deptford, where Captain Taylor invites Sir W: Batten, Sir John Robinson (who come in with a great deale of company from hunting, and brought in a hare alive and a great many silly stories they tell of their sport, which pleases them mightily, and me not at all, such is the different sense of pleasure in mankind), and others upon the score of a survey of his new ship; and strange to see how a good dinner and feasting reconciles everybody, Sir W. Batten and Sir J. Robinson being now as kind to him, and report well of his ship and proceedings, and promise money, and Sir W. Batten is a solicitor for him, but it is a strange thing to observe, they being the greatest enemys he had, and yet, I believe, hath in the world in their hearts. Thence after dinner stole away and to my office, where did a great deale of business till midnight, and then to Mrs. Clerk's, to lodge again, and going home W. Hewer did tell me my wife will be here to-morrow, and hath put away

Mary, which vexes me to the heart, I cannot helpe it, though it may be a folly in me, and when I think seriously on it, I think my wife means no ill design in it, or, if she do, I am a foole to be troubled at it, since I cannot helpe it. The Bill of Mortality, to all our griefs, is encreased 399 this week, and the encrease generally through the whole City and suburbs, which makes us all sad.

10th. Up, and entered all my Journall since the 28th of October, having every day's passages well in my head, though it troubles me to remember it, and which I was forced to, being kept from my lodging, where my books and papers are, for several days. So to my office, where till two or three o'clock busy before I could go to my lodging to dinner, then did it and to my office again. In the evening newes is brought me my wife is come: so I to her, and with her spent the evening, but with no great pleasure, I being vexed about her putting away of Mary in my absence, but yet I took no notice of it at all, but fell into other discourse, and she told me, having herself been this day at my house at London, which was boldly done, to see Mary have her things, that Mr. Harrington, our neighbour, an East country merchant, is dead at Epsum of the plague, and that another neighbour of ours, Mr. Hollworthy, a very able man, is also dead by a fall in the country from his horse, his foot hanging in the stirrup, and his brains beat out. Here we sat talking, and after supper to bed.

11th. I up and to the office (leaving my wife in bed) and there till noon, then to dinner and back again to the office, my wife going to Woolwich again, and I staying very late at my office, and so home to bed.

12th (Lord's day). Up, and invited by Captain Cocke to dinner. So after being ready I went to him, and there he and I and Mr. Yard (one of the Guinny Company) dined together and very merry. After dinner I by water to the Duke of Albemarle, and there had a little discourse and business with him, chiefly to receive his commands about pilotts to be got for our Hambro' ships, going now at this time of the year convoy to the merchant ships, that have lain at great pain and charge, some three, some four months at Harwich for a convoy. They hope here the plague will be less this weeke. Thence back by water to Captain Cocke's, and there he and I spent a great deale of the evening as we had done of the day reading and discoursing over part of Mr. Stillingfleet's "Origines Sacrae," wherein many things are very good and some frivolous. Thence by and by he and I to Mrs. Penington's, but she was gone to bed. So we back and walked a while, and then to his house and to supper, and then broke up, and I home to my lodging to bed.

13th. Up, and to my office, where busy all the morning, and at noon to Captain Cocke's to dinner as we had appointed in order to settle our business of accounts. But here came in an Alderman, a merchant, a very merry man, and we dined, and, he being gone, after dinner Cocke and I walked into the garden, and there after a little discourse he did undertake under his hand to secure me in L500 profit, for my share of the profit of what we have bought of the prize goods. We agreed upon the terms, which were easier on my side than I expected, and so with extraordinary inward joy we parted till the evening. So I to the office and among other business prepared a deed for him to sign and seale to me about our agreement, which at night I got him to come and sign and seale, and so he and I to Glanville's, and there he and I sat talking and playing with Mrs. Penington, whom we found undrest in her smocke and petticoats by the fireside, and there we drank and laughed, and she willingly suffered me to put my hand in her bosom very wantonly, and keep it there long. Which methought was very strange, and I looked upon myself as a man mightily deceived in a lady, for I could not have thought she could have suffered it, by her former discourse with me; so modest she seemed and I know not what. We staid here late, and so home after he and I had walked till past midnight, a bright moonshine, clear, cool night, before his door by the water, and so I home after one of the clock.

14th. Called up by break of day by Captain Cocke, by agreement, and he and I in his coach through Kent-streete (a sad place through the plague, people sitting sicke and with plaisters about them in the street begging) to Viner's and Colvill's about money business, and so to my house, and there I took L300 in order to the carrying it down to my Lord Sandwich in part of the money I am to pay for Captain Cocke by our agreement. So I took it down, and down I went to Greenwich to my office, and there sat busy till noon, and so home to dinner, and thence to the office again, and by and by to the Duke of Albemarle's by water late, where I find he had remembered that I had appointed to come to him this day about money, which I excused not doing sooner; but I see, a dull fellow, as he is, do sometimes remember what another thinks he mindeth not. My business was about getting money of the East India Company; but, Lord! to see how the Duke himself magnifies himself in what he had done with the Company; and my Lord Craven what the King could have done without my Lord Duke, and a deale of stir, but most mightily what a brave fellow I am. Back by water, it raining hard, and so to the office, and stopped my going, as I intended, to the buoy of the Nore, and great reason I had to rejoice at it, for it proved the night of as great a storme as was almost ever remembered. Late at the office, and so home to bed. This day, calling at Mr. Rawlinson's to know how all did there, I hear that my pretty grocer's wife, Mrs. Beversham, over the way there, her husband is lately dead of the plague at Bow, which I am sorry for, for fear of losing her neighbourhood.

15th. Up and all the morning at the office, busy, and at noon to the King's Head taverne, where all the Trinity House dined to-day, to choose a new Master in the room of Hurlestone, that is dead, and Captain Crispe is chosen. But, Lord! to see how Sir W. Batten governs all and tramples upon Hurlestone, but I am confident the Company will grow the worse for that man's death, for now Batten, and in him a lazy, corrupt, doating rogue, will have all the sway there. After dinner who comes in but my Lady Batten, and a troop of a dozen women almost, and expected, as I found afterward, to be made mighty much of, but nobody minded them; but the best jest was, that when they saw themselves not regarded, they would go away, and it was horrible foule weather; and my Lady Batten walking through the dirty lane with new spicke and span white shoes, she dropped one of her galoshes in the dirt, where it stuck, and she forced to go home without one, at which she was horribly vexed, and I led her; and after vexing her a little more in mirth, I parted, and to Glanville's, where I knew Sir John Robinson, Sir G. Smith, and Captain Cocke were gone, and there, with the company of Mrs. Penington, whose father, I hear, was one of the Court of justice, and died prisoner, of the stone, in the Tower, I made them, against their resolutions, to stay from houre to houre till it was almost midnight, and a furious, darke and rainy, and windy, stormy night, and, which was best, I, with drinking small beer, made them all drunk drinking wine, at which Sir John Robinson made great sport. But, they being gone, the lady and I very civilly sat an houre by the fireside observing the folly of this Robinson, that makes it his worke to praise himself, and all he say and do, like a heavy-headed coxcombe. The plague, blessed be God! is decreased 400; making the whole this week but 1300 and odd; for which the Lord be praised!

16th. Up, and fitted myself for my journey down to the fleete, and sending my money and boy down by water to Eriffe,--[Erith]--I borrowed a horse of Mr. Boreman's son, and after having sat an houre laughing with my Lady Batten and Mrs. Turner, and eat and drank with them, I took horse and rode to Eriffe, where, after making a little visit to Madam Williams, who did give me information of W. Howe's having bought eight bags of precious stones taken from about the Dutch Vice-Admirall's neck, of which there were eight dyamonds which cost him L60,000 sterling, in India, and hoped to have made L2000 here for them. And that this is told by one that sold him one of the bags, which hath nothing but rubys in it, which he had for 35s.; and that it will be proved he hath made L125 of one stone that he bought. This she desired, and I resolved I would give my Lord Sandwich notice of. So I on board my Lord Bruncker; and there he and Sir Edmund Pooly carried me down into the hold of the India shipp, and there did show me the greatest wealth lie in confusion that a man can see in the world. Pepper scattered through every chink, you trod upon it; and in cloves and nutmegs, I walked above the knees; whole rooms full. And silk in bales, and boxes of copper-plate, one of which I saw opened. Having seen this, which was as noble a sight as ever I saw in my life, I away on board the other ship in despair to get the pleasure-boat of the gentlemen there to carry me to the fleet. They were Mr. Ashburnham and Colonell Wyndham; but pleading the King's business, they did presently agree I should have it. So I presently on board, and got under sail, and had a good bedd by the shift, of Wyndham's; and so,

17th. Sailed all night, and got down to Quinbrough water, where all the great ships are now come, and there on board my Lord, and was soon received with great content. And after some little discourse, he and I on board Sir W. Pen; and there held a council of Warr about many wants of the fleete, but chiefly how to get slopps and victuals for the fleete now going out to convoy our Hambro' ships, that have been so long detained for four or five months for want of convoy, which we did accommodate one way or other, and so, after much chatt, Sir W. Pen did give us a very good and neat dinner, and better, I think, than ever I did see at his owne house at home in my life, and so was the other I eat with him. After dinner much talke, and about other things, he and I about his money for his prize goods, wherein I did give him a cool answer, but so as we did not disagree in words much, and so let that fall, and so followed my Lord Sandwich, who was gone a little before me on board the Royall James. And there spent an houre, my Lord playing upon the gittarr, which he now commends above all musique in the world, because it is base enough for a single voice, and is so portable and manageable without much trouble. That being done, I got my Lord to be alone, and so I fell to acquaint him with W. Howe's business, which he had before heard a little of from Captain Cocke, but made no great matter of it, but now he do, and resolves nothing less than to lay him by the heels, and seize on all he hath, saying that for this yeare or two he hath observed him so proud and conceited he could not endure him. But though I was not at all displeased with it, yet I prayed him to forbear doing anything therein till he heard from me again about it, and I had made more enquiry into the truth of it, which he agreed to. Then we fell to publique discourse, wherein was principally this: he cleared it to me beyond all doubt that Coventry is his enemy, and has been long so. So that I am over that, and my Lord told it me upon my proposal of a friendship between them, which he says is impossible, and methinks that my Lord's displeasure about the report in print of the first fight was not of his making, but I perceive my Lord cannot forget it, nor the other think he can. I shewed him how advisable it were upon almost any terms for him to get quite off the sea employment. He answers me again that he agrees to it, but thinks the King will not let him go off: He tells me he lacks now my Lord Orrery to solicit it for him, who is very great with the King. As an infinite secret, my Lord tells me, the factions are high between the King and the Duke, and all the Court are in an uproare with their loose amours; the Duke of Yorke being in love desperately with Mrs. Stewart. Nay, that the Duchesse herself is fallen in love with her new Master of the Horse, one Harry Sidney, and another, Harry Savill. So that God knows what will be the end of it. And that the Duke is not so obsequious as he used to be, but very high of late; and would be glad to be in the head of an army as Generall; and that it is said that he do propose to go and command under the King of Spayne, in Flanders. That his amours to Mrs. Stewart are told the King. So that all is like to be nought among them. That he knows that the Duke of Yorke do give leave to have him spoken slightly of in his owne hearing, and doth not oppose it, and told me from what time he hath observed this to begin. So that upon the whole my Lord do concur to wish with all his heart that he could with any honour get from off the imployment. After he had given thanks to me for my kind visit and good counsel, on which he seems to set much by, I left him, and so away to my Bezan againe, and there to read in a pretty French book, "La Nouvelle Allegorique," upon the strife between rhetorique and its enemies, very pleasant. So, after supper, to sleepe, and sayled all night, and came to Erith before break of day.

18th. About nine of the clock, I went on shore, there (calling by the way only to look upon my Lord Bruncker) to give Mrs. Williams an account of her matters, and so hired an ill-favoured horse, and away to Greenwich to my lodgings, where I hear how rude the souldiers have been in my absence, swearing what they would do with me, which troubled me, but, however, after eating a bit I to the office and there very late writing letters, and so home and to bed.

19th (Lord's day). Up, and after being trimmed, alone by water to Erith, all the way with my song book singing of Mr. Lawes's long recitative song in the beginning of his book. Being come there, on board my Lord Bruncker, I find Captain Cocke and other company, the lady not well, and mighty merry we were; Sir Edmund Pooly being very merry, and a right English gentleman, and one of the discontented Cavaliers, that think their loyalty is not considered. After dinner, all on shore to my Lady Williams, and there drank and talked; but, Lord! the most impertinent bold woman with my Lord that ever I did see. I did give her an account again of my business with my Lord touching W. Howe, and she did give me some more information about it, and examination taken about it, and so we parted and I took boat, and to Woolwich, where we found my wife not well of them, and I out of humour begun to dislike her paynting, the last things not pleasing me so well as the former, but I blame myself for my being so little complaisant. So without eating or drinking, there being no wine (which vexed me too), we walked with a lanthorne to Greenwich and eat something at his house, and so home to bed.

20th. Up before day, and wrote some letters to go to my Lord, among others that about W. Howe, which I believe will turn him out, and so took horse for Nonesuch, with two men with me, and the ways very bad, and the weather worse, for wind and rayne. But we got in good time thither, and I did get my tallys got ready, and thence, with as many as could go, to Yowell, and there dined very well, and I saw my Besse, a very well-favoured country lass there, and after being very merry and having spent a piece I took horse, and by another way met with a very good road, but it rained hard and blew, but got home very well. Here I find Mr. Deering come to trouble me about business, which I soon dispatched and parted, he telling me that Luellin hath been dead this fortnight, of the plague, in St. Martin's Lane, which much surprised me.

21st. Up, and to the office, where all the morning doing business, and at noon home to dinner and quickly back again to the office, where very busy all the evening and late sent a long discourse to Mr. Coventry by his desire about the regulating of the method of our payment of bills in the Navy, which will be very good, though, it may be, he did ayme principally at striking at Sir G. Carteret. So weary but pleased with this business being over I home to supper and to bed.

22nd. Up, and by water to the Duke of Albemarle, and there did some little business, but most to shew myself, and mightily I am yet in his and Lord Craven's books, and thence to the Swan and there drank and so down to the bridge, and so to the 'Change, where spoke with many people, and about a great deale of business, which kept me late. I heard this day that Mr. Harrington is not dead of the plague, as we believed, at which I was very glad, but most of all, to hear that the plague is come very low; that is, the whole under 1,000, and the plague 600 and odd: and great hopes of a further decrease, because of this day's being a very exceeding hard frost, and continues freezing. This day the first of the Oxford Gazettes come out, which is very pretty, full of newes, and no folly in it. Wrote by Williamson. Fear that our Hambro' ships at last cannot go, because of the great frost, which we believe it is there, nor are our ships cleared at the Pillow [Pillau], which will keepe them there too all this winter, I fear. From the 'Change, which is pretty full again, I to my office and there took some things, and so by water to my lodging at Greenwich and dined, and then to the office awhile and at night home to my lodgings, and took T. Willson and T. Hater with me, and there spent the evening till midnight discoursing and settling of our Victualling business, that thereby I might draw up instructions for the Surveyours and that we might be doing something to earne our money. This done I late to bed. Among other things it pleased me to have it demonstrated, that a Purser without professed cheating is a professed loser, twice as much as he gets.

23rd. Up betimes, and so, being trimmed, I to get papers ready against Sir H. Cholmly come to me by appointment, he being newly come over from Tangier. He did by and by come, and we settled all matters about his money, and he is a most satisfied man in me, and do declare his resolution to give me 200 per annum. It continuing to be a great frost, which gives us hope for a perfect cure of the plague, he and I to walk in the parke, and there discoursed with grief of the calamity of the times; how the King's service is performed, and how Tangier is governed by a man, who, though honourable, yet do mind his ways of getting and little else compared, which will never make the place flourish. I brought him and had a good dinner for him, and there come by chance Captain Cuttance, who tells me how W. Howe is laid by the heels, and confined to the Royall Katharine, and his things all seized and how, also, for a quarrel, which indeed the other night my Lord told me, Captain Ferrers, having cut all over the back of another of my Lord's servants, is parted from my Lord. I sent for little Mrs. Frances Tooker, and after they were gone I sat dallying with her an hour, doing what I would with my hands about her. And a very pretty creature it is. So in the evening to the office, where late writing letters, and at my lodging later writing for the last twelve days my Journall and so to bed. Great expectation what mischief more the French will do us, for we must fall out. We in extraordinary lacke of money and everything else to go to sea next year. My Lord Sandwich is gone from the fleete yesterday toward Oxford.

24th. Up, and after doing some business at the office, I to London, and there, in my way, at my old oyster shop in Gracious Streete, bought two barrels of my fine woman of the shop, who is alive after all the plague, which now is the first observation or inquiry we make at London concerning everybody we knew before it. So to the 'Change, where very busy with several people, and mightily glad to see the 'Change so full, and hopes of another abatement still the next week. Off the 'Change I went home with Sir G. Smith to dinner, sending for one of my barrels of oysters, which were good, though come from Colchester, where the plague hath been so much. Here a very brave dinner, though no invitation; and, Lord! to see how I am treated, that come from so mean a beginning, is matter of wonder to me. But it is God's great mercy to me, and His blessing upon my taking pains, and being punctual in my dealings. After dinner Captain Cocke and I about some business, and then with my other barrel of oysters home to Greenwich, sent them by water to Mrs. Penington, while he and I landed, and visited Mr. Evelyn, where most excellent discourse with him; among other things he showed me a ledger of a Treasurer of the Navy, his great grandfather, just 100 years old; which I seemed mighty fond of, and he did present me with it, which I take as a great rarity; and he hopes to find me more, older than it. He also shewed us several letters of the old Lord of Leicester's, in Queen Elizabeth's time, under the very hand-writing of Queen Elizabeth, and Queen Mary, Queen of Scotts; and others, very venerable names. But, Lord! how poorly, methinks, they wrote in those days, and in what plain uncut paper. Thence, Cocke having sent for his coach, we to Mrs. Penington, and there sat and talked and eat our oysters with great pleasure, and so home to my lodging late and to bed.

25th. Up, and busy at the office all day long, saving dinner time, and in the afternoon also very late at my office, and so home to bed. All our business is now about our Hambro fleete, whether it can go or no this yeare, the weather being set in frosty, and the whole stay being for want of Pilotts now, which I have wrote to the Trinity House about, but have so poor an account from them, that I did acquaint Sir W. Coventry with it this post.

26th (Lord's day). Up, though very late abed, yet before day to dress myself to go toward Erith, which I would do by land, it being a horrible cold frost to go by water: so borrowed two horses of Mr. Howell and his friend, and with much ado set out, after my horses being frosted

[Frosting means, having the horses' shoes turned up by the smith.]

(which I know not what it means to this day), and my boy having lost one of my spurs and stockings, carrying them to the smith's; but I borrowed a stocking, and so got up, and Mr. Tooker with me, and rode to Erith, and there on board my Lord Bruncker, met Sir W. Warren upon his business, among others, and did a great deale, Sir J. Minnes, as God would have it, not being there to hinder us with his impertinences. Business done, we to dinner very merry, there being there Sir Edmund Pooly, a very worthy gentleman. They are now come to the copper boxes in the prizes, and hope to have ended all this weeke. After dinner took leave, and on shore to Madam Williams, to give her an account of my Lord's letter to me about Howe, who he has clapped by the heels on suspicion of having the jewells, and she did give me my Lord Bruncker's examination of the fellow, that declares his having them; and so away, Sir W. Warren riding with me, and the way being very bad, that is, hard and slippery by reason of the frost, so we could not come to past Woolwich till night. However, having a great mind to have gone to the Duke of Albemarle, I endeavoured to have gone farther, but the night come on and no going, so I 'light and sent my horse by Tooker, and returned on foot to my wife at Woolwich, where I found, as I had directed, a good dinner to be made against to-morrow, and invited guests in the yarde, meaning to be merry, in order to her taking leave, for she intends to come in a day or two to me for altogether. But here, they tell me, one of the houses behind them is infected, and I was fain to stand there a great while, to have their back-door opened, but they could not, having locked them fast, against any passing through, so was forced to pass by them again, close to their sicke beds, which they were removing out of the house, which troubled me; so I made them uninvite their guests, and to resolve of coming all away to me to-morrow, and I walked with a lanthorne, weary as I was, to Greenwich; but it was a fine walke, it being a hard frost, and so to Captain Cocke's, but he I found had sent for me to come to him to Mrs. Penington's, and there I went, and we were very merry, and supped, and Cocke being sleepy he went away betimes. I stayed alone talking and playing with her till past midnight, she suffering me whatever 'ego voulais avec ses mamilles . . . . Much pleased with her company we parted, and I home to bed at past one, all people being in bed thinking I would have staid out of town all night.

27th. Up, and being to go to wait on the Duke of Albemarle, who is to go out of towne to Oxford to-morrow, and I being unwilling to go by water, it being bitter cold, walked it with my landlady's little boy Christopher to Lambeth, it being a very fine walke and calling at half the way and drank, and so to the Duke of Albemarle, who is visited by every body against his going; and mighty kind to me: and upon my desiring his grace to give me his kind word to the Duke of Yorke, if any occasion there were of speaking of me, he told me he had reason to do so; for there had been nothing done in the Navy without me. His going, I hear, is upon putting the sea business into order, and, as some say, and people of his owne family, that he is agog to go to sea himself the next year. Here I met with a letter from Sir G. Carteret, who is come to Cranborne, that he will be here this afternoon and desires me to be with him. So the Duke would have me dine with him. So it being not dinner time, I to the Swan, and there found Sarah all alone in the house . . . . So away to the Duke of Albemarle again, and there to dinner, he most exceeding kind to me to the observation of all that are there. At dinner comes Sir G. Carteret and dines with us. After dinner a great deal alone with Sir G. Carteret, who tells me that my Lord hath received still worse and worse usage from some base people about the Court. But the King is very kind, and the Duke do not appear the contrary; and my Lord Chancellor swore to him "by---I will not forsake my Lord of Sandwich." Our next discourse is upon this Act for money, about which Sir G. Carteret comes to see what money can be got upon it. But none can be got, which pleases him the thoughts of, for, if the Exchequer should succeede in this, his office would faile. But I am apt to think at this time of hurry and plague and want of trade, no money will be got upon a new way which few understand. We walked, Cocke and I, through the Parke with him, and so we being to meet the Vice-Chamberlayne to-morrow at Nonesuch, to treat with Sir Robert Long about the same business, I into London, it being dark night, by a hackney coach; the first I have durst to go in many a day, and with great pain now for fear. But it being unsafe to go by water in the dark and frosty cold, and unable being weary with my morning walke to go on foot, this was my only way. Few people yet in the streets, nor shops open, here and there twenty in a place almost; though not above five or sixe o'clock at night. So to Viner's, and there heard of Cocke, and found him at the Pope's Head, drinking with Temple. I to them, where the Goldsmiths do decry the new Act, for money to be all brought into the Exchequer, and paid out thence, saying they will not advance one farthing upon it; and indeed it is their interest to say and do so. Thence Cocke and I to Sir G. Smith's, it being now night, and there up to his chamber and sat talking, and I barbing--[shaving]--against to-morrow; and anon, at nine at night, comes to us Sir G. Smith and the Lieutenant of the Tower, and there they sat talking and drinking till past midnight, and mighty merry we were, the Lieutenant of the Tower being in a mighty vein of singing, and he hath a very good eare and strong voice, but no manner of skill. Sir G. Smith shewed me his lady's closett, which was very fine; and, after being very merry, here I lay in a noble chamber, and mighty highly treated, the first time I have lain in London a long time.

28th. Up before day, and Cocke and I took a hackney coach appointed with four horses to take us up, and so carried us over London Bridge. But there, thinking of some business, I did 'light at the foot of the bridge, and by helpe of a candle at a stall, where some payers were at work, I wrote a letter to Mr. Hater, and never knew so great an instance of the usefulness of carrying pen and ink and wax about one: so we, the way being very bad, to Nonesuch, and thence to Sir Robert Longs house; a fine place, and dinner time ere we got thither; but we had breakfasted a little at Mr. Gawden's, he being out of towne though, and there borrowed Dr. Taylor's sermons, and is a most excellent booke and worth my buying, where had a very good dinner, and curiously dressed, and here a couple of ladies, kinswomen of his, not handsome though, but rich, that knew me by report of The. Turner, and mighty merry we were. After dinner to talk of our business, the Act of Parliament, where in short I see Sir R. Long mighty fierce in the great good qualities of it. But in that and many other things he was stiff in, I think without much judgement, or the judgement I expected from him, and already they have evaded the necessity of bringing people into the Exchequer with their bills to be paid there. Sir G. Carteret is titched--[fretful, tetchy]--at this, yet resolves with me to make the best use we can of this Act for the King, but all our care, we think, will not render it as it should be. He did again here alone discourse with me about my Lord, and is himself strongly for my Lord's not going to sea, which I am glad to hear and did confirm him in it. He tells me too that he talked last night with the Duke of Albemarle about my Lord Sandwich, by the by making him sensible that it is his interest to preserve his old friends, which he confessed he had reason to do, for he knows that ill offices were doing of him, and that he honoured my Lord Sandwich with all his heart. After this discourse we parted, and all of us broke up and we parted. Captain Cocke and I through Wandsworth. Drank at Sir Allen Broderick's, a great friend and comrade of Cocke's, whom he values above the world for a witty companion, and I believe he is so. So to Fox-Hall and there took boat, and down to the Old Swan, and thence to Lumbard Streete, it being darke night, and thence to the Tower. Took boat and down to Greenwich, Cocke and I, he home and I to the office, where did a little business, and then to my lodgings, where my wife is come, and I am well pleased with it, only much trouble in those lodgings we have, the mistresse of the house being so deadly dear in everything we have; so that we do resolve to remove home soon as we know how the plague goes this weeke, which we hope will be a good decrease. So to bed.

29th. Up, my wife and I talking how to dispose of our goods, and resolved upon sending our two mayds Alce (who has been a day or two at Woolwich with my wife, thinking to have had a feast there) and Susan home. So my wife after dinner did take them to London with some goods, and I in the afternoon after doing other business did go also by agreement to meet Captain Cocke and from him to Sir Roger Cuttance, about the money due from Cocke to him for the late prize goods, wherein Sir Roger is troubled that he hath not payment as agreed, and the other, that he must pay without being secured in the quiett possession of them, but some accommodation to both, I think, will be found. But Cocke do tell me that several have begged so much of the King to be discovered out of stolen prize goods and so I am afeard we shall hereafter have trouble, therefore I will get myself free of them as soon as I can and my money paid. Thence home to my house, calling my wife, where the poor wretch is putting things in a way to be ready for our coming home, and so by water together to Greenwich, and so spent the night together.

30th. Up, and at the office all the morning. At noon comes Sir Thomas Allen, and I made him dine with me, and very friendly he is, and a good man, I think, but one that professes he loves to get and to save. He dined with my wife and me and Mrs. Barbary, whom my wife brings along with her from Woolwich for as long as she stays here. In the afternoon to the office, and there very late writing letters and then home, my wife and people sitting up for me, and after supper to bed. Great joy we have this week in the weekly Bill, it being come to 544 in all, and but 333 of the plague; so that we are encouraged to get to London soon as we can. And my father writes as great news of joy to them, that he saw Yorke's waggon go again this week to London, and was full of passengers; and tells me that my aunt Bell hath been dead of the plague these seven weeks.

DIARY OF SAMUEL PEPYS.

DECEMBER 1665

December 1st. This morning to the office, full of resolution to spend the whole day at business, and there, among other things, I did agree with Poynter to be my clerke for my Victualling business, and so all alone all the day long shut up in my little closett at my office, drawing up instructions, which I should long since have done for my Surveyours of the Ports, Sir W. Coventry desiring much to have them, and he might well have expected them long since. After dinner to it again, and at night had long discourse with Gibson, who is for Yarmouth, who makes me understand so much of the victualling business and the pursers' trade, that I am ashamed I should go about the concerning myself in a business which I understand so very very little of, and made me distrust all I had been doing to-day. So I did lay it by till to-morrow morning to think of it afresh, and so home by promise to my wife, to have mirth there. So we had our neighbours, little Miss Tooker and Mrs. Daniels, to dance, and after supper I to bed, and left them merry below, which they did not part from till two or three in the morning.

2nd. Up, and discoursing with my wife, who is resolved to go to London for good and all this day, we did agree upon giving Mr. Sheldon L10, and Mrs. Barbary two pieces, and so I left her to go down thither to fetch away the rest of the things and pay him the money, and so I to the office, where very busy setting Mr. Poynter to write out my last night's worke, which pleases me this day, but yet it is pretty to reflect how much I am out of confidence with what I had done upon Gibson's discourse with me, for fear I should have done it sillily, but Poynter likes them, and Mr. Hater also, but yet I am afeard lest they should do it out of flattery, so conscious I am of my ignorance. Dined with my wife at noon and took leave of her, she being to go to London, as I said, for altogether, and I to the office, busy till past one in the morning.

3rd. It being Lord's day, up and dressed and to church, thinking to have sat with Sir James Bunce to hear his daughter and her husband sing, that are so much commended, but was prevented by being invited into Coll. Cleggatt's pew. However, there I sat, near Mr. Laneare, with whom I spoke, and in sight, by chance, and very near my fat brown beauty of our Parish, the rich merchant's lady, a very noble woman, and Madame Pierce. A good sermon of Mr. Plume's, and so to Captain Cocke's, and there dined with him, and Colonell Wyndham, a worthy gentleman, whose wife was nurse to the present King, and one that while she lived governed him and every thing else, as Cocke says, as a minister of state; the old King putting mighty weight and trust upon her. They talked much of matters of State and persons, and particularly how my Lord Barkeley hath all along been a fortunate, though a passionate and but weak man as to policy; but as a kinsman brought in and promoted by my Lord of St. Alban's, and one that is the greatest vapourer in the world, this Colonell Wyndham says; and one to whom only, with Jacke Asheburnel and Colonel Legg, the King's removal to the Isle of Wight from Hampton Court was communicated; and (though betrayed by their knavery, or at best by their ignorance, insomuch that they have all solemnly charged one another with their failures therein, and have been at daggers-drawing publickly about it), yet now none greater friends in the world. We dined, and in comes Mrs. Owen, a kinswoman of my Lord Bruncker's, about getting a man discharged, which I did for her, and by and by Mrs. Pierce to speake with me (and Mary my wife's late maid, now gone to her) about her husband's business of money, and she tells us how she prevented Captain Fisher the other day in his purchase of all her husband's fine goods, as pearls and silks, that he had seized in an Apothecary's house, a friend of theirs, but she got in and broke them open and removed all before Captain Fisher came the next day to fetch them away, at which he is starke mad. She went home, and I to my lodgings. At night by agreement I fetched her again with Cocke's coach, and he come and we sat and talked together, thinking to have had Mrs. Coleman and my songsters, her husband and Laneare, but they failed me. So we to supper, and as merry as was sufficient, and my pretty little Miss with me; and so after supper walked [with] Pierce home, and so back and to bed. But, Lord! I stand admiring of the wittinesse of her little boy, which is one of the wittiest boys, but most confident that ever I did see of a child of 9 years old or under in all my life, or indeed one twice his age almost, but all for roguish wit. So to bed.

4th. Several people to me about business, among others Captain Taylor, intended Storekeeper for Harwich, whom I did give some assistance in his dispatch by lending him money. So out and by water to London and to the 'Change, and up and down about several businesses, and after the observing (God forgive me!) one or two of my neighbour Jason's women come to towne, which did please me very well, home to my house at the office, where my wife had got a dinner for me: and it was a joyfull thing for us to meet here, for which God be praised! Here was her brother come to see her, and speake with me about business. It seems my recommending of him hath not only obtained his presently being admitted into the Duke of Albemarle's guards, and present pay, but also by the Duke's and Sir Philip Howard's direction, to be put as a right-hand man, and other marks of special respect, at which I am very glad, partly for him, and partly to see that I am reckoned something in my recommendations, but wish he may carry himself that I may receive no disgrace by him. So to the 'Change. Up and down again in the evening about business and to meet Captain Cocke, who waited for Mrs. Pierce (with whom he is mightily stricken), to receive and hide for her her rich goods she saved the other day from seizure. Upon the 'Change to-day Colvill tells me, from Oxford, that the King in person hath justified my Lord Sandwich to the highest degree; and is right in his favour to the uttermost. So late by water home, taking a barrel of oysters with me, and at Greenwich went and sat with Madam Penington . . . . and made her undress her head and sit dishevilled all night sporting till two in the morning, and so away to my lodging and so to bed. Over-fasting all the morning hath filled me mightily with wind, and nothing else hath done it, that I fear a fit of the cholique.

5th. Up and to the office, where very busy about several businesses all the morning. At noon empty, yet without stomach to dinner, having spoiled myself with fasting yesterday, and so filled with wind. In the afternoon by water, calling Mr. Stevens (who is with great trouble paying of seamen of their tickets at Deptford) and to London, to look for Captain Kingdom whom we found at home about 5 o'clock. I tried him, and he promised to follow us presently to the East India House to sign papers to-night in order to the settling the business of my receiving money for Tangier. We went and stopt the officer there to shut up. He made us stay above an houre. I sent for him; he comes, but was not found at home, but abroad on other business, and brings a paper saying that he had been this houre looking for the Lord Ashley's order. When he looks for it, that is not the paper. He would go again to look; kept us waiting till almost 8 at night. Then was I to go home by water this weather and darke, and to write letters by the post, besides keeping the East India officers there so late. I sent for him again; at last he comes, and says he cannot find the paper (which is a pretty thing to lay orders for L100,000 no better). I was angry; he told me I ought to give people ease at night, and all business was to be done by day. I answered him sharply, that I did [not] make, nor any honest man, any difference between night and day in the King's business, and this was such, and my Lord Ashley should know. He answered me short. I told him I knew the time (meaning the Rump's time) when he did other men's business with more diligence. He cried, "Nay, say not so," and stopped his mouth, not one word after. We then did our business without the order in less than eight minutes, which he made me to no purpose stay above two hours for the doing. This made him mad, and so we exchanged notes, and I had notes for L14,000 of the Treasurer of the Company, and so away and by water to Greenwich and wrote my letters, and so home late to bed.

6th. Up betimes, it being fast-day; and by water to the Duke of Albemarle, who come to towne from Oxford last night. He is mighty brisk, and very kind to me, and asks my advice principally in every thing. He surprises me with the news that my Lord Sandwich goes Embassador to Spayne speedily; though I know not whence this arises, yet I am heartily glad of it. He did give me several directions what to do, and so I home by water again and to church a little, thinking to have met Mrs. Pierce in order to our meeting at night; but she not there, I home and dined, and comes presently by appointment my wife. I spent the afternoon upon a song of Solyman's words to Roxalana that I have set, and so with my wife walked and Mercer to Mrs. Pierce's, where Captain Rolt and Mrs. Knipp, Mr. Coleman and his wife, and Laneare, Mrs. Worshipp and her singing daughter, met; and by and by unexpectedly comes Mr. Pierce from Oxford. Here the best company for musique I ever was in, in my life, and wish I could live and die in it, both for musique and the face of Mrs. Pierce, and my wife and Knipp, who is pretty enough; but the most excellent, mad-humoured thing, and sings the noblest that ever I heard in my life, and Rolt, with her, some things together most excellently. I spent the night in extasy almost; and, having invited them to my house a day or two hence, we broke up, Pierce having told me that he is told how the King hath done my Lord Sandwich all the right imaginable, by shewing him his countenance before all the world on every occasion, to remove thoughts of discontent; and that he is to go Embassador, and that the Duke of Yorke is made generall of all forces by land and sea, and the Duke of Albemarle, lieutenant-generall. Whether the two latter alterations be so, true or no, he knows not, but he is told so; but my Lord is in full favour with the King. So all home and to bed.

7th. Up and to the office, where very busy all day. Sir G. Carteret's letter tells me my Lord Sandwich is, as I was told, declared Embassador Extraordinary to Spayne, and to go with all speed away, and that his enemies have done him as much good as he could wish. At noon late to dinner, and after dinner spent till night with Mr. Gibson and Hater discoursing and making myself more fully [know] the trade of pursers, and what fittest to be done in their business, and so to the office till midnight writing letters, and so home, and after supper with my wife about one o'clock to bed.

8th. Up, well pleased in my mind about my Lord Sandwich, about whom I shall know more anon from Sir G. Carteret, who will be in towne, and also that the Hambrough [ships] after all difficulties are got out. God send them good speed! So, after being trimmed, I by water to London, to the Navy office, there to give order to my mayde to buy things to send down to Greenwich for supper to-night; and I also to buy other things, as oysters, and lemons, 6d. per piece, and oranges, 3d. That done I to the 'Change, and among many other things, especially for getting of my Tangier money, I by appointment met Mr. Gawden, and he and I to the Pope's Head Taverne, and there he did give me alone a very pretty dinner. Our business to talk of his matters and his supply of money, which was necessary for us to talk on before the Duke of Albemarle this afternoon and Sir G. Carteret. After that I offered now to pay him the L4000 remaining of his L8000 for Tangier, which he took with great kindnesse, and prayed me most frankly to give him a note for L3500 and accept the other L500 for myself, which in good earnest was against my judgement to do, for [I] expected about L100 and no more, but however he would have me do it, and ownes very great obligations to me, and the man indeed I love, and he deserves it. This put me into great joy, though with a little stay to it till we have time to settle it, for for so great a sum I was fearfull any accident might by death or otherwise defeat me, having not now time to change papers. So we rose, and by water to White Hall, where we found Sir G. Carteret with the Duke, and also Sir G. Downing, whom I had not seen in many years before. He greeted me very kindly, and I him; though methinks I am touched, that it should be said that he was my master heretofore, as doubtless he will. So to talk of our Navy business, and particularly money business, of which there is little hopes of any present supply upon this new Act, the goldsmiths being here (and Alderman Backewell newly come from Flanders), and none offering any. So we rose without doing more than my stating the case of the Victualler, that whereas there is due to him on the last year's declaration L80,000, and the charge of this year's amounts to L420,000 and odd, he must be supplied between this and the end of January with L150,000, and the remainder in 40 weeks by weekly payments, or else he cannot go through his business. Thence after some discourse with Sir G. Carteret, who, though he tells me that he is glad of my Lord's being made Embassador, and that it is the greatest courtesy his enemies could do him; yet I find he is not heartily merry upon it, and that it was no design of my Lord's friends, but the prevalence of his enemies, and that the Duke of Albemarle and Prince Rupert are like to go to sea together the next year. I pray God, when my Lord is gone, they do not fall hard upon the Vice-Chamberlain, being alone, and in so envious a place, though by this late Act and the instructions now a brewing for our office as to method of payments will destroy the profit of his place of itself without more trouble. Thence by water down to Greenwich, and there found all my company come; that is, Mrs. Knipp, and an ill, melancholy, jealous-looking fellow, her husband, that spoke not a word to us all the night, Pierce and his wife, and Rolt, Mrs. Worshipp and her daughter, Coleman and his wife, and Laneare, and, to make us perfectly happy, there comes by chance to towne Mr. Hill to see us. Most excellent musique we had in abundance, and a good supper, dancing, and a pleasant scene of Mrs. Knipp's rising sicke from table, but whispered me it was for some hard word or other her husband gave her just now when she laughed and was more merry than ordinary. But we got her in humour again, and mighty merry; spending the night, till two in the morning, with most complete content as ever in my life, it being increased by my day's work with Gawden. Then broke up, and we to bed, Mr. Hill and I, whom I love more and more, and he us.

9th. Called up betimes by my Lord Bruncker, who is come to towne from his long water worke at Erith last night, to go with him to the Duke of Albemarle, which by his coach I did. Our discourse upon the ill posture of the times through lacke of money. At the Duke's did some business, and I believe he was not pleased to see all the Duke's discourse and applications to me and everybody else. Discoursed also with Sir G. Carteret about office business, but no money in view. Here my Lord and I staid and dined, the Vice-Chamberlain taking his leave. At table the Duchesse, a damned ill-looked woman, complaining of her Lord's going to sea the next year, said these cursed words: "If my Lord had been a coward he had gone to sea no more: it may be then he might have been excused, and made an Embassador" (meaning my Lord Sandwich).

[When Lord Sandwich was away a new commander had to be chosen, and rank and long service pointed out Prince Rupert for the office, it having been decided that the heir presumptive should be kept at home. It was thought, however, that the same confidence could not be placed in the prince's discretion as in his courage, and therefore the Duke of Albemarle was induced to take a joint command with him, "and so make one admiral of two persons" (see Lister's "Life of Clarendon," vol. ii., pp. 360,361).]

This made me mad, and I believed she perceived my countenance change, and blushed herself very much. I was in hopes others had not minded it, but my Lord Bruncker, after we were come away, took notice of the words to me with displeasure. Thence after dinner away by water, calling and taking leave of Sir G. Carteret, whom we found going through at White Hall, and so over to Lambeth and took coach and home, and so to the office, where late writing letters, and then home to Mr. Hill, and sang, among other things, my song of "Beauty retire," which he likes, only excepts against two notes in the base, but likes the whole very well. So late to bed.

10th (Lord's day). Lay long talking, Hill and I, with great pleasure, and then up, and being ready walked to Cocke's for some newes, but heard none, only they would have us stay their dinner, and sent for my wife, who come, and very merry we were, there being Sir Edmund Pooly and Mr. Evelyn. Before we had dined comes Mr. Andrews, whom we had sent for to Bow, and so after dinner home, and there we sang some things, but not with much pleasure, Mr. Andrews being in so great haste to go home, his wife looking every hour to be brought to bed. He gone Mr. Hill and I continued our musique, one thing after another, late till supper, and so to bed with great pleasure.

11th. Lay long with great pleasure talking. So I left him and to London to the 'Change, and after discoursed with several people about business; met Mr. Gawden at the Pope's Head, where he brought Mr. Lewes and T. Willson to discourse about the Victualling business, and the alterations of the pursers' trade, for something must be done to secure the King a little better, and yet that they may have wherewith to live. After dinner I took him aside, and perfected to my great joy my business with him, wherein he deals most nobly in giving me his hand for the L4,000, and would take my note but for L3500. This is a great blessing, and God make me thankfull truly for it. With him till it was darke putting in writing our discourse about victualling, and so parted, and I to Viner's, and there evened all accounts, and took up my notes setting all straight between us to this day. The like to Colvill, and paying several bills due from me on the Tangier account. Then late met Cocke and Temple at the Pope's Head, and there had good discourse with Temple, who tells me that of the L80,000 advanced already by the East India Company, they have had L5000 out of their hands. He discoursed largely of the quantity of money coyned, and what may be thought the real sum of money in the kingdom. He told me, too, as an instance of the thrift used in the King's business, that the tools and the interest of the money-using to the King for the money he borrowed while the new invention of the mill money was perfected, cost him L35,000, and in mirthe tells me that the new fashion money is good for nothing but to help the Prince if he can secretly get copper plates shut up in silver it shall never be discovered, at least not in his age. Thence Cocke and I by water, he home and I home, and there sat with Mr. Hill and my wife supping, talking and singing till midnight, and then to bed. [That I may remember it the more particularly, I thought fit to insert this additional memorandum of Temple's discourse this night with me, which I took in writing from his mouth. Before the Harp and Crosse money was cried down, he and his fellow goldsmiths did make some particular trials what proportion that money bore to the old King's money, and they found that generally it come to, one with another, about L25 in every L100. Of this money there was, upon the calling of it in, L650,000 at least brought into the Tower; and from thence he computes that the whole money of England must be full L6,250,000. But for all this believes that there is above L30,000,000; he supposing that about the King's coming in (when he begun to observe the quantity of the new money) people begun to be fearfull of this money's being cried down, and so picked it out and set it a-going as fast as they could, to be rid of it; and he thinks L30,000,000 the rather, because if there were but L16,250,000 the King having L2,000,000 every year, would have the whole money of the kingdom in his hands in eight years. He tells me about L350,000 sterling was coined out of the French money, the proceeds of Dunkirke; so that, with what was coined of the Crosse money, there is new coined about L1,000,000 besides the gold, which is guessed at L500,000. He tells me, that, though the King did deposit the French money in pawn all the while for the L350,000 he was forced to borrow thereupon till the tools could be made for the new Minting in the present form, yet the interest he paid for that time came to L35,000, Viner having to his knowledge L10,000 for the use of L100,000 of it.]--(The passage between brackets is from a piece of paper inserted in this place.)

12th. Up, and to the office, where my Lord Bruncker met, and among other things did finish a contract with Cocke for hemp, by which I hope to get my money due from him paid presently. At noon home to dinner, only eating a bit, and with much kindness taking leave of Mr. Hill who goes away to-day, and so I by water saving the tide through Bridge and to Sir G. Downing by appointment at Charing Crosse, who did at first mightily please me with informing me thoroughly the virtue and force of this Act, and indeed it is ten times better than ever I thought could have been said of it, but when he come to impose upon me that without more ado I must get by my credit people to serve in goods and lend money upon it and none could do it better than I, and the King should give me thanks particularly in it, and I could not get him to excuse me, but I must come to him though to no purpose on Saturday, and that he is sure I will bring him some bargains or other made upon this Act, it vexed me more than all the pleasure I took before, for I find he will be troublesome to me in it, if I will let him have as much of my time as he would have. So late I took leave and in the cold (the weather setting in cold) home to the office and, after my letters being wrote, home to supper and to bed, my wife being also gone to London.

13th. Up betimes and finished my journall for five days back, and then after being ready to my Lord Bruncker by appointment, there to order the disposing of some money that we have come into the office, and here to my great content I did get a bill of imprest to Captain Cocke to pay myself in part of what is coming to me from him for my Lord Sandwich's satisfaction and my owne, and also another payment or two wherein I am concerned, and having done that did go to Mr. Pierce's, where he and his wife made me drink some tea, and so he and I by water together to London. Here at a taverne in Cornhill he and I did agree upon my delivering up to him a bill of Captain Cocke's, put into my hand for Pierce's use upon evening of reckonings about the prize goods, and so away to the 'Change, and there hear the ill news, to my great and all our great trouble, that the plague is encreased again this week, notwithstanding there hath been a day or two great frosts; but we hope it is only the effects of the late close warm weather, and if the frosts continue the next week, may fall again; but the town do thicken so much with people, that it is much if the plague do not grow again upon us. Off the 'Change invited by Sheriff Hooker, who keeps the poorest, mean, dirty table in a dirty house that ever I did see any Sheriff of London; and a plain, ordinary, silly man I think he is, but rich; only his son, Mr. Lethulier, I like, for a pretty, civil, understanding merchant; and the more by much, because he happens to be husband to our noble, fat, brave lady in our parish, that I and my wife admire so. Thence away to the Pope's Head Taverne, and there met first with Captain Cocke, and dispatched my business with him to my content, he being ready to sign his bill of imprest of L2,000, and gives it me in part of his payment to me, which glads my heart. He being gone, comes Sir W. Warren, who advised with me about several things about getting money, and L100 I shall presently have of him. We advised about a business of insurance, wherein something may be saved to him and got to me, and to that end he and I did take a coach at night and to the Cockepitt, there to get the Duke of Albemarle's advice for our insuring some of our Sounde goods coming home under Harman's convoy, but he proved shy of doing it without knowledge of the Duke of Yorke, so we back again and calling at my house to see my wife, who is well; though my great trouble is that our poor little parish is the greatest number this weeke in all the city within the walls, having six, from one the last weeke; and so by water to Greenwich leaving Sir W. Warren at home, and I straight to my Lord Bruncker, it being late, and concluded upon insuring something and to send to that purpose to Sir W. Warren to come to us to-morrow morning. So I home and, my mind in great rest, to bed.

14th. Up, and to the office a while with my Lord Bruncker, where we directed Sir W. Warren in the business of the insurance as I desired, and ended some other businesses of his, and so at noon I to London, but the 'Change was done before I got thither, so I to the Pope's Head Taverne, and there find Mr. Gawden and Captain Beckford and Nick Osborne going to dinner, and I dined with them and very exceeding merry we were as I had [not] been a great while, and dinner being done I to the East India House and there had an assignment on Mr. Temple for the L2,000 of Cocke's, which joyed my heart; so, having seen my wife in the way, I home by water and to write my letters and then home to bed.

15th. Up, and spent all the morning with my Surveyors of the Ports for the Victualling, and there read to them what instructions I had provided for them and discoursed largely much of our business and the business of the pursers. I left them to dine with my people, and to my Lord Bruncker's where I met with a great good dinner and Sir T. Teddiman, with whom my Lord and I were to discourse about the bringing of W. Howe to a tryall for his jewells, and there till almost night, and so away toward the office and in my way met with Sir James Bunce; and after asking what newes, he cried "Ah!" says he (I know [not] whether in earnest or jest), "this is the time for you," says he, "that were for Oliver heretofore; you are full of employment, and we poor Cavaliers sit still and can get nothing;" which was a pretty reproach, I thought, but answered nothing to it, for fear of making it worse. So away and I to see Mrs. Penington, but company being to come to her, I staid not, but to the office a little and so home, and after supper to bed.

16th. Up, and met at the office; Sir W. Batten with us, who come from Portsmouth on Monday last, and hath not been with us to see or discourse with us about any business till this day. At noon to dinner, Sir W. Warren with me on boat, and thence I by water, it being a fearfull cold, snowing day to Westminster to White Hall stairs and thence to Sir G. Downing, to whom I brought the happy newes of my having contracted, as we did this day with Sir W. Warren, for a ship's lading of Norway goods here and another at Harwich to the value of above L3,000, which is the first that hath been got upon the New Act, and he is overjoyed with it and tells me he will do me all the right to Court about it in the world, and I am glad I have it to write to Sir W. Coventry to-night. He would fain have me come in L200 to lend upon the Act, but I desire to be excused in doing that, it being to little purpose for us that relate to the King to do it, for the sum gets the King no courtesy nor credit. So I parted from him and walked to Westminster Hall, where Sir W. Warren, who come along with me, staid for me, and there I did see Betty Howlet come after the sicknesse to the Hall. Had not opportunity to salute her, as I desired, but was glad to see her and a very pretty wench she is. Thence back, landing at the Old Swan and taking boat again at Billingsgate, and setting ashore we home and I to the office . . . . and there wrote my letters, and so home to supper and to bed, it being a great frost. Newes is come to-day of our Sounde fleete being come, but I do not know what Sir W. Warren hath insured.

17th (Lord's day). After being trimmed word brought me that Cutler's coach is, by appointment, come to the Isle of Doggs for me, and so I over the water; and in his coach to Hackney, a very fine, cold, clear, frosty day. At his house I find him with a plain little dinner, good wine, and welcome. He is still a prating man; and the more I know him, the less I find in him. A pretty house he hath here indeed, of his owne building. His old mother was an object at dinner that made me not like it; and, after dinner, to visit his sicke wife I did not also take much joy in, but very friendly he is to me, not for any kindnesse I think he hath to any man, but thinking me, I perceive, a man whose friendship is to be looked after. After dinner back again and to Deptford to Mr. Evelyn's, who was not within, but I had appointed my cozen Thos. Pepys of Hatcham to meet me there, to discourse about getting his L1000 of my Lord Sandwich, having now an opportunity of my having above that sum in my hands of his. I found this a dull fellow still in all his discourse, but in this he is ready enough to embrace what I counsel him to, which is, to write importunately to my Lord and me about it and I will look after it. I do again and again declare myself a man unfit to be security for such a sum. He walked with me as far as Deptford upper towne, being mighty respectfull to me, and there parted, he telling me that this towne is still very bad of the plague. I walked to Greenwich first, to make a short visit to my Lord Bruncker, and next to Mrs. Penington and spent all the evening with her with the same freedom I used to have and very pleasant company. With her till one of the clock in the morning and past, and so to my lodging to bed, and

18th. Betimes, up, it being a fine frost, and walked it to Redriffe, calling and drinking at Half-way house, thinking, indeed, to have overtaken some of the people of our house, the women, who were to walk the same walke, but I could not. So to London, and there visited my wife, and was a little displeased to find she is so forward all of a spurt to make much of her brother and sister since my last kindnesse to him in getting him a place, but all ended well presently, and I to the 'Change and up and down to Kingdon and the goldsmith's to meet Mr. Stephens, and did get all my money matters most excellently cleared to my complete satisfaction. Passing over Cornhill I spied young Mrs. Daniel and Sarah, my landlady's daughter, who are come, as I expected, to towne, and did say they spied me and I dogged them to St. Martin's, where I passed by them being shy, and walked down as low as Ducke Lane and enquired for some Spanish books, and so back again and they were gone. So to the 'Change, hoping to see them in the streete, and missing them, went back again thither and back to the 'Change, but no sight of them, so went after my business again, and, though late, was sent to by Sir W. Warren (who heard where I was) to intreat me to come dine with him, hearing that I lacked a dinner, at the Pope's Head; and there with Mr. Hinton, the goldsmith, and others, very merry; but, Lord! to see how Dr. Hinton come in with a gallant or two from Court, and do so call "Cozen" Mr. Hinton, the goldsmith, but I that know him to be a beggar and a knave, did make great sport in my mind at it.

[John Hinton, M.D., a strong royalist, who attended Henrietta Maria in her confinement at Exeter when she gave birth to the Princess Henrietta. He was knighted by Charles II., and appointed physician in ordinary to the king and queen. His knighthood was a reward for having procured a private advance of money from his kinsman, the goldsmith, to enable the Duke of Albemarle to pay the army (see "Memorial to King Charles II. from Sir John Hinton, A.D. 1679," printed in Ellis's "Original Letters," 3rd series, vol. iv., p 296).]

After dinner Sir W. Warren and I alone in another room a little while talking about business, and so parted, and I hence, my mind full of content in my day's worke, home by water to Greenwich, the river beginning to be very full of ice, so as I was a little frighted, but got home well, it being darke. So having no mind to do any business, went home to my lodgings, and there got little Mrs. Tooker, and Mrs. Daniel, the, daughter, and Sarah to my chamber to cards and sup with me, when in comes Mr. Pierce to me, who tells me how W. Howe has been examined on shipboard by my Lord Bruncker to-day, and others, and that he has charged him out of envy with sending goods under my Lord's seale and in my Lord Bruncker's name, thereby to get them safe passage, which, he tells me, is false, but that he did use my name to that purpose, and hath acknowledged it to my Lord Bruncker, but do also confess to me that one parcel he thinks he did use my Lord Bruncker's name, which do vexe me mightily that my name should be brought in question about such things, though I did not say much to him of my discontent till I have spoke with my Lord Bruncker about it. So he being gone, being to go to Oxford to-morrow, we to cards again late, and so broke up, I having great pleasure with my little girle, Mrs. Tooker.

19th. Up, and to the office, where all the morning. At noon by agreement comes Hatcham Pepys to dine with me. I thought to have had him to Sir J. Minnes to a good venison pasty with the rest of my fellows, being invited, but seeing much company I went away with him and had a good dinner at home. He did give me letters he hath wrote to my Lord and Moore about my Lord's money to get it paid to my cozen, which I will make good use of. I made mighty much of him, but a sorry dull fellow he is, fit for nothing that is ingenious, nor is there a turd of kindnesse or service to be had from him. So I shall neglect him if I could get but him satisfied about this money that I may be out of bonds for my Lord to him. To see that this fellow could desire me to helpe him to some employment, if it were but of L100 per annum: when he is not worth less than, I believe, L20,000. He gone, I to Sir J. Minnes, and thence with my Lord Bruncker on board the Bezan to examine W. Howe again, who I find upon this tryall one of much more wit and ingenuity in his answers than ever I expected, he being very cunning and discreet and well spoken in them. I said little to him or concerning him; but, Lord! to see how he writes to me a-days, and styles me "My Honour." So much is a man subjected and dejected under afflictions as to flatter me in that manner on this occasion. Back with my Lord to Sir J. Minnes, where I left him and the rest of a great deale of company, and so I to my office, where late writing letters and then home to bed.

20th. Up, and was trimmed, but not time enough to save my Lord Bruncker's coach or Sir J. Minnes's, and so was fain to walk to Lambeth on foot, but it was a very fine frosty walke, and great pleasure in it, but troublesome getting over the River for ice. I to the Duke of Albemarle, whither my brethren were all come, but I was not too late. There we sat in discourse upon our Navy business an houre, and thence in my Lord Bruncker's coach alone, he walking before (while I staid awhile talking with Sir G. Downing about the Act, in which he is horrid troublesome) to the Old Exchange. Thence I took Sir Ellis Layton to Captain Cocke's, where my Lord Bruncker and Lady Williams dine, and we all mighty merry; but Sir Ellis Layton one of the best companions at a meale in the world. After dinner I to the Exchange to see whether my pretty seamstress be come again or no, and I find she is, so I to her, saluted her over her counter in the open Exchange above, and mightily joyed to see her, poor pretty woman! I must confess I think her a great beauty. After laying out a little money there for two pair of thread stockings, cost 8s., I to Lumbard Streete to see some business to-night there at the goldsmith's, among others paying in L1258 to Viner for my Lord Sandwich's use upon Cocke's account. I was called by my Lord Bruncker in his coach with his mistresse, and Mr. Cottle the lawyer, our acquaintance at Greenwich, and so home to Greenwich, and thence I to Mrs. Penington, and had a supper from the King's Head for her, and there mighty merry and free as I used to be with her, and at last, late, I did pray her to undress herself into her nightgowne, that I might see how to have her picture drawne carelessly (for she is mighty proud of that conceit), and I would walk without in the streete till she had done. So I did walk forth, and whether I made too many turns or no in the darke cold frosty night between the two walls up to the Parke gate I know not, but she was gone to bed when I come again to the house, upon pretence of leaving some papers there, which I did on purpose by her consent. So I away home, and was there sat up for to be spoken with my young Mrs. Daniel, to pray me to speake for her husband to be a Lieutenant. I had the opportunity here of kissing her again and again, and did answer that I would be very willing to do him any kindnesse, and so parted, and I to bed, exceedingly pleased in all my matters of money this month or two, it having pleased God to bless me with several opportunities of good sums, and that I have them in effect all very well paid, or in my power to have. But two things trouble me; one, the sicknesse is increased above 80 this weeke (though in my owne parish not one has died, though six the last weeke); the other, most of all, which is, that I have so complexed an account for these last two months for variety of layings out upon Tangier, occasions and variety of gettings that I have not made even with myself now these 3 or 4 months, which do trouble me mightily, finding that I shall hardly ever come to understand them thoroughly again, as I used to do my accounts when I was at home.

21st. At the office all the morning. At noon all of us dined at Captain Cocke's at a good chine of beef, and other good meat; but, being all frost-bitten, was most of it unroast; but very merry, and a good dish of fowle we dressed ourselves. Mr. Evelyn there, in very good humour. All the afternoon till night pleasant, and then I took my leave of them and to the office, where I wrote my letters, and away home, my head full of business and some trouble for my letting my accounts go so far that I have made an oathe this night for the drinking no wine, &c., on such penalties till I have passed my accounts and cleared all. Coming home and going to bed, the boy tells me his sister Daniel has provided me a supper of little birds killed by her husband, and I made her sup with me, and after supper were alone a great while, and I had the pleasure of her lips, she being a pretty woman, and one whom a great belly becomes as well as ever I saw any. She gone, I to bed. This day I was come to by Mrs. Burrows, of Westminster, Lieutenant Burrows (lately dead) his wife, a most pretty woman and my old acquaintance; I had a kiss or two of her, and a most modest woman she is.

22nd. Up betimes and to my Lord Bruncker to consider the late instructions sent us for the method of our signing bills hereafter and paying them. By and by, by agreement, comes Sir J. Minnes and Sir W. Batten, and then to read them publicly and consider of putting them in execution. About this all the morning, and, it appearing necessary for the Controller to have another Clerke, I recommended Poynter to him, which he accepts, and I by that means rid of one that I fear would not have been fit for my turne, though he writes very well. At noon comes Mr. Hill to towne, and finds me out here, and brings Mr. Houbland, who met him here. So I was compelled to leave my Lord and his dinner and company, and with them to the Beare, and dined with them and their brothers, of which Hill had his and the other two of his, and mighty merry and very fine company they are, and I glad to see them. After dinner I forced to take leave of them by being called upon by Mr. Andrews, I having sent for him, and by a fine glosse did bring him to desire tallys for what orders I have to pay him and his company for Tangier victualls, and I by that means cleared to myself L210 coming to me upon their two orders, which is also a noble addition to my late profits, which have been very considerable of late, but how great I know not till I come to cast up my accounts, which burdens my mind that it should be so backward, but I am resolved to settle to nothing till I have done it. He gone, I to my Lord Bruncker's, and there spent the evening by my desire in seeing his Lordship open to pieces and make up again his watch, thereby being taught what I never knew before; and it is a thing very well worth my having seen, and am mightily pleased and satisfied with it. So I sat talking with him till late at night, somewhat vexed at a snappish answer Madam Williams did give me to herself, upon my speaking a free word to her in mirthe, calling her a mad jade. She answered, we were not so well acquainted yet. But I was more at a letter from my Lord Duke of Albemarle to-day, pressing us to continue our meetings for all Christmas, which, though every body intended not to have done, yet I am concluded in it, who intended nothing else. But I see it is necessary that I do make often visits to my Lord Duke, which nothing shall hinder after I have evened my accounts, and now the river is frozen I know not how to get to him. Thence to my lodging, making up my Journall for 8 or 9 days, and so my mind being eased of it, I to supper and to bed. The weather hath been frosty these eight or nine days, and so we hope for an abatement of the plague the next weeke, or else God have mercy upon us! for the plague will certainly continue the next year if it do not.

23rd. At my office all the morning and home to dinner, my head full of business, and there my wife finds me unexpectedly. But I not being at leisure to stay or talk with her, she went down by coach to Woolwich, thinking to fetch Mrs. Barbary to carry her to London to keep her Christmas with her, and I to the office. This day one come to me with four great turkies, as a present from Mr. Deane, at Harwich, three of which my wife carried in the evening home with her to London in her coach (Mrs. Barbary not being to be got so suddenly, but will come to her the next week), and I at my office late, and then to my lodgings to bed.

24th (Sunday). Up betimes, to my Lord Duke of Albemarle by water, and after some talke with him about business of the office with great content, and so back again and to dinner, my landlady and her daughters with me, and had mince-pies, and very merry at a mischance her young son had in tearing of his new coate quite down the outside of his sleeve in the whole cloth, one of the strangest mishaps that ever I saw in my life. Then to church, and placed myself in the Parson's pew under the pulpit, to hear Mrs. Chamberlain in the next pew sing, who is daughter to Sir James Bunch, of whom I have heard much, and indeed she sings very finely, and from church met with Sir W. Warren and he and I walked together talking about his and my businesses, getting of money as fairly as we can, and, having set him part of his way home, I walked to my Lord Bruncker, whom I heard was at Alderman Hooker's, hoping to see and salute Mrs. Lethulier, whom I did see in passing, but no opportunity of beginning acquaintance, but a very noble lady she is, however the silly alderman got her. Here we sat talking a great while, Sir The. Biddulph and Mr. Vaughan, a son-in-law of Alderman Hooker's. Hence with my Lord Bruncker home and sat a little with him and so home to bed.

25th (Christmas-day). To church in the morning, and there saw a wedding in the church, which I have not seen many a day; and the young people so merry one with another, and strange to see what delight we married people have to see these poor fools decoyed into our condition, every man and woman gazing and smiling at them. Here I saw again my beauty Lethulier. Thence to my Lord Bruncker's by invitation and dined there, and so home to look over and settle my papers, both of my accounts private, and those of Tangier, which I have let go so long that it were impossible for any soul, had I died, to understand them, or ever come to any good end in them. I hope God will never suffer me to come to that disorder again.

26th. Up, and to the office, where Sir J. Minnes and my Lord Bruncker and I met, to give our directions to the Commanders of all the ships in the river to bring in lists of their ships' companies, with entries, discharges, &c., all the last voyage, where young Seymour, among 20 that stood bare, stood with his hat on, a proud, saucy young man. Thence with them to Mr. Cuttle's, being invited, and dined nobly and neatly; with a very pretty house and a fine turret at top, with winding stairs and the finest prospect I know about all Greenwich, save the top of the hill, and yet in some respects better than that. Here I also saw some fine writing worke and flourishing of Mr. Hore, he one that I knew long ago, an acquaintance of Mr. Tomson's at Westminster, that is this man's clerk. It is the story of the several Archbishops of Canterbury, engrossed in vellum, to hang up in Canterbury Cathedrall in tables, in lieu of the old ones, which are almost worn out. Thence to the office a while, and so to Captain Cocke's and there talked, and home to look over my papers, and so to bed.

27th. Up, and with Cocke, by coach to London, there home to my wife, and angry about her desiring a mayde yet, before the plague is quite over. It seems Mercer is troubled that she hath not one under her, but I will not venture my family by increasing it before it be safe. Thence about many businesses, particularly with Sir W. Warren on the 'Change, and he and I dined together and settled our Tangier matters, wherein I get above L200 presently. We dined together at the Pope's Head to do this, and thence to the goldsmiths, I to examine the state of my matters there too, and so with him to my house, but my wife was gone abroad to Mrs. Mercer's, so we took boat, and it being darke and the thaw having broke the ice, but not carried it quite away, the boat did pass through so much of it all along, and that with the crackling and noise that it made me fearfull indeed. So I forced the watermen to land us on Redriffe side, and so walked together till Sir W. Warren and I parted near his house and thence I walked quite over the fields home by light of linke, one of my watermen carrying it, and I reading by the light of it, it being a very fine, clear, dry night. So to Captain Cocke's, and there sat and talked, especially with his Counsellor, about his prize goods, that hath done him good turne, being of the company with Captain Fisher, his name Godderson; here I supped and so home to bed, with great content that the plague is decreased to 152, the whole being but 330.

28th. Up and to the office, and thence with a great deal of business in my head, dined alone with Cocke. So home alone strictly about my accounts, wherein I made a good beginning, and so, after letters wrote by the post, to bed.

29th. Up betimes, and all day long within doors upon my accounts, publique and private, and find the ill effect of letting them go so long without evening, that no soul could have ever understood them but myself, and I with much ado. But, however, my regularity in all I did and spent do helpe me, and I hope to find them well. Late at them and to bed.

30th. Up and to the office, at noon home to dinner, and all the afternoon to my accounts again, and there find myself, to my great joy, a great deal worth above L4000, for which the Lord be praised! and is principally occasioned by my getting L500 of Cocke, for my profit in his bargains of prize goods, and from Mr. Gawden's making me a present of L500 more, when I paid him 8000 for Tangier. So to my office to write letters, then to my accounts again, and so to bed, being in great ease of mind.

31st (Lord's day). All the morning in my chamber, writing fair the state of my Tangier accounts, and so dined at home. In the afternoon to the Duke of Albemarle and thence back again by water, and so to my chamber to finish the entry of my accounts and to think of the business I am next to do, which is the stating my thoughts and putting in order my collections about the business of pursers, to see where the fault of our present constitution relating to them lies and what to propose to mend it, and upon this late and with my head full of this business to bed. Thus ends this year, to my great joy, in this manner. I have raised my estate from L1300 in this year to L4400. I have got myself greater interest, I think, by my diligence, and my employments encreased by that of Treasurer for Tangier, and Surveyour of the Victualls. It is true we have gone through great melancholy because of the great plague, and I put to great charges by it, by keeping my family long at Woolwich, and myself and another part of my family, my clerks, at my charge at Greenwich, and a mayde at London; but I hope the King will give us some satisfaction for that. But now the plague is abated almost to nothing, and I intending to get to London as fast as I can. My family, that is my wife and maids, having been there these two or three weeks. The Dutch war goes on very ill, by reason of lack of money; having none to hope for, all being put into disorder by a new Act that is made as an experiment to bring credit to the Exchequer, for goods and money to be advanced upon the credit of that Act. I have never lived so merrily (besides that I never got so much) as I have done this plague time, by my Lord Bruncker's and Captain Cocke's good company, and the acquaintance of Mrs. Knipp, Coleman and her husband, and Mr. Laneare, and great store of dancings we have had at my cost (which I was willing to indulge myself and wife) at my lodgings. The great evil of this year, and the only one indeed, is the fall of my Lord of Sandwich, whose mistake about the prizes hath undone him, I believe, as to interest at Court; though sent (for a little palliating it) Embassador into Spayne, which he is now fitting himself for. But the Duke of Albemarle goes with the Prince to sea this next year, and my Lord very meanly spoken of; and, indeed, his miscarriage about the prize goods is not to be excused, to suffer a company of rogues to go away with ten times as much as himself, and the blame of all to be deservedly laid upon him.

[According to Granville Penn ("Memorials of Sir W. Penn," ii. 488 n.) 2000 went to Lord Sandwich and L8000 among eight others.]

My whole family hath been well all this while, and all my friends I know of, saving my aunt Bell, who is dead, and some children of my cozen Sarah's, of the plague. But many of such as I know very well, dead; yet, to our great joy, the town fills apace, and shops begin to be open again. Pray God continue the plague's decrease! for that keeps the Court away from the place of business, and so all goes to rack as to publick matters, they at this distance not thinking of it.

The Echo Library
www.echo-library.com

Please visit our website to download a complete catalogue of our books. We specialise in out-of-copyright reprints in all subjects. We publish a range of Large Print Editions of classic titles.

Books for re-printing

Suggestions for re-printing can be sent to titles@echo-library.com. Titles must be out-of-copyright or you must own the copyright. They can be in digital or published form.

If we do not wish to add the title to our catalogue then we can reprint for you. Costs depend on the format of the manuscript or book and its size.

Feedback

Because we have no direct contact with our customers we would welcome constructive comments to feedback@echo-library.com

Complaints

If there is a serious error in the text or layout please advise us by sending details to complaints@echo-library.com and we will supply a corrected copy, usually within 15 working days (it may take longer outside the UK and USA).

If there is a printing fault or the book is damaged please refer to your supplier.